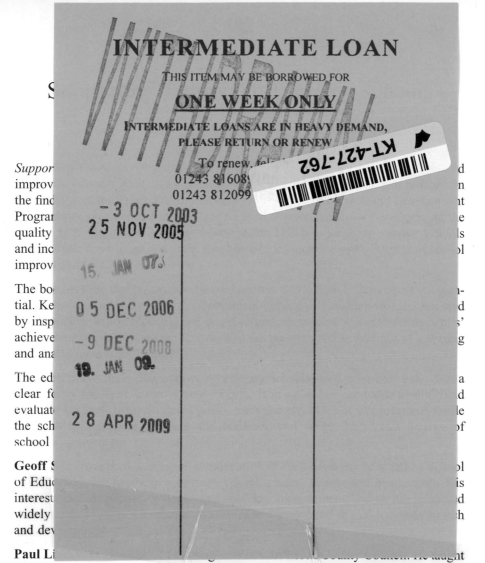

S

Suppor
improv
the find
Progra
quality
and inc
improv

The bo
tial. Ke
by insp
achieve
and ana

The ed
clear fo
evaluat
the sch
school

Geoff
of Educ
interest
widely
and dev

Paul Li ... for 19 years before joining the local education authority as an inspector. He was chair of the Essex Primary School Improvement Programme Steering Group and was closely involved with the programme throughout.

Supporting Improving Primary Schools

The Role of Heads and LEAs in Raising Standards

Edited by

Geoff Southworth and Paul Lincoln

First published 1999 by Falmer Press
11 New Fetter Lane, London EC4P 4EE

Simultaneously published in the USA and Canada
by Garland Inc., 19 Union Square West, New York, NY 10003

Falmer Press is an imprint of the Taylor & Francis Group

© 2000 Edited by Geoff Southworth and Paul Lincoln

Typeset in Times by Graphicraft Limited, Hong Kong
Printed and bound in Great Britain by Biddles Ltd, Guildford & Kings Lynn

British Library Cataloguing in Publication Data
A catalogue record for this book is available from the British Library

Library of Congress Cataloging in Publication Data are available

ISBN 0-750-71014-4 hbk
ISBN 0-750-71015-2 pbk

Contents

List of Figures and Tables   vii
Acknowledgments   ix

Introduction   1
Geoff Southworth and Paul Lincoln

Part 1:   **Overview and Main Findings**   7

Chapter 1   Overview of the EPSI Programme   9
                 Paul Lincoln and Geoff Southworth

Chapter 2   Main Findings   24
                 Pete Dudley, Tina Loose and Geoff Southworth

Part 2:   **School Insights**   67

Chapter 3   Headship, Leadership and School Improvement   69
                 Geoff Southworth

Chapter 4   Primary Schools and Pupil 'Data'   87
                 Pete Dudley

Chapter 5   Taking Pupil Perspectives Seriously: The Central
                 Place of Pupil Voice in Primary School Improvement 107
                 Michael Fielding, Alan Fuller and Tina Loose

Part 3:   **LEA Insights**   123

Chapter 6   The LEA and School Improvement   125
                 Sue Kerfoot and Gary Nethercott

Contents

Chapter 7   Process Consultancy: The Role of LEA Consultants
              in Supporting School Improvement   139
              Alan Fuller and Sue Fisher

Part 4:   **Wider Issues and Conclusions**   **153**

Chapter 8   Evaluating School Improvement   155
              Tina Loose and Judy Sebba

Chapter 9   Improvement Policies and LEA Strategies in Light
              of the EPSI Programme Findings   174
              Paul Lincoln

Chapter 10   Key Points and Conclusions   186
              Geoff Southworth and Paul Lincoln

Appendices   1. Programme Aims, Targets and Success Criteria   209
              2. Common Measures Agreed Across All EPSI
                 Programme Schools   213
              3. Pupil Attitude Survey   215
              4. EPSI Workshop Programmes   217
              5. The IQEA Six School Conditions   219

Notes on contributors   222

References   224
Index   229

List of Figures and Tables

Figures

2.1 Increases in gains in EPSI schools, as a percentage of gain in
     all Essex schools 1995–8   26
2.2 Gains in percentage of pupils at or above level 4 in KS2
     English tests for 11-year-olds   28
2.3 KS2 English test scores: EPSI v. Essex   29
2.4 EPSI schools KS2 English test results 1995–8   30
2.5 KS2 Mathematics tests: EPSI v. Essex   31
2.6 EPSI schools KS2 Mathematics test results 1995–8   31
2.7 KS2 Science tests: EPSI v. Essex   32
2.8 EPSI schools KS2 Science test results 1995–8   32
2.9 EPSI schools 'value added' 1996–7   33
4.1 Sample summary mark sheet   94
4.2 The perceived impact on improvement of the EPSI data sets   99
5.1 A climate conducive to learning   113
5.2 Feedback format   114
9.1 The Essex Quality Framework – the 12 quality dimensions   179
9.2 The Essex Quality Framework – the 12 questions   180

Tables

2.1 KS2 English tests, EPSI pupils and Essex pupils,
     percentages attaining level 4 and above   29
2.2 Percentages attaining level 4 and above in KS2
     Mathematics tests   30
2.3 KS2 Science tests, total EPSI and Essex pupils attaining
     level 4 and above   31
2.4 EPSI improvement targets   36–58
4.1 What EPSI schools identified as 'data sources', which were
     being monitored and analysed as a result of the EPSI focus   92

List of Figures and Tables

4.2   Contrasting patterns of results for three schools when
      expressed as percentages at level 4 and above, average levels
      and value added indicators   103
4.3   School data – triangulation of evidence of improvement   104

Acknowledgments

The Essex Primary School Improvement Programme was a partnership venture involving colleagues from schools, the Local Education Authority and the University of Cambridge School of Education. Consequently, thanks are due to many groups and individuals who participated in the programme or assisted those who did.

In particular we would like to thank the staff in all the primary schools that participated in the programme. Though we cannot name these schools, we do want to acknowledge them. Their cooperation and willingness to provide information on their work, efforts and ideas form the foundations of this programme and we are indebted to them.

Similarly we want to note the efforts of the LEA staff who were involved. The School Development Advisers, Senior Educational Psychologists and Special Educational Needs Team Leaders not only supported the schools, but also gathered a great deal of the data we present in this book. Their observations and views, which they shared during programme development days, have helped to inform and shape the outcomes and conclusions of this research.

There are three individuals whom we also want to thank. Ann Davies of Essex LEA throughout the programme played a vital role in terms of supporting the Steering Group, maintaining communication channels between all the partners and ensuring that all loose ends were tied together. We also want to thank Ruth Naunton of Essex LEA and Rosemary Jones of Reading University School of Education whose secretarial skills ensured that the manuscript of this book was put together and completed.

Introduction

Geoff Southworth and Paul Lincoln

The Essex Primary School Improvement Research and Development Programme (EPSI) was a partnership between Essex Local Education Authority (LEA) and a group of staff who then worked at the University of Cambridge School of Education (UCSE). The programme aimed to enable schools to develop strategies for improving the quality of teaching and learning, to increase the LEA's capacity to support schools and to increase knowledge and understanding of the processes and outcomes of school improvement.

The EPSI programme was a three-year-long initiative, formally commencing in September 1995 and closing in the summer of 1998. However, there was a lengthy period of project negotiation and design that occurred during 1994–5 when it was provisionally agreed who would be involved and supported, and that we would simultaneously research the process of primary school improvement.

The programme had two main elements. One was to offer LEA staff a programme of professional development to enhance their knowledge of school improvement research and practice, to increase their awareness of primary schooling and to build multi-disciplinary teams. The latter was an innovative feature of the programme, since it was decided that support for school improvement should forge new coalitions of LEA staff. Programme Teams were introduced, comprising School Development Advisers (SDAs), Special Needs Support Staff (SNSS) and senior educational psychologists. By combining these three different groups, it was intended that the teams and their schools would have a range of expertise available to them and that this range would assist their professional development.

The second element centred on how staff in the participating primary schools worked towards improving the quality of teaching and the pupils' learning and achievements and how they were supported by the programme teams. One objective of the programme was to work with and learn from the schools' experiences in using performance data to improve school outcomes and processes. Consequently each school was required to collect and analyse assessment information. In addition to end of key stage data from Year 6 pupils, schools were invited to use the then newly introduced Year 4

1

assessments. Key Stage 2 pupils were the focus for the EPSI programme. This was because there were national and LEA concerns about this key stage and because the programme was specifically designed to support primary schools.

The emphasis on primary schools arose from a number of sources. The LEA in the early 1990s experienced the switch of many secondary schools (as well as some primary) to grant maintained status. Grant maintained schools became totally independent of the LEA and were thus self-governing as well as self-managing. Consequently, the balance of the number of primary and secondary schools in the LEA tilted even more strongly in favour of primary schools. Yet the majority of senior staff in the LEA were from secondary school backgrounds and many of the school development advisers also only had secondary experience, although they would now be working in many more primary schools. Such a distribution of experience is not uncommon in other LEAs. What it reflects is a wider, structural issue that ensures that at policy-making levels and senior positions in LEAs there is a predominance of colleagues with secondary experience over those with primary phase expertise.

We say this not to infer a sectarian outlook, nor to imply that cross-phase working cannot take place, but to recognize a structural bias in parts of the educational system and to argue that it needs to be addressed. Since 1997, central government's reforms have been focused strongly on primary schools and this emphasis looks set to continue. Therefore, it is important that staff in LEAs, as well as national policy-makers and their advisers, remain keenly aware of the implications of their reforms for primary schools and how they improve and prosper.

Primary schools are not little big schools. They are different organizational units, often working in different ways and, sometimes, adopting different emphases and practices from their secondary phase counterparts. For example, class teaching remains the main structural arrangement, rather than subject-based teaching. Primary schools do not enjoy curriculum-led staffing, but must manage on teacher–pupil ratios. Yet, since the advent of the National Curriculum, primary teachers have had to teach a subject-based curriculum, which requires them to command knowledge of nine subject areas and a volume of content that would challenge the most able of polymaths.

It is also true that primary schools have not been well served by school improvement studies, which have generally favoured secondary schools, despite evidence from the Office for Standards in Education (OFSTED) indicating in 1994–5 some concerns about Key Stage 2 that warranted closer examination. These concerns probably related to the overloaded content of the National Curriculum and the lack of subject teaching specialists in primary schools, but whatever the specific reasons for them, these points also generally supported the case for studying primary schools.

Therefore, one of the significant features of the EPSI programme is that it was a research and development project that focused on *improving primary schools*. It was primary school orientated and concentrated on how staff in the participating schools went about improving the pupils' learning processes and outcomes. Moreover, this research and development programme was undertaken at a time when the educational reforms of the late 1980s and early 1990s had been implemented in schools and were becoming institutionalized. The National Curriculum and mandated assessment arrangements, as well as the regular inspection of all schools by OFSTED inspectors, had, by 1995, become established. Thus the EPSI programme was able not only to support primary school improvement, but also to study school staff's efforts and views in the contemporary context.

This book reports on the EPSI programme and what it has to tell us about supporting primary school improvement. Our findings and ideas are presented in 10 chapters, divided into four sections. Chapters 1 and 2 comprise Part 1 and offer an overview of the programme and set out the main findings. Chapters 3, 4 and 5 form Part 2 and report on the insights we developed about school improvement. In Part 3 Chapters 6 and 7 focus on the insights relevant to the work of LEAs. Part 4 consists of Chapters 8, 9 and 10, which separately and together consider some of the relevant wider issues in primary school improvement. As a brief introduction to each chapter, these are now reviewed in turn.

Chapter 1 provides an overview of the programme, setting out the context, the aims, the programme's strategy and rationale and the questions we wanted to explore and investigate. The chapter also outlines the benefits we anticipated and briefly describes whether and how these were realized.

Chapter 2 presents the evidence we collected and shows whether and how school improvement took place in the 22 schools that participated throughout the programme. The chapter relies on three sets of data. First, a series of graphs show the improvements the schools made. These graphs rely on quantitative data. Second, we present in tabular form the improvement targets each school selected and whether these were achieved. Two sources of data provide evidence of achievement. At the close of the programme each head wrote a report to the LEA on their schools' work and success. The schools' programme pair – that is the two members of LEA staff who supported each school – also compiled a report, independent of the headteachers' report. Third, a sample of 10 schools were revisited by an OFSTED inspector who reapplied OFSTED criteria to the schools' improvement focuses and targets and judged whether the schools had made progress in meeting these targets. Given that a condition of participating in the programme was that each school had to have been recently inspected by an OFSTED team, we were able to gauge whether this sample of schools had moved forward since their original inspection report.

Chapter 3 looks at headship, leadership and school improvement. It reports on what the headteachers of the programme schools had to say about school improvement and identifies common themes and issues from their accounts. It emerges from the heads' comments that all of them used the formal and what might today be called the 'official' model of school improvement. However, some heads also showed an awareness of the need to simultaneously develop the teacher cultures in the schools. The chapter offers four main conclusions. Two relate to the need for a clear focus for improvement and school leaders to sustain that focus, while also keeping many other features of the school in view. The chapter also concludes that while the programme schools developed a strong emphasis on pupils' learning, less emphasis was being given to pedagogy. Moreover, though many heads were aware of the need to develop the teacher cultures in their schools, there were no unambiguous signs that this cultural development was understood as contributing to a focus on pedagogy.

Chapter 4 describes why and how the programme focused on pupil data. It describes the ways schools used the data and examines some of the emerging issues relating to pupil data. The chapter offers a summary of the key points learned from the process and also what issues remain as challenges for schools and the LEA in the effort to make evidence-based school improvement effective in primary schools.

Chapter 5 concentrates on the pupil perception data. At the start and at the close of the programme schools were encouraged to collect pupils' perceptions on their learning and teaching. This chapter describes how this was done, why it is important to do this and what was discovered from the data collected. The chapter closes with some ideas about how pupil perceptions might figure in future school improvement projects and their contribution to transformative education.

Chapter 6 explores the implications of effective LEA support to schools, both in terms of the EPSI findings and the national agenda for school and LEA partnerships and the LEA code of practice. The chapter focuses on how the LEA created multi-disciplinary teams to work with the EPSI programme schools and how they offered a diverse range of advice and support.

Chapter 7 examines the role of the external LEA consultant in school improvement. The chapter describes the models of consultancy adopted and applied in the programme. The key lessons for LEA staff and schools are highlighted and the implications for the deployment of staff are noted.

Chapter 8 addresses how school improvement might be evaluated. The success criteria adopted and developed for the EPSI programme are reviewed and it is argued that these may offer a useful schedule for schools and LEAs to adopt as a starting point. It is also argued that school improvement is a complex process and one that cannot be evaluated by any single measure, because it is difficult to isolate the influences that bring about change.

Chapter 9 reviews improvement policies and strategies in the light of the EPSI programme. In particular, the impact of the programme on Essex LEA is discussed. The research questions relating to the LEA's role are reviewed. One conclusion is that rigour and consistency are needed within each school, across the LEA and by LEA staff if an evidence-based approach to improvement is to become reliable and valid.

Chapter 10 presents the emerging themes, issues and major conclusions. The chapter opens with a review of the programme team's views. Then the main points that emerge about primary school improvement are set out and discussed. In the following subsection the main points relevant to the LEA's role are discussed. Next, the value of a research and development approach to change is presented in the context of current criticism of the value of educational research. Finally, the findings and conclusions are summarized. It is argued that the EPSI programme was a success and, since this coincides with central government's model for school improvement, this model is viewed as one that works, although there are six important riders to add to this. These additional points are then listed and explained. The chapter and the book closes with the observation that more research and development work is needed if we are to improve our improvement efforts over time.

There are four other points we wish to make. First, school improvement in Essex primary schools did not start with the EPSI programme, nor cease when it stopped. Schools were improving before the programme and continue to grow today. We do not wish to imply, as we discuss the particulars of primary school improvement, that the programme holds a monopoly on improving practice.

Second, what we offer is not a formula. The broad framework we designed and its congruence with the now national framework – which occurred more by coincidence than anything else – appears to be helpful and successful. However, frameworks need to be respectful of school backgrounds and histories and flexible to context-determined needs.

Third, this research and development programme tracked *over time* how staff in 22 primary schools tried to improve the pupils' learning. What we have to offer is not based on limited visits to the schools, nor on the simple case examples favoured by the DfEE and OFSTED of practice in schools. Rather, we can provide sustained and detailed pictures of these schools' efforts using evidence drawn from multiple perspectives (e.g. LEA staff, HE staff, OFSTED inspectors, headteachers and teachers). Moreover, the data we collected include both quantitative information (e.g. end of Key Stage 2 outcome measures, as well as reading tests and Year 4 data) and qualitative data (e.g. the judgements of headteachers, OFSTED inspection data, LEA staff judgements, pupil perceptions). In other words, we have a rich store of information on which to draw.

Fourth, this book is about *self-improving* primary schools aided by external support. Throughout the book we have tried to sustain this dual focus and to respect both the theoretical and practical issues that relate to school improvement. What is certainly true is that the LEA has applied many of the lessons reported here and has used the programme to inform its own development. The programme was always regarded as a practical approach and so it has proved to be. Moreover, the LEA has demonstrated that it too is an improving organization. One lesson we have learned is that school improvement is enhanced when it occurs in an improving and learning Local Education Authority.

Part 1

Overview and Main Findings

Chapter 1

Overview of the EPSI Programme

Paul Lincoln and Geoff Southworth

Introduction

In this chapter we will set out the background and rationale for the Essex Primary School Improvement (EPSI) programme. The chapter is divided into five sections. In the first section we discuss the context in which the programme was conceived, planned and implemented. In the second, we outline the content of the programme, setting out the programme aims and how the project was organized. Included in this section is a review of the research questions we sought to address during the life of the programme as well as at its conclusion. Following on from this in the third section we describe the LEA focus and, in the fourth section, the anticipated benefits. In the last section we briefly review whether the programme actually helped us to address the research questions and whether the expected benefits accrued.

The Context

The national context continues to change. From 1988 through to 1997, Conservative governments introduced legislation and put in place a set of arrangements that established schools as separate units, largely managing their own affairs and competing against each other for clients. It introduced accountability by establishing the National Curriculum, a system of regular inspections undertaken to a standard framework, and the publication of league tables based on test and examination results. Their view was that these processes in themselves would make public the performance of individual schools, and thereby bring about school improvement. From May 1997, a Labour government with priorities of 'education, education, education' has continued the drive to raise standards of achievement with a regime of plans and target-setting at national, LEA and school levels. LEAs have been given a clearer role as an operational arm of central government to monitor performance and intervene in 'inverse proportion to success'.

School improvement, therefore, is a major priority in education. Though pupils' learning has always been a priority for educators, the current emphasis upon school *improvement*, in contrast to the notion of school *development*, suggests a more specific and outcome-orientated concern. Currently there is broad agreement that school improvement means the raising of pupils' achievements, enhancing the quality of pupils' learning, developing the quality of teaching and increasing the effectiveness of schools. Understood in these terms, school improvement includes a strong focus on pupils' learning outcomes, as well as on the processes of teaching and learning.

While we now have some reasonably clear ideas about the characteristics associated with more effective schools, the picture is less clear about how schools actually get to be like that. Two of the more influential factors in improving schools are the quality of teaching and the leadership provided by senior staff. It is also clear that establishing the organizational conditions that support innovation and development is important (Ainscow, Hopkins, Southworth and West, 1994a). Evidence from a number of studies demonstrates the importance of creating and sustaining 'moving' schools (e.g. Fullan, 1993; Fullan and Hargreaves, 1992; Hopkins, Ainscow and West, 1994; Nias, Southworth and Campbell, 1992; Rosenholtz, 1989). In moving schools a number of important workplace characteristics enable staff to manage successfully their improvement efforts and to learn with and from one another. Moving schools also appear able to draw upon external help and advice.

Yet, generally, much of our knowledge and understanding of how schools improve has not been systematically developed or updated in terms of the contemporary scene. Previous studies of school effectiveness and improvement have tended to work with those schools that already have the motivation and capacity to improve. Much of the emphasis now is on how to improve poorly performing schools with little or no capacity to move forward. The strategies required for these schools are likely to be very different. If our understanding of school improvement is somewhat unclear, it is further clouded by uncertainty about how recent changes in education have altered the nature and character of school improvement.

In addition, with a few exceptions such as 'Schools Matter' (Mortimore et al., 1988), much of what we know about school effectiveness and improvement is based on secondary school experience. At a point in time when the major challenge around raising achievement levels focuses on primary schools, there is little research on primary school improvement to inform and/or challenge policy and practice. It is important to understand how primary schools improve, because they are significantly different from secondary schools. Indeed, developing the quality of teaching in primary schools, with their commitment to class teaching, may be a quite different matter to enhancing the teaching of subject specialists in secondary schools.

Outline of the Programme

Such questions and concerns prompted the EPSI programme. The EPSI programme was initiated in September 1995, after many months of discussion, preparation and planning within the LEA, and between the LEA and colleagues at the University of Cambridge School of Education (UCSE).

The EPSI programme was a three-year-long initiative. It started in September 1995 and ended in the summer of 1998. The programme was designed as a collaborative venture involving staff from 22 primary and junior schools, the LEA's school development advisers (SDAs), senior educational psychologists, team leaders from the special needs support service, and lecturers from UCSE. All who were involved supported and simultaneously researched the process of primary school improvement. During the first year, LEA staff completed a programme led by UCSE lecturers focusing on research on school improvement, which provided a forum for team building. For each school, two LEA staff known as the 'programme pair' provided external support throughout the project. The pairs were clustered by geographical areas to enable broader teams to work together to provide support to one another and, sometimes, to encourage closer working between two or more schools.

The programme aims were to:

1   enable schools to develop strategies for improving the quality of teaching and learning provided for all pupils;
2   increase the LEA's capacity to support schools as they seek to improve the quality of education that they provide;
3   increase understanding of the processes and outcomes of school improvement.

For each of these aims, targets and success indicators were identified (see Appendix 1), and project data were related to each of the targets. The data were used to inform schools' future development, document the process of school improvement and explore the relative effectiveness of different measures in describing the process and outcomes. We defined school improvement in terms of pupils' learning outcomes. Using the data formatively therefore involved staff in schools in considering what the data suggested about effective strategies for improving pupils' learning. Schools were required to identify a 'focus' area, related to one or more key issues identified in their inspection reports, which addressed aspects of teaching and learning to pursue as their main improvement target. All 22 participating schools were recently inspected prior to participating in the programme, and the programme focused on Key Stage 2. Therefore, the schools that participated were either primary (JMI) or junior schools.

The programme established a Pupil Data Working Party to coordinate the collation of data. The working party comprised staff from the LEA, UCSE and a seconded headteacher. The working party was responsible for developing a strategy to encourage teachers individually and collectively to focus on pupil progress and act on the information on outcomes. In addition, the working party considered ways of evaluating the impact of the programme on the pupils, and of developing a longer-term strategy for evaluating school improvement. School staff, the programme teams from the LEA, and the university lecturers carried out data collection.

A Steering Group, which met regularly, managed the EPSI programme. The steering group included the Director of Education, the Principal Adviser (School Development), the Principal Educational Psychologist, the Senior Manager of Special Needs Support staff, Principal Inspector and two staff from UCSE. All members of the steering group were involved in analysing the summative data from the programme. These data included:

- the perceptions of staff in school, school governors and the programme teams as to the value and pertinence of the programme to them;
- staff and programme teams' views on whether the schools they worked in or with had improved;
- pupil learning outcome data, collected in January 1998, which were contrasted with the same types of data collected at the start of the programme;
- teacher assessment data; and
- pupil perceptions.

As has been made clear elsewhere (see Sebba and Loose, 1997; Southworth, 1997), a number of different types of data were collected and analysed so that the processes and outcomes of the schools' improvement efforts could be examined through a number of lines of enquiry and from a range of different perspectives (LEA, school staff, pupils, governors, university lecturers/researchers). In other words, the EPSI programme had many sources of evidence that could be used to examine and judge school improvement, and used multiple perspectives on the outcomes of these schools' improvement efforts, the LEA's support for the schools, and the quality of the insights the research strand of the programme had to offer.

From the outset, EPSI was a research and development programme. At a time when the value of much educational research is being strongly and rightly criticized because of its lack of impact on teacher practice, we believed that the model we adopted would help us to create an effective bridge between research and practice.

The programme deliberately aimed to develop:

- schools, by helping staff to enhance pupils' achievements;
- a data-driven approach to school improvement, which included action planning, establishing a clear focus, and target setting;
- teachers as researchers through their collection and analysis of Key Stage 2 pupil data; and
- LEA staff in terms of their understanding of what is currently known about the processes of school improvement, primary phase issues and using outcomes measures.

A vigorous debate was encouraged throughout the programme within the steering group, the teams of LEA staff, and the schools themselves, which brought about continuous learning.

The focus upon primary schools and, in particular, Key Stage 2 pupils, arose from a lack of interest in this phase of education in recent years. Though interest has been growing in baseline assessment and value added in Key Stage 1 and in the secondary sector, little work appears to be focused on Key Stage 2, yet it is here that recent inspection reports have identified some causes for concern.

The programme enabled us to investigate the following issues and questions as they related to the schools:

1 *What use do the schools make of pupil and school data?*

   Each school has collected starting point or programme entry data which include: pupil perceptions, reading data, pupils' writing data, a school conditions rating scale, as well as the OFSTED inspection report and the school's action plan.

2 *Whether and how such data lead to enhanced enquiry and reflection among the teaching staff?*

   Are staff, individually and collectively, looking more carefully at pupils' progress, achievement and learning gains? If they are, what are the consequences of this evidence-based enquiry and action research? If they are not, what are the reasons and/or explanations for this inaction?

3   *What are the characteristics of the schools' action plans?*

How well developed and sophisticated are the schools' approaches to action planning, target setting, the framing of success criteria, the implementing of classroom developments, and the monitoring and reviewing of progress?

4   *What emphasis is placed upon improving pedagogy?*

How do class teachers and senior staff interpret their evidence-based analyses of pupils' learning? Are connections made between what the pupils appear to be achieving and the pedagogic actions of teachers? In other words, are discussions about pupils' learning related to teachers' classroom practices? What monitoring of teaching is taking place in these schools?

5   *Has the OFSTED inspection motivated staff in these schools?*

What has been the teachers' response to the OFSTED inspection report and the main findings? How do the teachers describe its influence upon themselves and the school's development?

6   *What other significant features emerge?*

While we could anticipate some issues, we needed to leave scope for other issues to emerge. Although from the outset we could label some of these features, the precise nature of how they may play out in the schools was unpredictable. There may be some important school 'givens' that may need to be explored. These givens are characteristics previously established and rooted in the school, which may enable, or impede, the success of an individual school's improvement plan (e.g. experience and qualifications of staff; existing school policies, in particular, whole-school policies for teaching and learning, or policies for monitoring/use of subject coordinators; use of time; inter-staff communications, e.g. meetings, working groups; a school's previous experience in managing change; stability of staff group/turnover of teachers; the existence and presence of a 'culture of achievement' in the school).

By using these six focuses, we intended to develop a start-point picture of each school, to record and track what happened inside each of these schools, to gauge the pace and scale of improvements in each school (through the eyes of the staff, the perceptions of the programme teams and by using end-of-programme analyses of data and comparing them with the start-point data), and identify the barriers and drivers of school improvement both inside and outside these schools.

The LEA Focus

Essex LEA initiated the EPSI programme because it wanted to explore the potential of an LEA's role in school improvement within a national context that has been and continues to be ambivalent about the role of LEAs. The Essex commitment stemmed from its belief that if an LEA is not about improving learning for all then it has no reason to exist.

Through the programme the LEA wanted to reflect on and examine the following questions:

- How can an LEA best support schools in their improvement efforts?
- How can the focus on an individual pupil's learning and the focus on whole-school development processes complement each other?
- Can an LEA engage all schools in a systematic and cumulative programme of improvement?
- What sort of capacity and skills does an LEA require to achieve this?
- How can this work be 'built into' the normal activities of a school and an LEA rather than be seen as a 'bolt-on'?
- How can LEA staff from different professional backgrounds combine to support school improvement?
- How can pace and a sense of urgency be maintained at the same time as recognizing that school improvement takes time?

Anticipated Benefits

At the outset we anticipated the following benefits from this programme:

Benefits to Schools

- Inform the needs of pupils in Key Stage 2 in order to enhance learning.
- Help schools interpret the inspection report and develop action planning skills.

- Examine and develop the value of school inspection action planning and the implementation of the plan.
- Develop 'tool kits' for schools to enable them to make greater use of pupil data.
- Essex schools will have a major research programme resulting in coherent approaches to school improvement.
- The methodology will be available to all Essex schools.
- Opportunities for further professional development will be available to staff in participating schools.

Benefits to the LEA

- The school development advisers (SDA) team will develop consistent approaches to supporting school improvement in all schools.
- SDA team development will be enhanced.
- Special Educational Needs managers and staff in the LEA will have the opportunity to examine individual pupil progress in the context of the whole school and curriculum development.
- The benefits of the programme team approach will be evaluated.
- Opportunities for further professional development will be available to the programme team.
- Research findings will be disseminated widely among Education Department staff and schools.

Did we find answers to the research questions and were these benefits realized?

Two of the purposes of this book are to present our responses to the research questions and to describe whether the EPSI programme realized all the benefits we anticipated at the outset. In the following chapters we will explore our research findings, what the programme has to offer in terms of enhancing our understanding of primary school improvement and discuss in detail whether and how the programme benefited the schools and the LEA. In this section we can offer a flavour of the issues the programme has highlighted and the benefits that accrued from the programme, and sketch out what has proved more elusive to focus on and develop. We will begin by returning to the six questions we sought to address during the programme. Then we will present our views about the benefits that we believe the programme has provided.

1 What use did the schools make of pupil and school data?

It is clear, As chapters 3, 4 and 5 make plain, that the schools did make use of a range of information. Across the schools there was a range of practices that made use of performance data, and overall, all of the participating schools introduced or developed an evidence-based approach to school improvement. This marks a significant step forward not only in school improvement, but also in primary education.

Until recently, primary schools were, very generally and perhaps stereotypically, associated with a more process orientation to learning. The shift to include a 'product' orientation, through attention to pupils' learning outcomes, gains and progress has been underway for several years. Though it would be untrue to claim that the EPSI programme was solely responsible for such a shift of emphasis in the participating schools, there is sufficient evidence to warrant the claim that the programme supported, accelerated and extended this development in all the schools.

All the schools made use of pupil and school data. Some concentrated on National Curriculum levels and end of key stage assessment data. Others made use of reading test information and other test data, which they had been using for some time anyway. The writing data were seen as most valuable in those schools that gave priority to literacy projects. One general finding was that the schools valued the emphasis on Key Stage 2 and, more specifically, the attention to Year 4. All heads, along with ourselves, appreciated that Key Stage 2 was (and is) the longest key stage. It was clear to many that something was needed to bridge the time between Year 3 and Year 6 and that additional learning data was essential to enable staff to track pupils' progress throughout Key Stage 2, rather than just at the beginning and towards the end. All the schools were provided with Essex LEA value-added information and this helped most of the headteachers to look at pupil and school performance more closely than formerly.

It was also true that none of the senior staff accepted the data uncritically. It was clear from the teachers' and headteachers' comments that they saw these data as providing a partial picture of children's learning, rather than conclusive knowledge. Assessment and learning information was a helpful aid, but many questioned its validity and reliability.

The school conditions rating scale data provided some schools with a helpful audit of the school's capacity to improve, but few senior staff appeared to focus strongly on this information. Nor did many return to it later and reapply the rating scale to gauge whether and how their schools might be developing as organizations. One reason for the scales being used in a limited way was that the steering group offered them as a support rather than as something more substantial or necessary. Also, the school development advisers often took responsibility for administering them and analysing them and, though this was a sensible approach, it may have had the effect of blocking senior staff's feelings of ownership of the information.

2   Did the data enhance enquiry and reflection among the teaching staff?

The short answer to this question is yes! Though understandably staff were critical of some data, overall the use of learning outcome data gave staff, especially senior staff, much to think about. Without doubt the data enhanced reflection in these schools. Moreover, since the data were themselves often the result of teacher-led enquiries, they also increased the amount of monitoring and review taking place in the schools.

Chapters 4 and 5 in particular explore this question and between them they show three points. First, that collecting data, though an important task and one that needs to be conducted with care and diligence, is not as big a challenge as enabling staff to analyse data. Teachers undoubtedly need help in analysing performance information. Second, and following on from the first, not only do teachers' skills of analysis need support, but attention needs to be paid to how teachers and headteachers respond to these data. As is shown in Chapter 4, before analysis can be embarked on, teachers need to have dealt with the emotional impact of the data. Rejection and resistance to data are not uncommon responses. Within schools, a climate of readiness is important, otherwise the benefits of using data and of conducting classroom enquiries may be thwarted. Third, pupil perspective data proved to be particularly powerful information in some schools. The growing emphasis upon involving pupils in school improvement was shown by the EPSI programme to be as valid in primary schools as in secondary schools.

3   Characteristics of Schools' Action Plans

An analysis of 21 schools' inspection reports and action plans (Sebba and Loose, 1996) showed two related points. First, the action plans the schools had produced generally did not explicitly emphasize changes in teaching and learning. Second, and one reason for the first point, the OFSTED inspectors' list of key issues for action were not expressed as changes sought in teaching and learning. The inspectors' comments sometimes lacked clarity and precision, which made it difficult for senior staff and school governors to know with any certainty exactly what the school needed to do.

It was also the case that most schools did not express their success criteria for actions in terms of improvements in pupils' learning. Rather, the action plans judged success by the completion of tasks. These difficulties are not peculiar to schools in Essex LEA. Other analyses of post-inspection plans have shown similar weaknesses in schools elsewhere.

A positive characteristic of the EPSI programme and schools in the post-OFSTED inspection phase of improvement was that the programme enabled staff in the schools to monitor their progress and success in implementing their action plans. The programme pairs (made up of school development advisers and senior educational psychologists or special needs support staff) were able to draw attention to how the schools were proceeding with their action plans and many senior staff in the participating schools commented favourably on these additional perspectives.

4 The Emphasis Placed on Pedagogy

During the programme there was a strong emphasis on using evidence, monitoring pupils' learning outcomes and progress, classroom observation and school-based enquiry and reflection. These emphases were promoted and further developed by the programme pairs as they worked closely with their respective schools. Moreover, most schools were commencing work in these areas. For some, such developments were major changes in the schools' practices. For example, introducing monitoring by curriculum leaders was a significant change in itself in several schools. Similarly, the introduction of classroom observation was a considerable innovation in a number of the schools. Such changes altered the nature of teacher interaction and unless there were previously well established patterns and norms of teacher collaboration they needed to be introduced with care and managed sensitively by senior staff.

In other words, the emphases upon enquiry and evaluation of pupils' learning required changes in the teacher cultures in several schools. Changing teacher cultures is a major process in itself. Yet, the EPSI programme also aimed to change not only the nature of attention paid to learning, but also to pedagogy. The programme sought to enable staff not only to examine pupils' learning gains, but also to begin to identify what changes in teaching might be undertaken to better meet the children's learning needs.

There was only limited evidence that the latter attention to pedagogy was achieved in some schools. Several heads said, when interviewed, that they were working towards this emphasis themselves, but within the time-scale of the programme they had not accomplished this. Implicitly these and other heads saw this emphasis as a medium- to long-term goal. One explanation for such a seemingly distant time horizon is that dealing with learning data was a sufficiently challenging task to be going on with.

Another reason is that changing teachers' pedagogy was tacitly acknow-ledged to be a task requiring very careful management and leadership and was best conducted when organizational conditions had been developed and the teachers' culture made more amenable to investigating pedagogy.

5 Did the OFSTED inspection motivate staff in these schools?

The answer to this question is complex and the findings that relate to it are dispersed across a number of the chapters including 3, 8 and 9.

Most of the headteachers regarded OFSTED as a factor in their schools' improvement efforts. Those heads who saw the OFSTED inspection as im-portant or very important tended to be leaders of schools whose perform-ance was lower than other programme schools. The other heads did not see the inspection process as revealing anything they had not already been aware of, although some felt the confirmation of their perceptions was helpful.

However, given previous comments about the lack of clarity in the articulation of key issues for action in some of the schools' inspection reports, it is also true that the process may have caused some uncertainty. In common with many others, a number of headteachers felt the process had been very time-consuming and had depleted staffs' energy levels.

It also seems that the inspection itself had not been particularly motiv-ating for most schools. What appears to have been as important, if not more so, was how the headteacher and senior staff used the inspection report as an audit of the schools' strengths and development needs.

6 Other Emerging Features

Here is not the best place to identify these. Many emerge in the subsequent chapters. Also, in Chapter 10 we will highlight these and discuss them in greater detail than we could here. Therefore, readers interested in finding out about them should refer now to that chapter.

Turning to the benefits, we grouped these under two headings – benefits for schools and to the LEA. We will discuss the benefits under these two headings.

Benefits to the Schools

The programme did deliver all the benefits to schools we anticipated at the outset. However, it remains an open question whether the programme did this to the levels everyone expected or hoped for. Some staff in some schools undoubtedly hoped for greater benefits than they experienced. Three reasons can be given for this state of affairs.

First, the programme was probably over ambitious. We make no apology for this, because we wanted to raise levels of achievement and knew that to do this we needed high expectations.

Second, it is now clear from the outset that the steering group should have provided more and clearer information about the programme and tried to resolve some of the questions that colleagues in schools wanted answering. There are many reasons why we were unable to be as clear as some wanted, but certainly some participants' hopes were not always well matched to what the programme was actually aiming to do and how we were going about realizing these goals.

Third, when the programme was starting, most primary schools had only just come to terms with the fact that they were self-managing organizations and several still looked to the LEA for direct guidance. Yet this programme marked a further move for schools in that it paved the way for them to become self-improving institutions. At the time of embarking on the programme, this idea was only just being introduced. It is only in the past two years that the idea has been made explicit that it is schools who are responsible for their improvements. Therefore, many colleagues in schools (as well as in some parts of the LEA's service agencies) were only just becoming aware of this development and what it meant for their roles. Consequently, some colleagues probably applied to the programme ideas and expectations that were becoming outmoded and that were inconsistent with the programme's rationale.

As for the specific benefits listed earlier, we can briefly offer our views on each in turn. The programme certainly helped schools to examine the needs of pupils in Key Stage 2 and the schools did enhance their pupils' learning and achievements.

The programme pairs and SDAs worked closely with staff in school to help them interpret their inspection reports and develop action planning skills. Numerous instances of this took place and many headteachers were grateful for the skill and support these pairs and individuals offered them. Also, as noted above, we have examined the value and use of school inspection action planning and been able to provide some insights to strengthen the process.

The LEA is now developing some 'tool kits' for schools, which draw extensively on materials developed during the programme. These tool kits enable schools to make greater use of pupil data. It is also worth adding that the IT software package developed by the LEA was warmly received by the programme schools, who were among some of the first schools in

the LEA to use it. This package, though not a product of the EPSI programme, is nevertheless an example of how the LEA is more generally
meeting the needs of schools as they develop an evidence-based approach
to improvement.

The EPSI programme was a major project within the LEA's portfolio
of research. It contributed to the LEA's knowledge base about school
improvement and has played a part in developing the LEA's strategy of
becoming a research-based organization. The methodology of the EPSI
programme has been made available to all Essex schools through the work
of SDAs, the use of the 'tool kit' and the more general orientation towards
school improvement across the LEA.

Benefits to the LEA

Before considering these it is worth noting that when the schools have
benefited from the EPSI programme, then by definition so too has the LEA,
because the schools are an integral and large part of the LEA. The EPSI
programme was formative for the LEA in developing our approaches to the
effective use of pupil data in primary schools. As such, it has had a major
and powerful impact on what we do.

The more specific benefits set out earlier in the chapter were that
the SDA team would develop consistent approaches to supporting school
improvement in all schools. There is evidence that the programme provided
both focus and time for SDAs to share approaches and practice and that, as
a result, greater consistency and a stronger sense of teamwork is now in
place. One outcome is that we are now producing protocols, for example,
around the SDAs' role with schools on target-setting in order to clarify
expectations.

Special Educational Needs managers did have the opportunity to
examine individual pupil progress in the context of whole school development. They valued highly the professional development opportunities this
provided. The Director has built on this success by ensuring that advisory
and SEN staff work together regularly now on a range of activities.

The benefits of the programme team approach were evaluated and this
process showed that not only did LEA staff value this way of working, but
so too did many of the schools. Again this has caused us to provide more
opportunities for multi-disciplinary working as part of our normal practice.

Opportunities for further professional development were available for
the programme team. Some individuals embarked on, or were already
engaged in, higher degree programmes. Others chose not to undertake formal CPD work. However, it is worth noting that the initial development

programme for LEA staff (SDAs and Learning Support managers) was itself an important part of professional learning, as were the feedback sessions held during the programme. Moreover, the very processes of working in partnership with colleagues provided opportunities for peer learning. Indeed, there is considerable evidence that this kind of on-the-job research and development is much more influential on staff practice than 'off-the-job' development opportunities.

In the following chapters these benefits and many other ideas and insights are identified and discussed. It was clear when we set out on this programme that there was much to discover and explore in terms of improving primary schools. This undoubtedly proved to be true for all of us, whether we work outside schools or inside them. What now follows tries to capture and record some of the lessons we have learned about school improvement. We begin in Chapter 2 by setting out the main findings.

Main Findings

Pete Dudley, Tina Loose and Geoff Southworth

Introduction

In this chapter we present the main programme findings. As will become clear in the following chapters, the EPSI programme generated and made use of a wealth of data. From the outset each school's OFSTED inspection report was available as a start-of-programme review of the schools' strengths and weaknesses. Also, all schools were asked to collect assessment data on pupils' reading ages, to use the newly introduced Year 4 assessments and to apply a writing test, which some of the SDAs developed specifically for EPSI. Furthermore, the schools were required to administer the annual end of key stage assessments and these data were available to us and the schools to use to evaluate school progress and performance.

Qualitative data were also collected throughout the programme. Members of the steering group interviewed headteachers and teachers, chairs of governors and the programme teams to gather in their respective views on the schools' improvement efforts and success. School condition rating scales, developed from the IQEA project (see Ainscow et al., 1994a) were used in many schools, as were pupil perception data. At the close of the programme some schools were also revisited by a freelance OFSTED Registered Inspector to judge whether there had been improvements in the school according to the OFSTED criteria. Headteachers were also asked to complete an end-of-programme report on their schools, as were the programme teams.

Some of these data are reported in specific chapters in the book, so we have not included them here. In Chapter 3 the headteacher data are discussed. In Chapter 5 the pupil perception data are examined, and in Chapter 8 a careful analysis of several sources of data is presented in order to consider what they have to say about tracking and evaluating school improvement.

In this chapter we have restricted ourselves to the following data sets:

- end of key stage data;
- the headteacher and programme pairs' reports on whether the schools achieved their targets; and
- the re-application of OFSTED criteria to a sample of schools.

We have limited the discussion to these findings because they offer three different but complementary perspectives on the schools' improvements. Together they show that the EPSI schools did improve and that most made significant progress. These findings are most noticeable in the first section of this chapter (Quantitative data findings), where the graphical data show the scale of improvement in the schools and how these compare with other schools.

The qualitative data in the second and third sections of this chapter also show that the schools improved, but here the picture becomes more differentiated and complex. The range of school targets is set out in the second section and the strategies and approaches adopted by the schools described in the headteacher and programme pairs reports. This section shows the variety and breadth of activity even in a relatively small sample of schools.

At the start of the EPSI programme 25 schools agreed to participate. At the close of the programme 22 schools remained. Those that did not complete the programme were schools where there was a very high staff turnover or a change of headteacher, which caused such discontinuities that it was unhelpful to continue or because the governors and parents elected to adopt grant maintained status.

The sample of schools, whether at the start or close of the programme, covered a range of school types, sizes and locations. The smallest school had 47 pupils, the largest 488. The schools were a mix of county and denominational (Church of England and Roman Catholic) and located in urban, suburban and rural settings and communities. Some schools had very low percentages of pupils eligible for free school meals (e.g. 2.8%, 3%, 3.4%) while others had far higher numbers (e.g. 61%, 45%, 43%).

Quantitative Data Findings

This first part of the chapter summarizes quantitative school performance data from the end of Key Stage 2 national tests in English, mathematics and science.

The data are from the 22 schools that completed the programme. Each school had a very different starting point, certainly as judged and reported by OFTSED inspectors. The sample contained high-attaining and low-attaining schools, schools that were successful and schools that were coasting or struggling. One school was judged at the time of its inspection to require special measures and two were judged to require much improvement in several aspects. A further three were also causing some concern at the outset of the programme.

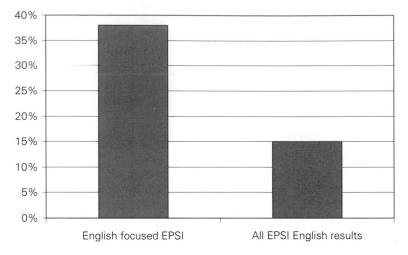

Figure 2.1 Increases in gains in EPSI schools, as a percentage of gain in all Essex schools 1995–8

This section will detail the following points:

- the overall performance of the EPSI schools in the end of key stage tests for 11-year-olds;
- how gains made by EPSI programme schools in the end of key stage tests for 11-year-olds compare with the gains made by other schools in the LEA;
- how gains made by groups of schools with improvements focusing in similar areas of learning compared with all EPSI schools and all LEA schools.

We will then go on to detail some of the more qualitative school-level data.

The findings show that in the three subjects of English, mathematics and science, EPSI programme schools performed as a group ahead of other LEA schools in the end of Key Stage 2 tests for 11-year-olds. The participating 22 programme schools adopted a variety of improvement focuses often related to management or particular groups of learner rather than curricular focuses, but when the results of the programme schools with a clear focus on literacy or mathematics are considered separately, the gains are significant. For instance Figure 2.1 shows the gains in pupils achieving level 4 and above in Key Stage 2 English tests made by all EPSI schools alongside EPSI schools *with an English-based focus* as a percentage of the 17 per cent overall gain made by all Essex schools during the same period.

Analyses were made during the first two years of the programme, which controlled for differences attributable to term of birth and gender and affluence profiles of a wider sample of Essex LEA schools that included all 22 EPSI programme schools. Consequently, it is possible to make comparisons using these 'value added' scores. In these analyses, the EPSI group of schools perform significantly ahead of other schools in the sample.

The combined average level for the three core subjects rises for EPSI schools slightly (0.1 level) ahead of all Essex schools. (One National Curriculum level currently represents over two years' progress.)

During the two terms immediately following the close of the programme, schools set formal targets for attainment of 11-year-olds in English tests and mathematics tests. These targets tell us something about expectations and confidence of schools. They show that programme schools were targeting to make progress well ahead of the rate of LEA schools in mathematics and at the same rate as LEA schools in English between 1998 and 2000, preserving the gains built up during the programme.

Detailed Summary of Programme School Performance Data

Eleven-year-olds in England first took end of Key Stage National Curriculum Tests in the summer of 1995. The overall national results of these first tests were published, but school-by-school results were not published, as happened in subsequent years with the publication of performance tables.

Since 1997, the results of National Curriculum Tests and teacher assessments of 11-year-olds in English, mathematics and science have been published in performance tables. The results of these tables form the basis of much media coverage locally and nationally. School inspection reports are also published. Between 1994 and 1998 every primary school in England was inspected by OFSTED.

Schools have generally found that the performance tables have not been very helpful. Many have experienced large rises or falls in the two sets so far published at the time of writing. These variations are due to the fact that the percentages quoted in the tables may be based on a year group cohort size of no more than 11 pupils. (Where ten or fewer pupils are in the cohort the school's results are not listed in the public tables in order to protect the identity of individuals.) This is true of a number of schools in the programme. (See school by school data in Table 2.4.)

The following information summarizes the performance of EPSI programme schools collectively and individually over the three years from May 1995 before the programme began to May 1998 after the programme closed. The year 1995 may be regarded as a baseline. The formative work with EPSI schools was going on between 1995 and 1997 when schools were identifying their focuses and drawing up and implementing action plans. Most schools continued to work on their focuses for the 1998 academic year, but with the same support as all other LEA schools.

It can be seen later in this chapter that the focuses schools identified were diverse, stemming from their inspection reports. Many focused on requirements to improve monitoring and management and as such were linked with pedagogy and learning outcomes indirectly. Thus, the results for pupils in English, mathematics and science that follow are only directly related to the schools' improvement focuses in some cases. Data is provided for those programme schools that had a direct link with performance in English (11 of the 22 schools) or mathematics (3 of the 22 schools). No schools focused particularly upon science. Because these results focus upon test scores, the results of assessments of pupils' investigational and applied skills development are not reflected.

Results for English

Figure 2.2 shows the gains made by the 50 per cent of EPSI schools with an English-based focus and the gains made by all EPSI schools compared with the gains made by all Essex schools over the same period (1995–8).

Over the four years from 1995 to 1998 the percentages of pupils in EPSI programme schools attaining level 4 and above, rose by almost 20 per cent. These gains were a little ahead of the gains made by schools in the LEA as a whole and schools nationally.

The moves in the percentages of pupils at level 4 and above in the 11 EPSI programme schools that had a focus aimed at improving English were from 38 per cent in May 1995 to 63 per cent in May 1998. This is an

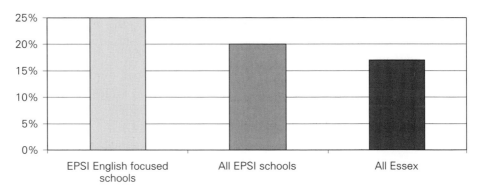

Figure 2.2   Gains in percentage of pupils at or above level 4 in KS2 English tests for 11-year-olds

*Table 2.1   KS2 English tests, EPSI pupils and Essex pupils,
percentages attaining level 4 and above*

	EPSI	Essex
1995	47%	48%
1996	58%	56.1%
1997	64%	62.9%
1998	67%	65.1%

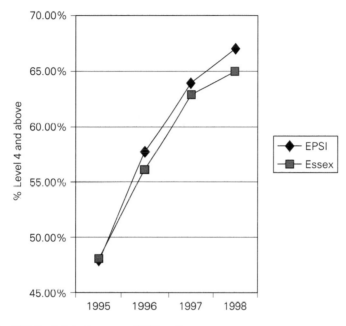

Figure 2.3   KS2 English test scores: EPSI v. Essex

increase of 25 per cent over the three years, representing a gain 5 per cent
ahead of EPSI schools and 7 per cent ahead of all Essex schools.

The percentages of pupils attaining level 4 and above for the EPSI
schools compared with the averages for the whole of the LEA are given in
Table 2.1 for each year.

Figure 2.3 shows the results for 11-year-olds in English for EPSI
schools compared with the results of other Essex schools. It can be seen
that the EPSI sample in 1995 was slightly (1%) below that of the LEA.
Over subsequent years the EPSI schools made small gains ahead of the
gains made by LEA schools. The overall gains made by the total pupils
in EPSI schools in English were around 3 per cent ahead of the gains made
by Essex schools.

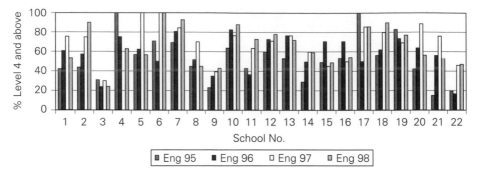

Figure 2.4   EPSI schools KS2 English test results 1995–8

Figure 2.4 shows the performance of individual EPSI schools over the three years from May 1995 to May 1998.

Mathematics Results

Pupils in EPSI schools also made steady gains each year and the total gains were a little ahead of those for the LEA overall (Table 2.2). The total gain over the four years for EPSI schools was 17 per cent. This is 1 per cent ahead of the 15.9 per cent gain for the LEA over the same period. EPSI schools did not suffer the same reversal in attainment as did LEA schools and national results in 1998 (Figure 2.5).

Figure 2.6 shows the performance year by year for the individual schools in the programme.

Three schools in the programme had a focus particularly relating to mathematics. Their performance was ahead of LEA schools and reached higher attainment than other EPSI schools. The schools started from a base-line of 62 per cent at level 4 and above in 1995 – 20 per cent above the all-EPSI baseline. Attainment at level 4 and above rose in these schools by 11 per cent over the three years with a 1998 percentage at 73 per cent – 15 per cent above the Essex 1998 percentage and 13 per cent above the EPSI 1998 percentage.

Table 2.2   Percentages attaining level 4 and above in KS2 Mathematics tests

	EPSI	Essex
1995	43%	42.2%
1996	54%	53.1%
1997	60%	61.4%
1998	60%	58.1%

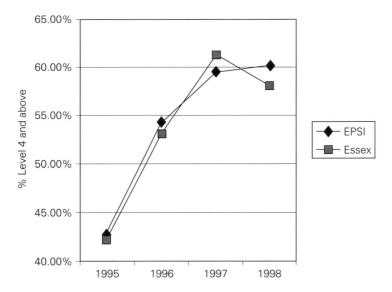

Figure 2.5   KS2 Mathematics tests: EPSI v. Essex

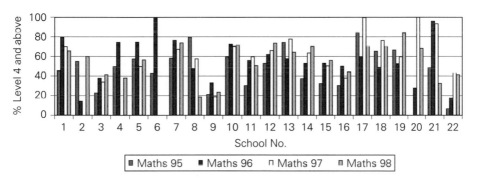

Figure 2.6   EPSI schools KS2 Mathematics test results 1995–8

Science scores

Despite beginning the process only half a per cent above the LEA average 1995 percentage, the gains made by pupils in EPSI schools were 3 per cent ahead of those made by the rest of the LEA.

Table 2.3   KS2 Science tests, total EPSI and Essex pupils attaining level 4 and above

	EPSI	Essex
1995	69%	68.70%
1996	67%	60.10%
1997	71%	66.90%
1998	72%	68.70%

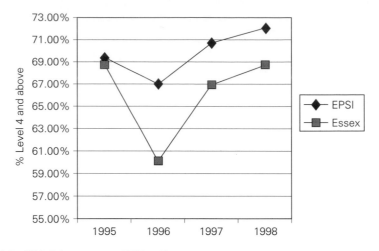

Figure 2.7   KS2 Science tests: EPSI v. Essex

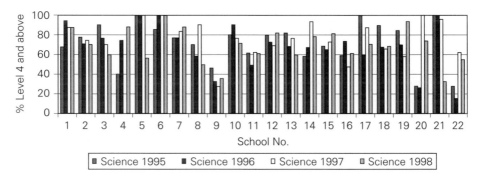

Figure 2.8   EPSI schools KS2 Science test results 1995–8

It should be noted, however, that the attainment in the science tests has not been uniform. Nationally 70 per cent of pupils attained level 4 and above in 1995, 60 per cent attained that level in 1996, and in 1997 and 1998 69 per cent of pupils attained level 4 and above (Figure 2.7).

Figure 2.8 shows the performance over the three years of each school in the programme.

Essex School Improvement and Value Added Network Data

In 1996 Essex LEA began to provide primary schools with contextualized analyses of these data both for the performance of 11-year-olds and for the performance of 7-year-olds. These analyses were intended to help schools

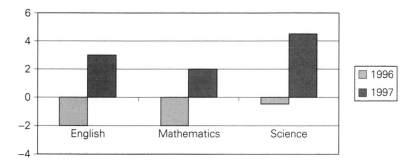

Figure 2.9 EPSI schools 'value added' 1996–7

use the 'raw results' data. The national tables of results list the percentages of 11-year-olds in each school attaining National Curriculum level 4 and above in each of the three subjects. Schools found these tables unhelpful in evaluating performance, as they took no account of a range of external *given* factors that affect pupil progress.

Contextualized analyses have been found helpful by schools because they are based on the average levels of all pupils, not only the percentages attaining and above the level 4 threshold. They also take account of the effect of certain 'givens' – most notably the effect of deprivation as indicated by the percentage of pupils entitled to receive free school meals, the effect of the term of children's birth and the proportion of boys and girls in the cohort. These data are only available for the years 1996 and 1997. Figure 2.9 shows programme schools moving over these two years from a position in 1996 below what would be predicted from the sample when account is taken of the background factors, to a position broadly above in each of the three core subjects.

Point 0 on the vertical axis represents the 'predicted' attainment for each school once account has been taken for affluence, gender and term of birth factors. The zero point on this axis represents the point at which a school's actual results match those predicted by the model accounting for the external variables. A score below 0 is lower than would be predicted by the model and a score above 0 indicates performance above that which the model predicted.

Improvement of Schools in Difficulties

The one school requiring special measures made good progress on its focus and key issues during the time intensive LEA support was provided. Pupils' attitudes to learning also improved. However, the improvements were judged by HMI not to be sufficiently sustained by the school when support was withdrawn. The school was closed in August 1998. Attainment in English in the two schools requiring much improvement rose significantly – 38 per cent in one school and 20 per cent in the other – but attainments in mathematics and science have been more variable. Teaching has been judged to have improved in both schools, although recruitment and retention of staff in one – a school struggling to succeed in difficult circumstances – has proved difficult. Only one of the schools causing concerns was continuing doing so by the end of the programme.

Overall Summary

In the three core subjects the results of EPSI schools are consistently, though not dramatically, seen to rise in advance of LEA schools. The progress in the large proportion of schools with an English focus is significant. In mathematics the improvements are more marginal. The schools focusing on mathematics in the EPSI sample were starting from a point significantly (20%) above the EPSI baseline and therefore it is to be expected that the gains would be less dramatic. Few EPSI schools had a mathematics-based focus and it is therefore to be expected that the gains in mathematics might be lower than in English in which half the schools had a broad focus. In two years there were dips in performance in Essex schools – 1996 in science and 1998 in mathematics – but EPSI schools did not dip in line with the LEA schools. The value added indicators also indicate improvement in all three subjects for EPSI schools ahead of LEA schools. There is also a gain in the combined average level for the schools, but this is very marginal.

The EPSI process was not geared to any specific curriculum area. Many schools had a focus geared towards management improvements or meta-cognitive cross-curricular learning issues, which would not be expected to impact immediately on test scores. The data would certainly seem to indicate no specific areas suffered as a result of the EPSI focus, as all indicators showed gains of one order or another. It is also worth noting that EPSI schools Key Stage 1 results showed no significant change during the programme.

Although these gains are in no way dramatic, overall we should be satisfied that, consistently, gains were made against the agreed range of indicators, and where the improvement focuses were in areas more directly addressed by the indicators, the gains were more notable. It is probably true that some of the changes brought about by EPSI activity will only become apparent in test data later on. The true test of EPSI's success will be the degree of continued self-improvement of schools for some time after the interventions of the programme have ceased.

Qualitative Data Findings

In addition to the quantitative data, we collected a wealth of qualitative information about the schools, including each school's OFSTED report, school brochures, interview data from headteachers, teachers, governors and the programme teams and pairs. We also collected pupil perspective data, observed classrooms in some schools, made formal field notes and reports on the schools and invited the headteachers and programme pairs to complete end-of-project reports. Taken together, this amounts to a great volume of information, far too much to include in this book. Therefore, we have had to be very selective about what to include here.

We have chosen in this section to include summaries of each school's specific EPSI targets and the comments the headteachers made at the close of the programme as part of the headteachers' final report (Table 2.4). Three schools did not complete the form. In two of these schools this was because the headteachers had left the school in the preceding term and the acting heads did not feel able to complete them.

When completing their forms, the headteachers were aware that the programme pairs would also be making their independent assessments of the schools' improvement efforts and success. Therefore, after reproducing what each head had to say about her or his school's improvements, we have included what the programme pair had to say, since this acts either as a validity check, or shows differences in judgements. There are no programme pair reports for three schools. Various factors account for this. During the programme there were personnel changes within the LEA because of promotions and the creation of unitary authorities. In addition there were also some absences because of ill health. These factors combined in the case of three schools to such an extent that it was not possible for a viable report to be compiled.

Some of the following details also show what the schools focused on, since much of the data presented here illustrates the schools' project targets and how they worked towards them in a variety of ways. Thus quite a lot of what follows provides some details of what the programme looked like in the schools. It is also worth remembering that many of these schools were simultaneously working on other school-based developments. Therefore, what follows is by no means a full record of the schools' improvement activities.

Table 2.4 EPSI improvement targets
SCHOOL 1 Number of pupils: 229 Percentage eligible for free school meals: 10

EPSI improvement targets	Extent to which targets were met? Headteacher's comments:	Programme pairs' report:
To improve the role of the curriculum coordinators in supporting improvements in teaching and learning. Re-evaluating assessment, recording and reporting procedures, including the marking policy to improve teaching and learning.	The role of the coordinator changed significantly during the project. All teachers have a clear idea of their role in relation to other members of staff and are developing both a confidence in supporting other teachers and in ways of researching effectiveness of teaching, children's attitudes and learning. We have introduced a clear structure for their role with systems for financial control, reporting to governors and influencing the school's development plan. The evidence for this change is not easily quantifiable and it is too early to discern impact on children's achievements. However, there is evidence of a culture change in the school, a willingness to collect data and interpret results, a greater confidence about the role of coordinator and a reaffirmation of the importance of the work they do in relation to their subject. There has been greater enjoyment in developing the work and much has been achieved by individuals. However, it has to be said that the future development of this work is being hampered by lack of funds. The only non-contact time available to the teachers is when the headteacher takes the class. The budget is so tight that presently the headteacher covers for the first three days of a teacher's absence and when teachers attend courses. It has therefore not been possible for the coordinator role to be further developed and the situation will be more difficult in the next academic year when the headteacher will have a part-time teaching responsibility for a class. Assessment work is still in progress and will not be complete for some time. We have introduced pupil self-assessment, subject coordinators are working on banks of assessment tasks related to the learning objectives identified in our taught curriculum. We are using assessment data to inform planning. We regularly moderate examples of children's work from each class. We routinely test reading and mathematics each year and analyse the results, looking for trends, gender or teaching group bias, as well as individual attainment matched against teacher assessment and expectations. We are introducing non-verbal tests for Years 3 and 5.	The school has met its EPSI targets to a considerable degree. They have developed a model for a successful coordinator's role and have been re-evaluating assessment, recording and reporting procedures in the school.

Table 2.4 (cont'd)
SCHOOL 2 Number of pupils: 63 Percentage eligible for free school meals: 3

EPSI improvement targets	Extent to which targets were met? Headteacher's comments:	Programme pairs' report:
Developing independence in learning, alongside improving the quality of teaching and learning, improving pupils' behaviour – especially at lunchtime – and developing an assignment book.	We have taken a more structured approach in reviewing policies. Staff have been aware of the need for review and responded positively. Work on pupil behaviour with staff and MDAs has been most beneficial – success criteria indicate very few poor behaviour incidents at lunchtime. The assignment books allowing pupils to record, evaluate and reflect on their work have been positively used by most children and their families. We have set strategies in place to continue our improvement since we always saw the project as a start.	The school has made sporadic progress against the targets. Initially there was significant progress in pupils' levels of independence. During the following year little further progress.

Table 2.4 (cont'd)
SCHOOL 3 Number of pupils: 197 Percentage eligible for free school meals: 43

EPSI improvement targets	Extent to which targets were met? Headteacher's comments:	Programme pairs' report:
Improve teachers' planning and increase teachers' expectations, matching more closely pupils' ability and providing them with more challenge.	N/A	Staff have now adopted systems for medium and long term planning and there are improvements in consistency and continuity throughout the school. This has been noted by ourselves, during a school review visit and by HMI in a follow-up visit to the school's inspection. HMI said in their report: 'Good progress has been made. A thorough and manageable system is now in place and it is used well by all teachers. In the majority of lessons learning objectives are clearly defined and followed. 'The headteacher scrutinises the teachers' weekly plans and their evaluations of previous lessons. Work is now planned for pupils of differing ability and appropriate support is given when needed. . . . Planning ensures continuity and progression of the curriculum throughout the school. All staff meet together to do long term planning. The subject co-ordinators are able to oversee the quality.'

Table 2.4 (cont'd)
SCHOOL 4   *Number of pupils: 29   Percentage eligible for free school meals: 0*

EPSI improvement targets	Extent to which targets were met? Headteacher's comments:	Programme pairs' report:
Overall to identify, develop and improve the independent learning skills of all pupils, with a focus on Key Stage 2 and Years 4 and 5 in particular: *Target 1*: to improve the ability of pupils in Years 4 and 5 to select appropriate resources from the library independently. *Target 2*: to improve the ability of pupils to select, locate and return resources appropriate to the task. *Target 3*: to develop the skills of pupils as listeners. *Target 4*: to identify and develop the skills required by pupils to work collaboratively.	*Target 1*: met – children were assessed individually on a range of tasks before and after the project. *Target 2*: partially met. *Target 3*: progress made – observations were used initially to establish to what extent pupils listened/took part. We have made pupils more aware of the need to listen and how to show they are listening. They enjoy circle time activities, show they are listening, summarise instructions and main points of discussions. The class teachers' observations and comments from visitors show that listening skills have improved. *Target 4*: A lot of progress has been achieved – We started with a questionnaire to establish the children's point of view about group work and identified from this the key areas for development: 1. Composition of the group; 2. Leadership of the group; 3. Time management; 4. Allocation of tasks. Evidence from observation of activities, pupils' views and teachers' comments is that there has been a big improvement in the pupils' ability to work as a group.	N/A

39

Table 2.4 (cont'd)
SCHOOL 5   Number of pupils: 71   Percentage eligible for free school meals: 14

EPSI improvement targets	Extent to which targets were met? Headteacher's comments:	Programme pairs' report:
Focus never clearly established beyond developing pupils' research skills.	Change of headteacher, unable to complete end of project report.	Conditions rating scale completed. Good OFSTED report, 1996. School looked, to a limited extent, at independent learning. Pair observed pupils' research skills – these judged as good. 2.5 teachers + head; KS1 teacher left during project; sudden death of KS2 teacher in mid-project. Plus headteacher resigned Easter 1997.

Table 2.4 (cont'd)
SCHOOL 6 Number of pupils: 47 Percentage eligible for free school meals: 15

EPSI improvement targets	Extent to which targets were met? Headteacher's comments	Programme pairs' report:
To increase pupils' independence as learners.	I would regard our school to have largely achieved our target. Evidence for success can be found in pupils' work samples evaluations by staff, Governors and HMI. Pupils now work well in groups, individually and as a whole. Pupils regularly monitor their own progress in achieving targets set by themselves, they are enthusiastic learners who have developed good research skills and are much less adult-dependent than witnessed in the OFSTED inspection. Evidence of gaining reflection and independence can be seen in pupil perceptions and half-term evaluations, as well as tracking progress in literacy skills.	Through the six monthly HMI visits and LEA monitoring of the school, as part of the special measures support, there have been clear progress checks against the focus issues. When the school was provided with active SDA support, for four days each week the school made progress, as acknowledged by HMI. When this support was withdrawn the school was unable to sustain the improvements and this was noted by HMI and the LEA. The pupils have had a range of teachers, one of whom has been constant – the headteacher. During a period of extensive professional support the pupils' attainments and independence has significantly developed.

Table 2.4 (cont'd)
SCHOOL 7   Number of pupils: 421   Percentage eligible for free school meals: 5

EPSI improvement targets	Extent to which targets were met? Headteacher's comments:	Programme pairs' report:
To focus on the needs of the more able pupils in mathematics.	The provision itself has been improved, both in material and human resources and in organisational structures and techniques. Year 6 SATs results were improved in Maths, in terms of those pupils scoring above level 4, despite a cohort perceived to be of generally lower ability [1996 results: 77%; 1997 results: 84%]. Headteacher observation and interaction with more able pupils indicates conceptual development of pupils has improved.	The school has met with some success in meeting its improvement targets. The focus has been applied across both key stages, but the evidence shows that the impact has been more marked in Year 6 than in other groups, using evidence from the programme adviser's observations and pupil interviews.

Table 2.4 (cont'd)
SCHOOL 8 Number of pupils: 169 Percentage eligible for free school meals: 19

EPSI improvement targets	Extent to which targets were met? Headteacher's comments:	Programme pairs' report:
Raising standards in reading. Developing and extending parental involvement.	Improvements in SAT results from 1995–1997 [enhanced attainment in English, maths and science]. Writing data shows an improvement in writing over a two year period. Year 4 pupils attaining higher scores than Year 4 pupils in 1995. Reading test data shows improvement in Reading Ages over Chronological Ages. Value added data indicates a trend of improvement in all core subjects but especially in English and science	Significant rise in the levels of achievement in pupils' reading scores against their chronological age for the majority of pupils across both Key Stages. Increase in the proportion of pupils gaining higher level SATs scores in all subjects, particularly English. Quality of pupils' work improved in terms of presentation skills, technical accuracy, fluency of writing, quality of work produced. Increased parental involvement in supporting children's learning and their understanding of the curriculum, particularly the focus areas of language and reading.

Table 2.4 *(cont'd)*
SCHOOL 9 *Number of pupils: 198 Percentage eligible for free school meals: 38.4*

EPSI improvement targets	Extent to which targets were met? Headteacher's comments:	Programme pairs' report:
English: reading and writing. Behaviour management. In particular to raise self-esteem of pupils and staff; to improve planning and assessment; to involve the school community in teaching and learning; to use data to track progress; to set targets for improvement.	English: reading ages level with or above chronological age have increased by 6% between September and December 1997, following the introduction of a structured 45 minute, daily reading session. Self-esteem and morale of staff has increased, although there has been a 50% change in the teaching staff. Through training in behaviour management staff confidence has increased. New behaviour policy and anti-bullying policy appear to be showing a positive rather than negative approach to behaviour. Data from value-added project shows a picture of enhanced attainment.	Staff were slow to change, but the 50% turnover of staff has led to improvement. Headteacher is using data to track progress, target setting is helping to focus teaching, but uncertain how far this is influencing staff in raising expectations. Improvements in writing less certain and secure than those in reading. Pupil behaviour appears better and staff self-esteem has risen.

Table 2.4 *(cont'd)*
SCHOOL 10 *Number of pupils: 214   Percentage eligible for free school meals: 2.8*

EPSI improvement targets	Extent to which targets were met? headteacher's comments:	Programme pairs' report:
The establishment of more consistently good quality teaching throughout the school. Targets include: agreed common vocabulary to describe good teaching; teachers to use more open-ended questions in core subjects; children to become more independent learners and reach higher standards.	We feel we have developed through training and our policy for teaching a basis for a common language. The expectations we have laid down are central to the quality of teaching and learning. Some monitoring strategies are in place and where staff are not applying consistency of practice (e.g. classroom organisation, or direct teaching strategy) they are being asked to comply. I feel intuitively that there is some more open-ended work going on because I have seen and heard teaching discussions. No hard evidence about the independent learning except I know from examining pupils' work and classroom observation that children in two Key Stage classes are producing higher quality work than previously.	Overall the school has worked to achieve its target of establishing more consistency in good quality teaching across the school. It has achieved some success in that the main strategy for achieving this has been paired classroom observations by teachers which has led to an awareness of the need to have a shared language for what constitutes good teaching. Teachers were asked by the head to write their reflections and thoughts on the EPSI programme. All staff have been positive about classroom observation and their comments demonstrate what an effective strategy it has been to stimulate reflection on their own quality of teaching. The analysis of the writing data developed a more specific focus to raise the quality of teaching. Staff used the information from the writing task to focus on the development of creative writing and teachers planned and were observed by their peers implementing lessons for creative writing.

Table 2.4 (cont'd)
SCHOOL 11 Number of pupils: 337 Percentage eligible for free school meals: 25

EPSI improvement targets	*Extent to which targets were met?* *Headteacher's comments:*	*Programme pairs' report:*
Coordinator development and reading in Key Stage 2. The targets were: that the coordinator role be understood and accepted by all teachers; a pilot group be set up; in-service training in monitoring and evaluation for coordinators and governors; monitoring and evaluation be carried out and reported.	All staff now involved in monitoring and evaluating progress. Four coordinators were trained and supported others. Reports are being prepared for the governing body. The reading target has yet to be assessed by testing.	There has been some evidence of improvement. The school agreed whole staff teaching and learning indicators which form the backdrop for classroom observation. After considerable INSET and focus from the programme pair observations were carried out by 3 coordinators. Reports of progress were compiled and presented to the governors. These reports were not focused particularly on levels of attainment or progress and there was only incidental reference to the agreed classroom teaching and learning indicators. The 1998 conditions rating scale shows a significant improvement on the 1996 one in terms of the senior managers' perceptions about coordination, but only a slight improvement from the point of view of the teachers. There is evidence of increased monitoring of pupils' progress in that the headteacher is using the Hertfordshire reading test and National Curriculum Year 4 assessments.

Table 2.4 (cont'd)

EPSI improvement targets	Extent to which targets were met? Headteacher's comments:	Programme pairs' report:
		There is evidence of considerable improvement in the 1997 NC English results from 36% in 1996 to 63% in 1997.
		Attitudes in the school remain fixed, although there are signs of the school being influenced by outside thought – there has been attendance on INSET by senior coordinators and the deputy is in the first NPQH cohort. Signs of improvement in terms of coordination and enquiry and reflection.
		Reviewing the range of efforts and support to develop the school over the last 2 years it seems that not much has been taken up by the school which seems to have viewed EPSI as a school improvement 'course' rather than a supported school self-improvement programme.

Table 2.4 *(cont'd)*
SCHOOL 12 *Number of pupils: 488 Percentage eligible for free school meals: 7.6*

EPSI improvement targets	*Extent to which targets were met? Headteacher's comments:*	*Programme pairs' report:*
Teaching of maths.	Held a maths week to raise awareness of mathematics across the curriculum. Carried out two surveys of all children to gather evidence about their attitudes to maths scheme of work we have produced. Maths policy has been written and monitoring of maths in place.	Scheme of work for maths established and being implemented. Consistent use of short-term planning format. Recognition among staff of need to improve assessment procedures and practices. No assessment data available as yet.

Table 2.4 (cont'd)
SCHOOL 13 *Number of pupils: 206   Percentage eligible for free school meals: 10*

EPSI improvement targets	Extent to which targets were met? *Headteacher's comments:*	*Programme pairs' report:*
To improve teaching and learning in Key Stages 1 and 2 to ensure that pupils have appropriate opportunities to experience investigational work in mathematics.	The headteacher left the school in December as the programme drew to a close in the following Spring term. No headteacher report was submitted.	Staff interpretation of what constitutes investigational work has altered over time. Initially some of the investigations were 'bolted on' activities. More recently staff have recognised that a vital ingredient of genuine investigational work is that it involves a degree of problem solving and discovery which is in part or totally independent of teacher support.

From an analysis of the observations of the investigational work across the school and from staff discussions it is evident that pupils' approaches to investigational tasks have improved. They are less intent on finding the right answer and more willing to try different approaches.

Evidence from the pupil perception questionnaire indicates that pupils have a clear understanding of the advantage of collaborative work and their roles within. |

Table 2.4 (cont'd)
SCHOOL 14 Number of pupils: 178 Percentage eligible for free school meals: 17

EPSI improvement targets	Extent to which targets were met? Headteacher's comments:	Programme pairs' report:
To improve standards of achievement by increasing the range and repertoire of appropriate teaching skills and learning strategies, including pupils' ability to learn independently.	Consistency of approach is evident from classroom observation, short and medium term planning, in-service training, monitoring of learning, regular evaluation of specific learning objectives and the purchase of appropriate resources. We have also drafted a teaching and learning policy. Shared understanding of standards and progression evidence through classroom observation, evaluation of teachers' plans by the headteacher, staff meetings to evaluate outcomes and agree appropriate assessment criteria. Independent learning takes place in all year groups.	The EPSI targets have all been met. The school has developed a clear system for describing, planning, monitoring and evaluating pupil learning. The teachers regularly review pupil learning outcomes and each other's teaching in order to identify areas for improvement and to share best practice. This was developed through paired observation. Targets for individual pupils have been set. Evidence from pupil perceptions, staff perceptions, and harder data such as value-added data all indicate that the school has increased its capacity to improve, and the commitment of pupils to achieve and their awareness of achievements have improved. The school's end of Key Stage 2 assessment outcomes over the past three years reveal a dramatic upward trend.

Table 2.4   (cont'd)
SCHOOL 15   Number of pupils: 59   Percentage eligible for free school meals: 3.4

EPSI improvement targets	Extent to which targets were met? Headteacher's comments:	Programme pairs' report:
For pupils to know how well they are doing, for them to reflect on their learning and to have a positive attitude to their work.	Children are more independent in the classroom. They are able to select their own materials and resources and are less dependent on the teacher. There is more group work and collaborative planning. Children are planning and taking assemblies, are more confident, articulate about their work and have enthusiasm and motivation towards their work. Children are more closely monitored. Teachers' planning includes teaching strategies and differentiation. The reward system is one children respond to and children are taking more pride in their work so that the level of presentation is now much higher.	The school has had a great deal of success in meeting the targets set as shown by the pupil perception data, classroom observations of teaching and learning, the school conditions rating scale, observation of pupils' behaviour and teacher attitudes. Two different collections of data from the pupil perception survey show that over a period of two years pupil attitudes have improved. Their understanding of the learning process and their part in this has developed. They realise they have a responsibility towards their own learning which they did not realise before. They believe it is their place to comment on and criticise their own and others' work 'to help them'. Classroom observations showed teachers' planning, classroom organisation, displays, use of resources, comments to groups of pupils and individuals to aid learning, strategies to encourage thinking, questioning, the setting of individual targets. Praise and assessment procedures were either now in place or improved. The ethos of the whole school has changed over two years.

Table 2.4 (cont'd)
SCHOOL 16   Number of pupils: 226   Percentage eligible for free school meals: 61

EPSI improvement targets	Extent to which targets were met? Headteacher's comments:	Programme pairs' report:
To raise the standard of the teaching of English.	As a school we found the follow-up support at the end of the first stage of the EPSI programme to be unfocused. This left us with a great deal of information and no visible means of moving forward. We had to look beyond the support structure of the EPSI programme to find direction and advice on how to move forward. As a staff group we have adopted the National Literacy Strategy and are building a scheme of work for English around that. The enthusiasm of the staff towards this whole school way of working, planning and evaluating is in itself a success indicator, but at the moment, apart from continuing to collect samples of children's work we have not collated any further evidence.	N/A

Table 2.4 (cont'd)
SCHOOL 17 Number of pupils: 229 Percentage eligible for free school meals: 3.6

EPSI improvement targets	Extent to which targets were met? Headteacher's comments	Programme pairs' report:
Meeting individual needs [SEN]; key issue 4 in the OFSTED Inspection Report.	We fully met our first target insofar as the SEN register in 1995 contained 69 pupils and the 1998 register contains 26. SEN support is now largely classroom based. Withdrawals are rare. Teachers and SENCO planning show evidence of support for SEN pupils for a range of targets. A review of existing resources has been undertaken and the audit showed reliance on one published scheme. Financial limitations have prevented provision of some resources for SEN but priority list exists for future expenditure. The IEPs show targets are being set for a range of needs, not just literacy. The SENCO involves older pupils in target setting and evaluations. Plans to develop this with more able pupils in the future.	1. Significant Development – teachers in KS2 use assessment information to identify targets. Children are involved in the process. Differentiation is evident in planning. 2. Fully developed – Key indicators used to inform planning – the staff have levelled the learning outcomes against benchmarks, to raise expectations of attainment. 3. Evidence of increased attainment only at the end of KS2 not in KS1 and only in English at KS2. Evidence of raised achievement mostly in English for the cohort of children (Year 4 at beginning of project – current Year 6). See data on Reading scores, Writing tasks, Maths etc. There has been a real focus of management and staff as to why the dip in performance and this remains an issue. HT has completed sociograms and monitors the performance of children in Years 3 and 4 very closely. New teachers in this phase and a change in organisation of leadership indicate some progress here.

53

Table 2.4 (cont'd)
SCHOOL 18 Number of pupils: 317 Percentage eligible for free school meals: 37.9

EPSI improvement targets	Extent to which targets were met? *Headteacher's comments:*	*Programme pairs' report:*
To identify and establish strategies to develop pupils' independence and responsibility.	We feel it is too early to quantify to what extent the improvement targets have been met. This is due to the way our EPSI adviser tried to establish a means by which hard evidence could be gained and then analysed using software packages. Our judgement about the level of success is based on changed attitudes, perspectives and approaches by both pupils and staff which we feel begin to show the improvements in learning outcomes we hoped would be the result. We do not feel we have met the improvement targets throughout Key Stage 2. The focus began in Years 3 & 4 and certainly there are signs of success there. We also feel our current Year 5 who started the project as part of the Y 3/4 team are reflecting behaviour and learning patterns we can attribute to the EPSI programme.	N/A

Table 2.4 (cont'd)
SCHOOL 19 Number of pupils: 71 Percentage eligible for free school meals: 19.7

EPSI improvement targets	Extent to which targets were met? Headteacher's comments:	Programme pairs' report:
The targets were: To improve the children's abilities to tackle writing unaided. To encourage improvement by setting individual pupil targets following a half-termly piece of writing.	The EPSI programme was on hold when I arrived in the school because staff were unsure whether the new headteacher would want to be involved. I decided to take the opportunity that the project offered. We have examined pupils' writing in staff meetings, teachers have looked at their practice and we have developed a new English scheme of work. As a key area to develop staff decided to set individual targets for pupils, which would then be reviewed by the teacher and child and new targets set. This process has been uncertaken and the children's writing is improving. Judgements are based on the level descriptors and the marking key used in the SATs.	Targets relating to raising pupils' standards in writing have been met. Evidence comes from the EPSI writing tasks which show pupils improved. Also confirmed by classroom observation.

Table 2.4 (cont'd)
SCHOOL 20 Number of pupils: 149 Percentage eligible for free school meals: 45

EPSI improvement targets	Extent to which targets were met? *Headteacher's comments:*	*Programme pairs' report:*
Raising standards of achievement by pupils across both key stages with particular emphasis on reading and writing. Raising the quality of teaching by improved systems of planning, monitoring and recording. Refine systems of data collection.	The headteacher left before the report was issued.	The EPSI targets lacked precision and are difficult to quantify. The quality of teaching has improved, based upon my judgements in visiting the school over a period of time. However, teaching is still characterised by a lack of pace, continuity and challenge. Planning, recording and data collection systems have been introduced, largely through our efforts. The new headteacher will move forward on this.

Table 2.4 (cont'd)
SCHOOL 21 Number of pupils: 31 Percentage eligible for free school meals: 38.5

EPSI improvement targets	Extent to which targets were met? Headteacher's comments:	Programme pairs' report:
Writing standards – teaching and learning.	An assessment package for writing has been developed and put into practice. We have used it to identify pupils' learning needs. Not yet a part of all teachers' practice. Yet to see any major improvement in writing attainments throughout the school. However, 1997 SATs results up by 20%. Reading ages improved on average and compare favourably to previous results. New coordinator using test data to track progress made every six months in each class.	Initial analysis of Year 4 writing task data identified concerns in the teaching and learning of writing. New schemes of work introduced in September 1996. Regular biannual assessment of all pupils now established. There have been many changes in leadership and a radical change in school organisation. SATs results show significant improvement 1996–7.

Table 2.4 *(cont's)*
SCHOOL 22 *Number of pupils: 260 Percentage eligible for free school meals: 30*

EPSI improvement targets	*Extent to which targets were met?* *Headteacher's comments:*	*Programme pairs' report:*
Develop target setting. Increase the percentage of Year 2 and 6 pupils reaching levels 2 and 4 respectively. Reduce the dip in attainments noted in Years 3 and 4 by OFSTED.	An increase in the percentage of pupils achieving level 4 in Year 6; from 62% to 83%. The dip in achievement in Years 3 and 4: we know from data analysed that Year 3 in 1996 was a problematic cohort. Working in a focused way, their English and mathematics have shown improvement – but the important target of being able to identify low achievement has been achieved. We are now better placed to respond to information about improvement.	Significant development – teachers in Key Stage 2 use assessment information to identify targets. Children are involved in the process. Differentiation is evident in planning. Evidence of increased attainment at the end of Key Stage.

OFSTED Revisits to a Sample of EPSI Schools

Each of the schools was visited at the close of the programme in the summer term 1998 by an OFSTED registered inspector for between half a day and one day. In some cases the OFSTED registered inspector was assisted by the school's long-term school development adviser and in other cases by a newly appointed school development adviser, thus providing additional time for the review of the school's progress. In some instances the assistant was also an OFSTED registered inspector. In two cases the registered inspector had been the original registered inspector for the OFSTED inspection and in five other cases the registered inspector had been following the progress of the school through a range of roles. This role had necessitated previous visits to four of these schools. There had been no direct contact with five of the schools prior to the revisit.

Because of the limited time available for each revisit, it focused in some schools on aspects for which we had limited data. In others the time was used to corroborate the evidence offered by other data sources. In all instances there was a detailed discussion with the headteacher or staff who had been highly active in the improvement programme. In half the schools substantial Key Stage 2 classroom observations were undertaken. In two other schools in-depth discussions and review of children's work took place. In the remainder more modest classroom observations and discussions with pupils and other staff were made to confirm the reported outcomes and clarify certain issues. Documentary evidence relating to improvements was also scrutinized. These included, for example, materials devised to increase parental interest and involvement in the children's learning, materials to support new approaches to assessment, detailed records of data and their analysis and tools produced by schools to help them research areas of personal importance.

In one of the schools where substantial classroom observations were undertaken, the quality ranged from satisfactory to very good, with the achievement culture of the pupils varying in the classes visited. There was evidence of some very high quality work going on with pupils reaching high levels of attainment. There were, however, some inconsistencies in the experiences of pupils, which were partly as a result of staff changes and the introduction of the literacy strategy training, which appeared to be deflecting work from the focus. There was evidence of substantial improvements brought about by target-setting involving staff and pupils. This was supported by a move towards more careful differentiation of work in relation to set targets. Some very careful assessment work undertaken as a closely focused longitudinal study of individual pupil progress represented one of the successful ways staff were using assessment to inform future planning.

This school had successfully addressed a range of tasks associated with its chosen focus and had raised end of Key Stage 2 English test results.

In three of the five schools where substantial lesson observations were made, all lessons were at least good in quality, with a number being very good. This was matched by very high quality learning experiences for the pupils, who had very good attitudes. They made obvious progress in the lessons, sometimes at a rapid rate, and often had above-average levels of attainment in the areas being addressed. Although in each case the schools were focusing on different matters, for example independent learning, raising attainment of high-ability pupils or increasing the range of teaching skills, improvement was not confined to this area. Discussions suggested that this was partly because some aims could not be achieved without effort on a wider front and in some cases because the improvement in one aspect influenced others. The observations and other evidence in these three schools demonstrated the improvements and consistently high quality practice that can be achieved when the right areas are targeted, the best mix of people come together, they are encouraged to work as a team and they are committed to success. Some of the other schools might well have had the same degree of success had they not had some clearly identifiable factor, often beyond their control, that interfered with their progress and therefore their success.

In the fifth school in which substantial classroom observations occurred the practice was wide-ranging with there being some significant teaching weaknesses. However, the programme had been of value to at least one person, who had come to understand better the key features of good quality teaching and significantly improved the quality of both teaching and learning within the classroom. In other classes the teaching and learning observed ranged from unsatisfactory to satisfactory, with both strong and weak features in the latter. There was less evidence of a whole-class achievement culture than found in some of the other schools. Other observations, carried out by school staff, describe positive teaching and learning. Though in some respects this was confirmed, it was the lack of clear identification of weaknesses and action needed to address them that may have resulted in less progress than the school would have wished for. A shift in focus during the programme appeared to have also reduced the rate of progress.

In some of the other schools, brief classroom observations were carried out. Some situations were satisfactory and many more were at least good. In these schools the focus was on the changing views of the staff and the responses and competencies of the pupils in relation to the chosen focus. These showed a similar range of responses to those from schools where more time had been spent on classroom observations. Discussions were held with pupils in six schools and these concentrated on their improved skills and what they recognized as improvements to their learning and teaching over the period of the programme. In all cases they were highly conscious of changes and the benefits these had brought to their learning. Their comments covered such areas as setting in groups, being forced to take leadership roles, working collaboratively, being prepared to seek help, having more opportunities to extend their skills, for example in ICT, having parents more involved in their work, school projects to improve standards in specific areas, knowing the levels of their performance and knowing how long it took them to make specific gains in reading. Some also commented eloquently about the improvements to teaching and their teachers' skills.

Discussions with staff indicated differing understanding and appreciation of the programme. In a few cases staff really did not have a grasp of EPSI or how it had influenced the school. One expressed this in terms of a lack of sharing of valuable information that might benefit all the pupils.

Not all schools felt that the external help had been as valuable as it could have been, as they felt that their agenda and that of their external supporters were slightly different. A few felt that they had been manipulated, although it may have been due to lack of confidence on both sides concerning what they were doing and where they were going. Some schools felt they had been extremely well supported by some external help while others felt much of the progress had been made on their own. There appeared to be little correlation between the amount of progress made and the degree to which they felt supported from without the school. They could all identify significant benefits for school improvement of one kind or another from the programme.

Most had found the opportunities offered by the conferences for some staff and governors to be valuable. However, early on, one headteacher found this aspect 'profoundly disappointing', with the accompanying governor having 'no idea what they were talking about'. Though this school had made some good use of the programme, the strong comments using terms such as 'bitter resentment' and 'angry' relating to deadlines and subsequent exclusion from another project because of inclusion in this programme, seemed to link to some of the problems experienced in getting the programme underway and through to a satisfactory conclusion. The climate and conditions for success appeared to be weaker in some schools than in others.

Some schools felt that they would need, in the future, to set more precise success criteria when embarking on a project so that they could measure success in terms of learning outcomes. Others felt that, without the support of EPSI, they eventually would have made the same progress but at a slower rate. Some felt it had given them greater power to move the school forward and a few felt that they now had new skills to help them address school improvement in the future. A few would have valued greater links with schools pursuing similar aspects of school improvement. A number had produced tools to help with measuring where they were, so that their actions could be more appropriately targeted. In the main, greater value was now placed on pupils' views of the school and their learning experiences and a number of the schools had taken these views into account when planning action. The pupils valued this respect shown to their views.

Involvement in the programme appeared, overall, to encourage teachers to be more considered and thoughtful about aspects of their work other than the focus. This was clearly articulated by almost all the staff who were interviewed. Some teachers realize that although they have made great progress, there is still much to be done, especially for those who have found improvement most difficult. The most successful schools in the sample appeared to have moved to a position where there was a unified and agreed understanding of what constitutes good quality learning. They had also established what contributes to this, for example good quality teaching, understanding progression and assessment and appreciating the importance of an achievement culture where expectations are high. Using the initial OFSTED report against which to judge the outcomes of the revisit, it is clear that for some of the schools the teaching and learning have dramatically improved over the time of the programme. For others there has been good progress. In a few there has been some progress but not as much as was expected, with an occasional fall-back in some aspect of their development.

These revisits to schools highlighted the wide range of conditions needed for effective school improvement and the fact that in one school something may succeed while in another it may not. Personalities have a powerful part to play, as do the basic teaching skills and capacity and will for improvement of all the players. A respected leading school improvement figure with an intelligent understanding of change and the tools that can be used to bring it about seem to be key features. Single features such as an individual member of staff can seriously hamper achieving consistency in the improvement area. Change of staff in such a situation can radically improve the rate of improvement, while in others it can hamper it. Strangely, however, there was an example of a school having made good progress in spite of almost total staff changes. Only a part-time teacher remained and she was initially the least involved teacher, but she competently carried the work through to bring about marked improvement in the target area. The fragility of improvement cannot be underestimated where staffing plays such a crucial role. Whatever a school pursues in order to underpin good quality teaching and learning, the final key rests with the quality of the teacher. The provision he or she makes, in the light of all the improvements, for the children in his or her daily care is part of the key. This was clearly demonstrated on the revisits to the schools.

Overall, all schools had developed, with some making limited progress, and in others the improvements were stunning. In these cases all the right conditions had come together or been fought for in a dedicated effort to improve opportunities for children in their care. Their starting points had been different at the time of their OFSTED inspection. A few of the schools are prime examples of outstanding school improvement, as they started from a very low base. They have achieved everything they set out to achieve in a little over two years and in some cases are very different schools from those initially inspected by OFSTED.

Twelve schools were not revisited. Based on the substantial evidence gathered before the revisits, a direct comparison could be made between the schools to provide a representative sample for revisiting. As a result of the revisit, four schools were deemed to have improved even more than all their other evidence of improvement suggested. In the group of 12 schools not revisited, the evidence suggested that none had made only limited improvement and more had made considerable improvements than in the group to be revisited. These schools appear to have also included examples of uneven development, some fragility in sustainability and occasional regression. However, the dominant picture is one in which progress and improvement have undoubtedly been made. Had these schools had the opportunity to be revisited, they may have mirrored the pattern of the revisited schools with evidence of some exceptional levels of improvement being discovered. In the group not revisited there were more schools who had started at a very low base and three of these had made good progress in their work on improvement. The matching of schools across the two samples and consideration of the evidence collected suggests that the improvements seen in the revisited schools are likely to have been replicated in the rest of the schools.

Conclusions

In this chapter we have shown that the EPSI programme did make a positive difference to the participating schools, both in terms of quantitative and qualitative measures.

The quantitative measures showed that in the three core subjects, results in the EPSI schools rose in advance of other LEA schools. Neither did the programme schools dip in common with LEA schools in science in 1996 and mathematics in 1998. Progress in those schools focusing on English work was significant. The value added indicators also indicate improvement in all three subjects for EPSI schools ahead of LEA schools. It is also worth noting that in EPSI schools Key Stage 1 results showed no significant trends during the process.

The EPSI programme was not geared to any specific curriculum area. Schools were rightly free to choose their own focuses. Many schools had a focus geared towards management improvements or meta-cognitive cross-curricular learning issues, which would not be expected to impact immediately on test scores.

Overall gains were made against the agreed range of indicators and where the improvement focuses were in areas more directly addressed by the indicators, the gains were more notable. It is likely that some of the changes brought about by EPSI activity will only become apparent in test data later on.

In qualitative terms, the evidence collected from a number of sources showed that there were process gains in the schools. In short, the schools improved their internal capacities to improve. In all the schools their capacity to use pupil data and learning outcome information developed. The heads and teachers became better at using an evidence-based approach to pupil and school performance. The staff also became more able and willing to enquire and reflect on performance information and to act on this. The visit by the OFSTED registered inspector suggested that several schools had accelerated their rates of improvement because of their involvement in the programme.

Overall, these indicators show that these schools were improving the quality of education they provided for the pupils across a range of success criteria. To a more limited extent there was also evidence that the quality of teaching was improving, although this varied from school to school.

We have not included in this chapter the benefits the programme provided to the LEA as an organization. Clearly, benefits to the schools are gains for the LEA, but there were also many advances in the LEA's ways of working. These are specifically addressed in Chapter 9.

The comments of the registered inspector also highlight the fragility of improvement efforts in primary schools. For a number of reasons, primary schools are prone to organizational 'instability'. The most obvious reason is when staff are absent or when there are major changes in staff. Such changes occurred in most programme schools and in some to a great degree. For example, during the summer of 1997 there was an unusually high number of staff retirements because of central government's revisions to the teacher early retirement scheme. Therefore, in noting the improvements these schools made, it should not be ignored that the staff in these schools made great efforts to minimize the impact of staff turnover, where they created discontinuities and adversely affected the staffing strengths by altering the balance of teacher expertise and experience in the school. It would be all too easy to draw from the information presented in this chapter a static view of school improvement, whereby schools are assumed to be unchanging and 'steady-state' organizations. Schools are not always stable institutions because they rely on their teaching staff and school leaders so much and are affected by changes to their personnel. Managing the equilibrium of the school is a key feature in school improvement and one that it is too easy to ignore when focusing solely on performance and outcomes.

For this reason, as well as to provide greater detail about what went on in the schools, the next part now looks at three specific aspects of the schools' efforts.

Part 2

School Insights

Chapter 3

Headship, Leadership and School Improvement

Geoff Southworth

Introduction

In this chapter I report what the headteachers of the programme schools had to say about school improvement. A series of interviews were conducted with the heads during the life of the project in order to capture and record their observations about the processes and outcomes of improvement in primary and junior schools. From their individual accounts common issues and themes were identified, which will be discussed in this chapter.

It is both a strength and a limitation that in this chapter our evidence relies on what the headteachers said. One of the strengths is that the data are headteachers' perceptions, and the emerging issues are their views about the processes of school improvement. It is important to examine what heads have to say about school improvement. Their experiential knowledge and understanding of school improvement are central to the whole exercise. How heads actually regard school improvement is a key factor influencing the direction of school improvement efforts in individual schools. Moreover, what the heads said about their schools' improvement strategies illuminates what they believe helps and hinders the process. The in-school barriers and drivers of school improvement need to be investigated, particularly when central government is so determined to raise educational standards and schools' levels of performance. Such high-level priorities need to be matched by more detailed awareness of what school improvement looks like to those who actually manage and lead it in schools. Though government can provide a panoramic agenda, because it is the responsibility of individual, self-managing schools to improve, there is also an urgent, concomitant need to explore what school improvement looks like on the ground, inside schools.

If it is a strength that this chapter contributes to understanding headteachers' *interests* in school improvement, that is their concerns, pre-occupations and insights, it is also the case that these are also limitations. In research terms, the heads' statements are a set of claims and as such, perhaps, provide only a sense of headteachers' rhetoric about school improvement. Mindful of this, we have contrasted their interview comments with their end-of-programme written reports, to see if there is consistency between their oral and written accounts. Also, and perhaps more telling, we have compared the heads' written and verbal accounts with the programme pairs' report on each school. In these ways we have cross-checked and triangulated the data. We also reported back to the heads and to the LEA school support staff the emerging findings and encouraged them to comment on them. This further refined our understandings and helped to validate the findings.

Four sets of interviews were conducted with the heads of the programme schools. These interviews took place during the first term of their participation, at the close of the programme and twice during the intervening period. The interviews were semi-structured, using a prepared schedule of questions, but we also left scope for the heads to raise issues. The great majority of interviews were conducted face-to-face in the heads' schools, although some were conducted off-site or by telephone.

The chapter is organized into three sub-sections. First, the main findings will be presented. Second, the major themes to emerge from these findings will be discussed. In the third section, three conclusions will be highlighted and developed.

Main Findings

From analysing what all the heads said, in each of the four interviews conducted with them, it was apparent that the heads differed in the reasons why they wanted to be involved in the programme at the outset. Some wanted closer ties with the LEA, while others wanted external help with their school improvement efforts. Some of the heads specifically wanted support in following up their recent school inspection.

Though the heads' comments showed that a range of motives underlay their, and the governors' and staffs', willingness to be involved in the programme, it was quite clear that each school had a different starting point in the programme. The majority of the schools adopted a school-specific improvement focus and dissimilarity in focus rather than similarity was the norm. A major reason why this was the case was because each of the heads was aware that they were dealing with school improvement in *this* school. The heads described in their early interviews where they saw 'their' schools coming from and what specific challenges they faced.

At the close of the programme a similar state of affairs existed. Each head referred to where they thought the school now was, what they had achieved and how far they thought the school had travelled. According to these heads' testimonies, the schools had moved in different directions and at different rates.

The heads' comments point to two interrelated issues. First, school improvement is a differentiated exercise. For example, it is differentiated by an individual school's needs and priorities and the pace at which the staff and governors work towards these goals. Second, these heads regarded their leadership and management of school improvement as a highly specific activity. Leading the school's improvement efforts was very largely dependent on the school's situation. The heads told us about the environmental factors they saw influencing the work of the school – its history, recent and current levels of performance, the pupils and their home backgrounds, parental support or apathy, the teaching staff's experience and strengths, staff attitudes to change and so on. In short, leading school improvement was context-specific. Consequently, these heads saw leadership as contingent on their schools' circumstances. Therefore, these heads tacitly adopted a contingency theory of school leadership.

All of the programme schools had recently been inspected by teams of OFSTED inspectors. One of the potential benefits of joining the programme was that the schools would gain some assistance with their post-inspection developments. Therefore, we were interested to see whether, and in what ways, the OFSTED inspections contributed to the schools' improvement efforts.

When asked about the influence of the OFSTED inspection on the schools' developments, 18 of the 22 heads regarded it as a factor. Four of these 18 heads saw the inspection as important and another five reported it as a major factor. These nine heads who saw the OFSTED inspection as important or very important tended to be leaders of schools whose performance was lower than other programme schools. However, several heads also said that the inspection report 'did not tell us anything we did not already know'. In other words, the inspectors' judgements were confirmatory rather than revelatory. Nevertheless, for some of the heads the inspectors' views were a useful external validation of their own perceptions.

One difficulty encountered by some of the heads was the fact that the inspection reports were not always clearly written. Some heads struggled to understand exactly what was being said in some parts of the report, while others had to draw on external help to interpret what was being said. These difficulties tended to unsettle the post-OFSTED action planning process since some heads were unsure, or unclear, about the action points they should address.

Overall, the OFSTED inspection process played a part in these schools' improvement efforts. More often than not, the inspection provided a useful contribution, but the degree of usefulness varied from school to school.

Also, occasionally, the lack of clarity in some of the inspection reports inhibited or delayed post-inspection action.

The EPSI programme placed a strong emphasis on using pupil data. One reason for this emphasis was the perceived need, both by LEA staff and those of us interested in studying school improvement, to support schools as they made the transition into the 'new age' of information-based school self-evaluation, analysis and improvement. Another reason centred on the LEA and the HE staffs' belief in teaching as a research-based profession and the value of teachers conducting action research into their classroom and school tasks and into trying to see more clearly than otherwise what learning looks like and means for the pupils.

The EPSI programme was constructed, in part, in the belief that teachers and governors of self-managing and improving schools should adopt a data-driven approach to developing their schools. Experience within the IQEA school improvement work (see Hopkins et al., 1994; Ainscow et al., 1994b) demonstrated the value of schools using a range of data to inform their improvement priority setting and planning. The IQEA project recognized that improving schools are not only moving schools (Rosenholtz, 1989), but that they also need to have a clear sense of the direction they are working towards. Furthermore, we appreciated that improving schools set targets so that they know where they are going, when they want to get there and how they will know they have arrived (Barber, 1996, p. 134). Therefore, the EPSI programme stressed the importance of staff in the participating schools, supported by the LEA, developing evidence-based analyses of their work and their improvements.

When the heads and teachers in the participating schools were interviewed about using data, their responses were almost entirely positive. For example, one head thought that using pupil learning data 'helped the staff to be more reflective'. Others said such data:

> Gives me information of what is really happening. I can track progress and [pupils'] learning gains.
> Provide us with a safety net for our own judgements.
> Help us to identify issues.

Several of the interviewees were aware that they had embarked on a relatively new and different professional task when they collected and, particularly, when they analysed and interpreted the data. One head saw his own and the school's efforts as 'All very embryonic at the moment'.

Another head was concerned that the 'data were not always intelligible' because he and the staff found it difficult, sometimes, to discern what the data actually meant. Another described the challenge in this way:

My problem is I don't know how to act on the data. Take the spelling data, we do not have the expertise [in the school] to act on it. What do we do instead? What new strategies [in spelling] do we employ? How do we make connections between the data and teaching?

There seemed to be two related aspects to meeting the challenge of analysing and understanding data. First, as one head himself said, 'staff data handling skills are an issue'. Some heads and teachers expressed low confidence or uncertainty in handling data. In a sense, the research skills of collecting and analysing data, both quantitative and qualitative, and of developing interpretations or speculating about possible meanings, were not skills which heads and teachers felt greatly confident about.

Second, and following on from the first, several interviewees highlighted the need for help, advice and support. One head asked, 'How do we develop the expertise to use data?' His reply was to insist, 'We need external support.' Another said, 'There are limits to how much schools can do with data on their own.' There was a general belief that teachers need to be supported when collecting, analysing and interpreting data.

Moreover, where external help and advice was available, this had been well received. In one school, the SDA had supported the staff's analysis of the pupil data and had been an active player in the process. This had been very well received by the senior staff, who regarded it as a learning process for everyone. Also, the computer software that the LEA provided for schools to collate and present data was greatly appreciated by staff in the schools because the software not only allowed them to collate the data, but offered an efficient and speedy way of categorizing the data in a variety of ways.

One data set the programme schools were required to collect was the pupil perception or attitude information. These data were collected from groups of pupils in Years 4 and 6 (see Chapter 5). Using a prescribed set of questions prepared by a sub-group of participating LEA staff, pupils' views on their work, their learning and the school in general were sought. Through the questions and pupils' responses it was hoped that the children's attitudes to their learning, teaching and achievement would be indicated.

These data proved to be of considerable fascination to the staff in several of the schools. From the outset we noted that the pupil attitude data seemed to be the most interesting of all the data sets to the staff. For some schools these data continue to be the most powerful and perplexing. For example, one head believed:

The pupil attitude data has been an important aspect for us. We are working towards developing our insights. We have looked at these data . . . the results were alarming.

What is being alluded to here was the fact that the pupils' comments were sharply at odds with what the teachers expected. The children's comments 'shocked' the staff and the head because they were much more negative than they expected.

In other schools the impact of the pupil attitude data subsided a little as time went by. Nevertheless, what emerged from this aspect of schools using pupil data was the fact that staff have found children's views to be so very interesting. Possibly this is because the children's comments offer another and sometimes surprising view of classroom life and learning. It seems that asking teachers to consider the pupils' perspectives is rather like 'turning round the telescope': suddenly by looking from the other end of the lens, things look quite different. In other words, pupils' perceptions supplemented the otherwise egocentric view of teaching and learning that some teachers hold. Pupils' perceptions overthrow the monocular view of teaching that often prevails in schools and, by contrast, provide a 'binocular perspective'.

Though pupils' views about their learning and schooling engaged many of the teachers and headteachers, there was little evidence of staff in the programme schools making strong connections between any of the pupil learning data sets they collected and analysing them in terms of what they might imply for developing the quality of teaching. Throughout the interviews we conducted there was very little unsolicited comment about teaching. There was much discussion about collecting data, the value of being in the EPSI programme, action planning and priorities each school had set or was struggling to focus on. But very, very little was heard about developing teaching.

The third round of interviews focused explicitly on pedagogy and whether the EPSI pupil data had influenced teaching in the school, and what emerged was that there was less attention to teaching than to other things. For example, where schools developed targets from the data these favoured targets for pupils rather than targets for teachers and their pedagogy.

However, there were some exceptions to this general view. In two schools there were signs of staff looking closely at how they taught as well as at how the pupils were progressing. In one school both the head and deputy said that the data had been 'revelatory' to staff. The SAT levels had raised questions about what makes a good writer and had stimulated discussions about the staff's criteria for 'good writing'. Teachers were becoming 'much more focused in teaching criteria for writing'. There had also been some developments in the staff's approaches to planning and marking children's written work:

> Our planning is much more specific, criterion referenced. Our plans [for teaching] are much more target based. (Head)

Everyone is beginning to work from learning objectives and this has made us more focused in our planning and teaching. When we observed each other teaching we asked the children: What are you doing and why? We found that the children did know what and why they were doing things and that the learning objectives were being used by teachers. Teaching is more targeted and focused. We are shifting our teaching and becoming clearer and sharing more among ourselves.   (Deputy)

In the second school the headteacher described how an increased attention had been paid to teaching styles, particularly in Key Stage 2. Efforts in science were striving to develop more open-ended activity. The head and science coordinator saw a need for more practical and concrete experiences for pupils in Key Stage 2 and they were beginning to lead staff in this direction. There was too much didactic teaching in Years 3 and 4 and this needed to be looked at and reconsidered.

Therefore, though in some schools there was a dual focus on learning and teaching, in most schools there was a stronger emphasis on looking at the learning data without any direct connections with teaching. As the head of a school that comes within this latter category said:

I would like the pupil data to inform our teaching. It should be diagnostic, but so far it is not.

One reason why this was the case may be, as another head said, because he had been concerned with 'getting classroom monitoring going and looking at learning, rather than at teaching'. This was certainly the case in several of the other schools as well. Most of the heads, when asked, said that monitoring in their schools had increased during the period of the programme, although the nature of the monitoring varied from school to school, with some introducing peer observation in classrooms, others deploying coordinators to monitor subjects and others examining samples of pupils' work and learning data. In other words, certain activities, namely classroom visiting, monitoring and looking at pupils' learning, took precedence over attention to pedagogy. Whatever the reasons, the finding remains that there was certainly less attention to teaching than to pupils' learning in these schools.

The EPSI programme played a part in enabling these schools to develop an evidence-based approach to school improvement. By the end of the programme staff, particularly senior staff, in all the schools were embarked on monitoring activities and the collation of pupil outcome data, which they were analysing in order to examine pupils' achievements and progress. Of course, many other factors influenced this development as well. For example, central government's target-setting initiatives, the publication of key stage data, OFSTED inspectors' emphasis on monitoring and the introduction of ICT systems in school management were undoubtedly contributory factors. Also, in some of the programme schools use was already being made of pupil learning data.

Notwithstanding these other factors, it seems that the EPSI programme played a major role in assisting staff in the programme schools to make greater use of pupil learning data than formerly. This was recognized by many of the heads when they considered the benefits of participating in the EPSI programme, as the following responses from four different headteachers illustrate:

> The EPSI programme has helped me over two years to see more clearly what school improvement means . . . It means improving from a starting point and moving from there. We have used data and targets to inform our work on differentiation. The idea of target setting is important. We are becoming more structured in our use of targets. [Overall] we have a better grip on school improvement, on using data, assessments and key indicators. The programme has given us the tools to improve – data handling, being able to make judgements about the data and acting on it. We have started to have a longitudinal perspective on pupils which staff accept. Staff acceptance speeds up action – there is less defensiveness, less concern and more interest in action.

> The programme got us going with Year 4 assessments – we have seen the value of this and we will keep on doing it. The programme has, in effect, trained the two Year 4 teachers to assess. It has also helped us to think about progression in Key Stage 2.

> [Using pupil data was valuable] because of the whole staff discussion of standards [which followed]. From the discussion came the backbone for the school's development plan, which was continuity and progression across the school. The data helped staff to start to understand what was happening in the school as a whole. This was supported by peer observation and coordinators monitoring the use of resources in classrooms and picking things up about teaching and learning.

> . . . Now got data coming in on pupils' achievement levels. We've bought a computer for the staff room which will be dedicated to providing teachers with access to pupil data since it will be networked to the Office machine. It all helps staff to appreciate that an evidence-base is central to improvement.

When the heads reflected on the benefits of the EPSI programme, they all spoke about how important it was to have a clear focus for improvement.

Indeed, *focus* was a much used word by the heads during all the interviews with them. For some, focusing on Key Stage 2 had been important, for others the emphasis on Year 4 had helped. However, the word 'focus' was most commonly used in relation to the improvement priorities each school identified and worked on throughout the programme. The heads believed it was very important to identify a clear focus at the outset and then to try steadfastly to work towards successfully achieving those goals. Focus in this sense meant identifying explicit aspects of the schools' work that would be attended to. They were sometimes expressed as goals, targets or action points. They were identified by the OFSTED inspectors, heads, teachers' concerns and pupils' comments and often stemmed from both an audit of the school and/or pupil learning data. Whatever the means by which a focus was established, the heads were unanimous in recognizing the need for one.

Furthermore, the EPSI programme not only helped heads and teachers to develop a clear focus, but it played a part in enabling staff in the participating schools to keep their focuses in view throughout the life of the programme. Both establishing and *sustaining* a clear focus were important. When both were accomplished, the heads believed they had a greater chance of achieving success, because finite school resources and staff efforts could be directed to agreed and explicit goals and staff would know when and whether they had accomplished what they had set out to achieve.

The importance these heads attached to the need for a focus for school improvement also has wider implications, because it relates to how the heads tacitly conceptualized school improvement. When their comments were analysed in terms of what they were generally saying about improving primary schools, two implicit models of improvement could be detected. In the next section these two models will be identified and discussed because they offer a broader interpretation of the heads' understanding of the school improvement process.

Emerging Themes

The heads' comments about establishing a clear focus, monitoring, using data and action planning showed that all of them had adopted the 'formal' model of school improvement. The naming of this particular model has proved something of a challenge to us and we eventually settled on this particular label in order to show that the schools, in particular the head-teachers, used a systematic approach to their improvement efforts. They adopted the five-stage model of evaluation and improvement promoted by the DfEE and OFSTED and used it reasonably regularly and methodically. Although there was some variation between schools, in broad terms each

was monitoring and collecting learning data, each had a school development plan and an action plan, and many were setting targets.

The EPSI programme encouraged such an approach, but it would be
wrong to say that EPSI alone was responsible for the formal model being
implemented in these schools. At least two other forces played a part in
persuading heads and others to follow this model. For one thing, as noted
above, the model is very much in line with 'official' assumptions and prescriptions concerning school improvement. The DfEE's (1997) cycle of
school self-evaluation embodies much of the foregoing, and so too does
OFSTED's credo that inspection is for school improvement, particularly when
this is coupled with the inspectors' advocacy for monitoring, auditing and
action planning. Second, the formal model is consistent with the principles
and traditions of scientific management. Scientific management includes a
rational planning process that is sequential, involves management by objectives and adopts cyclic systems of audit, planning, prioritizing, implementing and evaluating (see Levacic, Glover, Bennett and Crawford, 1998).
Such systems have long been promoted by adherents in business schools
and by organizational management theorists and they have also latterly been
promoted by the Audit Commission (1993) and educationists who have
promoted development planning (e.g. Hargreaves and Hopkins, 1991; West
and Ainscow, 1991) and school self-evaluation (e.g. Holly and Southworth,
1989). Therefore, it is unsurprising that this formal model of institutional
improvement was evident in the heads' comments and in their work in
schools.

Though all the heads demonstrated an awareness of this model, it was
also the case that they were using it in varying ways. In particular, they
differed in how they used external LEA support and guidance, with some
schools making greater use than others of the programme pairs. Also, the
headteachers reported a number of barriers to adopting this model. The lack
of data-handling skills was one such barrier to establishing an evidence-
based approach. Another was the lack of time for monitoring classroom
practice. School budgets were sometimes so constrained that the heads said
they could not afford the financial costs of releasing staff, usually subject
coordinators, to monitor colleagues' classwork in order to develop an across-
school perspective on teaching and learning in their subject area. Also,
several of the heads said that they had to deal with so many other demands
themselves that they could not always release staff by personally providing
cover teaching for them. One further constraint on developing the formal
model was staff turnover. While changes in staffing were sometimes helpful to the heads' and to the schools' development, on other occasions they
were an impediment to improvement efforts as valued colleagues and key
individuals left the school and less experienced staff replaced them. Staff

turnover created turbulence in some of the programme schools and this, in turn, slowed the pace of development and progress.

Yet, alongside the formal model we detected another one that was implicit in the remarks of some, but not all, of the heads. This approach to school improvement can be labelled the 'cultural' model. The model is essentially founded on an anthropological definition of culture, where culture means the values, customs, rituals, symbols and language of a group as a 'way of life', or at the very least, as a way of doing things in a particular school, or unit of a school.

The heads who demonstrated this awareness spoke of how, during the programme, teachers' interactions and exchanges had altered and how staff meetings had developed. They reflected on the nature and content of teachers' collaborations, the quality and focus of teamwork, key stage and whole-school cohesion and teachers' professional learning and development. For example, one head, when asked what she thought had most helped the school to develop, answered:

> Talking in various groups. The year group pairs of teachers talk every week to plan. I sit in on at least one such meeting with every pair, every term. The talk focuses on the teaching techniques, pupils' learning, practical stuff. We debate, we argue – that is when we grow, that is staff development of a high order.

Another head reflecting on the school's improvement said:

> I think the school has improved . . . Staff are better informed, up to date, aware of national and local debates on education and this has had an effect on the teachers. They feel they know what they are doing. There is a continuous debate here on school improvement. We have never had that before. There's a cultural change here.

The cultural model embodies an approach that acknowledges that as well as employing rational systems and formalized structures and processes, school leaders need to take account of human relationships. This is an important point. Those heads who implied that they were aware of teacher cultures suggested that they saw both models as existing side-by-side. This is an important point because we do not wish to imply that the two are necessarily separate. Our experience suggests that the two can be connected and in some circumstances are iterative. Nor in highlighting them in this section is there any suggestion that one is somehow 'better' than the other. Rather, the first point to make is that we saw evidence of both models underscoring the assumptions and perspectives of several of the headteachers.

Closer analysis of this finding failed to highlight any other specific patterns. For example, expression of a cultural awareness was not confined to the more experienced headteachers. Nor was it always associated with the more successful schools. However, there was a suggestion in the data that in those schools that were most severely criticized by the OFSTED inspectors, the heads adopted a more strongly formal approach to school improvement. Whether this pattern is a function of the schools' needs, the headteachers' leadership style, or some combination of the two, is unclear. There was a suggestion from one of the heads who used the formal model in a school with severe weaknesses, that she had adopted a more direct approach than formerly because of the time pressures she and the staff were under and which had been imposed by HMI following up the school's OFSTED inspection. When asked if her approach as a headteacher had changed over the two years of the programme, in terms of improving the school, she replied:

> My approach, in some ways, has hardened. I have become more straight, more frank with staff, especially when monitoring lessons. I accentuate the positive, but also what I think. If things have not been quite right I have said so . . . We are also making more specific, systematic use of learning objectives by staff in their teaching.

These comments suggest that heads whose schools need to improve quickly and from a relatively low point, are likely to adopt the formal model and be more direct and plain-speaking in their approach than colleagues in schools in different circumstances.

There may also be some implications in these two models about the pace of school improvement. In the poorer-performing schools there was a sense of urgency that was less noticeable in some of the others. This was probably because most of the programme schools were not under the same time pressures as those with severe weaknesses, even though all the programme schools wanted and knew they were expected to show improvements over the two-year project period. Nevertheless, the heads in those schools that had been judged sound or better by OFSTED were not as concerned with accelerating their schools' rates of progress as those judged to have significant difficulties. Of course, it might also be the case that using the formal model with a 'human touch' is itself a slower-paced approach because it requires attention to more rather than fewer aspects of the school.

It is not clear precisely why some heads implied an awareness of teacher cultures. Was this another manifestation of a contingency approach to school leadership as noted earlier? Was it that they recognized, in line with Fullan's (1991) thinking, that at the heart of school improvement lies the need to build organizational capacity to manage change? One of the tools schools were offered early on in the programme was a 'conditions rating scale' (Ainscow et al., 1994a), which helped senior staff to reflect on a set of organizational capacities associated with more successful management of change and school improvement. Heads and others were made aware that at the same time as they were working on the curricular and other priorities for improvement, they also needed to pay attention to those internal features of a school and ways of working that enabled it to get the work done. Schools do need to focus on and create the internal conditions that facilitate development (Ainscow et al., 1994b). Therefore, when some of the heads spoke about their organizational cultures they may have been reflecting on whether they had created and sustained the internal capacity to make improvements happen.

Clearly there is more to discuss about the co-existence of these two models. In the next section we shall return to it, but in drawing this section to a close, it is worth highlighting two further points. First, it seems that while both models may operate simultaneously, this does not seem to mean that the two are always (if ever) applied equally. In some circumstances a more formal and direct approach may take precedence over the cultural model. This, in turn, points towards the idea that a single approach to school improvement and leadership is inappropriate.

Second, we have come to the conclusion that the formal model is a necessary strategy (or set of strategies) for improving schools. The model offers a common set of processes which, when managed appropriately, provides a basic level of competence in school improvement. In other words, the formal model provides a common denominator for all schools to work from and is one that the cultural model can build on and around. This argument parallels the research of Fullan (1992) into successful school improvement because he says that school improvement requires:

> A radical change in the culture of schools and the conception of teaching as a profession . . . Cultural change requires strong, persistent efforts because much of current practice is embedded in structures and routines and internalised in individuals . . . Bureaucratic reforms may be able to guarantee minimal performance, but not excellence in teaching. (p. 121)

The formal model offers schools a basic framework to develop a set of conditions and sufficient organizational capacity to improve. The cultural model, however, may be essential if schools are to achieve excellence.

So saying, it is important to note that our research also suggests that these two models do not operate one after the other, but in a more complex and symbiotic way. For example, the formal model can contribute to cultural development because the formal model's processes will simultaneously impact on cultural norms and patterns. The two are intertwined and closely related. Therefore, it is not simply a case of senior staff putting the formal model in place and then working on the teacher culture. The two can be developed alongside each other.

Conclusions

There are three conclusions to note from the findings presented above. First, although these schools improved and some made significant gains in terms of pupils' learning outcomes, rather less emphasis was placed on teaching and developing pedagogy than on pupils' learning. This was true both in the general sense and in terms of the heads' leadership.

Across all the schools monitoring took place and there was a move towards an evidence-based approach to school improvement, yet the evidence staff in the programme schools collected was primarily pupil learning data and rarely included information on teaching. Much the same was true for the heads' actions. They played a key role in helping their schools to use evidence and broadly supported an action research approach. Many actively encouraged and participated in classroom monitoring. However, their efforts were more commonly and explicitly focused on pupils' learning achievements and progress than on pedagogy.

This bald conclusion needs to be softened somewhat, because there was some evidence of pedagogy being examined, mainly in those schools deemed to have severe weaknesses. Nevertheless, the overall conclusion raises questions as to why there was less attention to pedagogy than to other aspects of the school.

We suggested earlier that one reason why this pattern occurred was because the heads in several of the schools were trying to establish the principle of an evidence-based approach before extending this to include teaching. In other words, these heads were taking a sequential approach and saw attention to teaching as a later development, after monitoring had been adopted and after the analysis of pupil learning data had become common practice.

This may be a wise way forward. The idea of 'working towards' attending to pedagogy allows heads to prepare the ground with teachers, helps to lower some of the barriers to observing teaching and offers time for trust and openness to develop before teachers' feel they are being directly judged. These 'barriers' to focusing on teaching are well known. There still lingers in some schools a teacher culture of independence and 'autonomy', which is often reinforced by the workplace creating a social milieu that undermines professional openness and the sharing of pedagogic knowledge and skills (see Fullan and Hargreaves, 1992; Hargreaves, 1994). Heads in such schools understood that they had to take a lead and transform the teacher culture into one that supported professional dialogue and practical assistance.

However, while a sense of 'working towards' pedagogy seems a sensible strategy, there is the danger that some may never ever reach this destination. Millett (1998) was plainly aware of this when she remarked:

> I am always struck by how difficult teachers find it to talk about teaching – or rather the nature of teaching – and how unwilling some of them are to talk about teaching at all. They prefer to talk about learning.
>
> By contrast they can talk with great clarity about matters such as the curriculum, assessment and testing, classroom organisation, examination structures – almost anything except teaching itself. . . . Since 1944 we have tackled most educational issues but ignored the most important one because of a British reluctance to tread on teachers' professional toes. (p. 28)

Millett's last point may further explain why most of the heads' pedagogic or instructional leadership was lacking. Although several of the heads cited other factors such as their lack of time to visit classrooms, it needs to be recognized, as Millett argues, that a professional tradition in looking at teaching has not been present until recently. The introduction by OFSTED of a strong focus on the quality of teaching during school inspections has been a major shift. So too has the work of the Teacher Training Agency (TTA), which Millett herself leads. Moreover, others have been calling for greater attention to pedagogy (Reynolds, 1998; Southworth, 1996, 1998).

While the case for focusing on pedagogy is now being articulated and bolstered, the EPSI programme findings suggest that this emphasis is lagging behind the emphasis now being placed on pupils' learning. The latter appears to be taking precedence over the former. Furthermore, primary headteachers in the programme schools were, on balance, not playing a major, direct or active part in leading the development of pedagogy in their schools. Instructional leadership, certainly at the headteacher level, but probably at other levels as well (e.g. deputy, subject coordinators), was largely invisible.

The second conclusion relates to the first and to the discussion in the previous section about school cultures. Clearly a number of the programme heads, certainly more than half, were aware that the teacher cultures in their schools needed to be transformed. Most who referred to these cultures generally seemed aware of the need to reduce teacher isolation and independence and were striving to enhance the quality of teacher interdependence. Classroom monitoring was a significant step in this direction for some staff groups and the heads. In terms of teacher cultures, these heads were seeking to develop a stronger sense of organizational cohesion and professional collaboration. The heads were also encouraging colleagues to look beyond their own classrooms and to take a wider view of learning and teaching.

These are all important characteristics and conditions to develop and maintain, as many research projects have shown and commentators have argued (e.g. Ainscow et al., 1994a; Fullan and Hargreaves, 1992; MacGilchrist et al., 1997; Mortimore et al., 1988; Nias et al., 1992; Nias, Southworth and Yeomans, 1989; Rosenholtz, 1989). Nevertheless, an additional point needs to be added to this finding, which connects to the previous conclusion.

Though the heads were tacitly concerned about creating and maintaining a culture of collaboration, there were no unambiguous signs that this was understood as contributing to focusing on pedagogy. A collaborative culture was implied to be a 'good thing' because of the benefits that can accrue from teacher interdependence and organizational coherence. However, it was not directly seen to be a workplace characteristic that would enable a stronger emphasis on pedagogy to flourish. This may have happened because the heads were not directly asked about this issue, but whatever the reason for this under-emphasis, it is worth highlighting that the heads' observations about teacher cultures appeared to omit reference to any links between teacher culture and improving pedagogy.

Given the increasing number of calls for teachers to examine the nature of their teaching, for them to talk about pedagogy and for heads to challenge the idea that the classroom is every teacher's castle and to establish a climate of enquiry among staff into teaching (Millett, 1998), some heads may need to modify their assumptions and understanding of culture. These heads need to become more aware that workplace conditions and norms should be developed in order to create the institutional capacity for staff to learn with and from one another about their individual teaching strategies and repertoires. In short, culture should serve as the means to an end and not an end in itself.

This outlook is evident in the thinking of Loose (1997), who has argued that schools should create an 'achievement culture', which is a teacher culture characterized by norms of continuous school improvement and the development of pedagogy.

The programme heads' comments and implicit assumptions about culture and school improvement suggest that existing thinking about primary school cultures and workplace conditions needs to be further refined. Just as attention to whole-school curriculum development enhanced the initial understanding of collaborative cultures (Nias et al., 1992), so has this programme advanced our thinking again. It now seems that although the existence of a culture of collaboration is a necessary condition for whole-school development because it creates trust, security and openness, these are not sufficient conditions for growth. For growth to take place teachers must be constantly learning (Nias et al., 1992, p. 247). Moreover, for schools to improve, there has to be a concerted effort to examine and act on pupils' learning outcomes and children's perspectives on their learning and schooling. At the same time, if improvement is to become continuous and if pedagogy is to be included in improvement efforts, then staff need to monitor, discuss and develop their pedagogy. Collaborative cultures and teachers' professional learning are important insofar as they facilitate the growth of teachers as pedagogues and help them to assess and understand pupils' achievements and progress.

Therefore, there are two important additional points to make about the formal and cultural models. First, while the formal model provides a basic framework for school improvement, the cultural model is necessary to enhance the power and efficacy of the formal model, because it will enable teachers to work together in stronger ways and to learn from each other. Second, the cultural model needs to move beyond enabling stronger professional ties between teachers and to create the conditions for teachers to focus more keenly on their pedagogy. Only when the cultural model embraces attention to pedagogy will it increase the school's capacity to achieve excellence in teaching.

The third conclusion relates to the notion of 'focus' that was so commonly used by the heads throughout their interviews. The heads were almost unanimous in their belief that one of the benefits of the EPSI programme had been helping them and their staffs to identify a clear focus and to stick to it throughout. This finding suggests that since clear objectives are an important early step in rational planning and systematic improvement, establishing a clear focus is not only important in its own terms, but also because so much of the formal model of school improvement rests on developing a sharp focus. Another interpretation of what these headteachers said is that unless school leaders and teachers are clear about what they trying to improve, their chances of success may be significantly reduced.

However, in this chapter we have also suggested that a clear focus is but one thing among several others that school leaders need to attend to. School staff need a clear focus for their improvement efforts, but heads also need to attend to a number of dualities. They have to consider both learning gains and the quality of teaching. They have to consider the performance of individual pupils and the development of colleagues. They need to consider process and outcome issues. They also have to consider how improvements relate to the school's mission and the head and staff's vision for the school.

We could continue with the list, but the point we seek to make here is that while focus matters, heads and other leaders need, at the very least, to have bifocal vision.

Leading school improvement involves attending to many things at once and heads need to be able to focus on each and all of these at different points, as well as at the same time. Though the notion of vision is a much vaunted concept in leadership theorizing, what the practice of these heads suggests is that the ability to see many things and the skills of looking closely and from a distance also matter. Bifocal vision matters because professional perception is a key skill for leaders of improving primary schools.

Chapter 4

Primary Schools and Pupil 'Data'

Pete Dudley

Introduction

Because the EPSI programme was committed to a definition of school
improvement rooted in improved learning and achievement, pupil data was
a focus from the outset. The importance of pupil data grew steadily throughout
the programme's duration, becoming a dominant feature of what schools
reported they had learned from involvement in EPSI and, equally, a formative learning experience for the LEA.

In the first part of this chapter we describe why and how the programme focused upon pupil data. We go on to describe the ways schools
developed their use of pupil data in practice, as well as how the use of these
data evolved at programme level in helping both the evaluation of school
performance as well as having an impact of the programme itself. We then
examine some of the issues relating to pupil data emerging from EPSI
schools and from the wider programme.

In recent years, more attention has been paid to primary school performance data than ever before. This is happening in a national context
where research on school effectiveness and school improvement is dominat-
ing government education policy and also at a time when developments
in ICT are making complex statistical procedures accessible to increasing
numbers of people at all levels of the education system.

The EPSI programme provided a sustained focus and consequently a
powerful learning experience for us all in pupil data issues. I will set out at
the close, a summary of both the key points the LEA has learned from the
process, and what issues remain as challenges for schools and LEA in the
effort to make evidence-based, school improvement effective in primary
schools over the longer term.

Pupil Data Used in the EPSI Programme

The pupil data used at programme level was to serve two purposes:

1   to help provide an evidential basis of how outcomes for learners in EPSI schools were changing; and
2   to help evaluate the impact of the programme itself.

A Pupil Data Working Group was established at the beginning of the EPSI programme, principally to advise on pupil data issues. It comprised members of the LEA school development adviser team, psychology and assessment service, the principal school development adviser, a seconded head teacher and members of UCSE – one of whom chaired the group. From the outset, it became clear that the remit was more complex and formative than may have been envisaged and the group's meetings each term were a forum for vigorous debate, much of which greatly influenced the development of the wider programme.

One decision immediately confronting the group was how prescriptive the requirements on pupil data should be made for schools. It is certain that some of the decisions taken by the group raised the profile of certain data sets and thus influenced the actions taken by some schools, presenting what might be viewed as a problem for a programme committed to supporting and studying school *self*-improvement. These matters are examined in detail later in this chapter.

The group identified data sets which, it was intended, would allow appropriate school self-improvement, while also allowing for some comparative analysis. These data were chosen:

- in the light of early indications of the schools' improvement focuses;
- with a clear intention to use existing data sources where possible;
- with an intention to use measures that were curriculum based and that would allow for formative and diagnostic responses as well as summative judgements;
- with an intention, where new data were to be gathered, to minimize the burden of collection or generation of data that may not be of *direct* relevance to the school's improvement focus; and
- in the light of the degree to which the data may subsequently be used to triangulate or validate judgements and perceptions.

Steering Group Pupil and School Level Data Sets

The rationale for the data sets collected from EPSI schools and a description of the measures themselves are given below. Each data set was collected at the outset of the programme in Spring 1996 as a baseline measure, and again in Spring 1998 as part of a composite programme-outcome measure.

It was not intended that judgements about the programme schools' perform-ance against these would be the sole bases for judgements about school improvement. However, the measures later became important components in that profile of data. The data comprised two broad categories:

1   pupil learning outcome data, and
2   other qualitative data.

The learning outcome data were largely concerned with cognitive learning. The other qualitative measures were concerned with affective factors.

Pupil Learning Outcome Data

Three main kinds of learning outcome measures were used across all schools and related to the national curriculum, as discussed below.

(1) End Key Stage 2 (11-year-olds) English, mathematics and science test data. These data were expressed in three different ways:

1   the percentage of pupils attaining level 4 and above;
2   the average level for the cohort;
3   a 'value added' comparative measure for all schools in EPSI along-side a wider network of schools, where an analysis of the results data controls for the effects of three variables across a wider sample of schools including EPSI schools. These variables are: deprivation/affluence, gender and term of birth. A full description and commentary is given in Appendix 2.

(2) Reading test data. No single reading test instrument was prescribed for use in the programme. At the start of the programme there was a lack of historical data held by the LEA because reading data collected in the past had been abandoned in the light of National Curriculum assessment. Many schools, however, had their own sets of reading data from tests adminis-tered at school level – although these tests varied from school to school. It was felt likely that prescribing a specific test for the purposes of the pro-gramme might disrupt existing data sets being used by schools for their own self-evaluation as well as adding to workload and pressure on curriculum time. Consequently, schools were asked to continue to use the data they already collected. Where there were no reading data, schools were asked to begin to administer a standardized reading test.

(3) Year 4 EPSI writing test data. In view of the four-year duration of Key Stage 2, a longer programme of study than is demanded of learners or

teachers at any other phase of education, it was decided to collect data from the cohort of 8- and 9-year-old pupils who were in Year 4 at the time the programme began. This cohort would have their end of key stage assessment in 1998, at the close of the programme. A writing assessment was agreed because it represented little intrusion into good teaching practice and therefore had 'ecological validity' (Black and Wiliam, 1998, p. 8) as well as representing a skill essential to effective learning. An instrument was devised for the purpose, which assessed pupils using criterion marking which was also convertible into National Curriculum levels.

Other Qualitative Data

It needs to be recognized that schools used a range of learning and outcome data not collected centrally by the programme. Teacher assessments, curriculum plans, pupils' work, marking, progress records, and individual education plans (IEPs) are all central to the process of evidence-based self-evaluation and improvement. These data were important to the ongoing developmental work being done by schools and programme pairs. Nevertheless, a number of more qualitative data sets were collected at programme level.

Pupil Perception Data

The working group on pupil data added two key measures to the learning outcome data sets originally envisaged for the programme. One was a set of data intended to capture pupils' perceptions of their learning and schooling. This was intended to be set alongside the perceptions of heads and school and LEA staff in order to provide first-hand 'user' information about changes at pupil and classroom level. A pupil survey approach, such as those developed by MacBeath and Mortimore (ISEP, 1996), and Keele University (Keele, 1994) or that used in Essex's Tilbury initiative was considered. While such an approach enables the views of a large sample of pupils to be captured, quantitative pupil survey data have been found to be less effective in triggering debate and action (Dudley, 1997), and it was decided to adopt an interview approach at school level with smaller but consistent samples of pupils. The development and use of this data set were of exceptional importance to the programme. A full account is given in Chapter 5.

Staff Perception Data

One feature of many early school improvement initiatives was a tendency to focus on whole-school management issues, with a failure to engage a range of teaching staff at an early stage, resulting in little emphasis on and aware-ness of teaching and learning in classrooms.

> We remain concerned that the impact of school improvement efforts goes behind the classroom door. Unfortunately, many school improvement projects underestimate the difficulty of affecting classroom practice. (Ainscow et al., 1994a, p. 23)

Consequently, the 'Improving the Quality of Education for All (IQEA) Conditions Rating Scale' (Ainscow et al., 1994a) was administered in all programme schools near the outset of the programme and again after the close. Programme pairs (the LEA officers working with the school) and schools used the information within the context of the school's specific improvement focus and, more generally, the instrument highlighted the importance of school capacity for improvement. The survey sampled staff perceptions of six conditions for school improvement, which are: enquiry and reflection, planning, coordination, involvement, leadership and staff development (see Appendix 5). The data were later reviewed as a back-ground indicator at programme level. In practice, schools and programme pairs also monitored and reported on staff perceptions informally.

How the Data Were Used in Practice

One thing is certain. Pupil data were a focus to a greater or lesser extent in every school involved in the programme.

> The most important strategy has been the adoption of the research tool, to question . . . to carry out school based research and find practical solutions. (EPSI school headteacher reflecting on the programme)

A change common to all schools involved in EPSI has been the increased use of 'data' – whether generated in school or externally. One English coordinator described graphically how 'mucking about with data' from Year 4 English tests provided a defining moment that generated stark questions about teacher and school expectations of pupil attainment, shaping the school's improvement strategy. Nearly every school involved in the pro-gramme reported analysis of assessment and test data as having a significant impact on improvement planning. The great majority used a range of data at different times during the programme for different purposes (see Table 4.1).

OFSTED inspection reports have always contained judgements based on a range of qualitative as well as quantitative data, but these judgements

Table 4.1   What EPSI schools identified as 'data sources', which were being monitored and analysed as a result of the EPSI focus

Data sources	Percentage of schools reporting use
National Curriculum Test, value added and other test data	95%
Assessment data	90%
Classroom observation data	70%
Data from teaching plans	95%
Samples of pupils' work and learning outcomes	70%
Data relating to targets for achievement	40%
Data relating to collaboration and independence in learning	30%
Pupil self-assessment data	30%
Pupil perceptions	100%
Staff perceptions (informally or formally)	100%

Source: school and LEA pair programme reports

have been made for schools by external agents rather than by the schools themselves. An aim of EPSI was to improve schools' abilities to make such judgements through self-evaluation. More recently, and hard on the heels of EPSI, summaries and analyses of learning outcome data and inspection judgements have come into schools in the form of OFSTED Performance and Attainment (PANDA) summaries and QCA benchmarks. It is fair to say that a number of the data sources listed above go well beyond the narrow ranges offered to schools through these external summaries and would not have been overtly perceived as sources of 'data' back in 1995 when the programme was beginning. Programme schools were sensitized to 'data' issues earlier than many primary schools across the country, and have perhaps – as the above list would suggest – developed a broader concept of 'data': one which goes beyond the notion of aggregate, summative quantitative – largely outcome focused – measures, and as such may be able to provide a more accessible purchase at school level for improvement planning and evaluation. As one of the participating heads said when reflecting on the programme: 'One of the most significant changes during EPSI has been an "improved awareness and understanding about the collection and use of data".'

How Schools Used the EPSI Data Sets

Schools used the learning outcome measures in a variety of ways. The 1996 Key Stage 2 outcomes were analysed and fed back to schools using unique school identification codes, which prevented the schools from being identified. EPSI schools were able to view their average levels and performance in each subject at level 4 and in comparison with other schools. For many this analysis came late – in the November following the assessments in May. What was found more useful and was used more by schools and programme pairs, was the value added analysis, which took account of contextual background factors. This was felt to be fairer and was therefore something around which schools and programme pairs could more readily unite. Percentages of pupils attaining at or above level 4 (which appear in government performance tables) for some schools were depressingly low, while for others attaining 100 per cent, the measure provided little incentive to improve further. These issues are discussed in detail later in the chapter.

For some, the comparative feedback on the percentages of pupils at level 4 and above provided a helpful preparation for the national publication of this data four months later in the first primary school performance tables. For a significant number of schools, the outcome data became much more interesting when the data generated by the Year 4 writing assessments were added to the picture.

It had not been possible at programme level to provide schools with data on pupil progress. The 11-year-old pupils being statutorily assessed in 1996 and 1997 had been assessed at age 7 on an earlier version of the curriculum and at a time of national boycotting of the process – so there was a lack of prior attainment data. At school level many teachers at the time did not see a connection between the statutory assessments at end of Key Stage 1 with those at the end of Key Stage 2. The processes themselves were often felt by teachers to be so different as not to warrant fair comparison. The writing assessments carried out with Year 4 pupils generated interesting outcomes.

An overall comparison between the 1996 and 1998 writing assessments does not reveal any significant changes or trends in terms of improved outcomes. But an analysis of the assessments carried out in 1996 – and of the impact on the behaviours of schools – shows that for many Year 4 teachers, criterion-referenced assessment of pupil writing in the National Curriculum was still a relatively new experience. Many found great variance between their teacher assessments and the levels generated by the mark scheme. Most had not used such a mark scheme before (see Figure 4.1).

As part of the process, Year 4 teachers were brought together for moderation meetings and evaluation of the impact of the exercise. They were also asked to record the pupils' views of the process and to negotiate a target for improvement with the pupils individually.

The exercise was important for teachers in that it:

• brought Year 4 teachers into the programme activities – they felt much involved as a result; and

Pete Dudley

Mark sheet No .... of ....   *Please bring copy of mark sheets on 2 May.*

Name	DoB	M/F	Story Total marks	Letter Desc. Expln marks	Pupil evaluation – key words	Spell marks	Hand-writing. Level

Figure 4.1 Sample summary mark sheet. Marks were converted to national curriculum levels.

- highlighted an area in the middle of Key Stage 2 where there was clear lack of teacher experience of assessment or progress issues.

It was significant for a number of headteachers also. The summary results were fed back to schools, giving comparative information for the EPSI sample. They were classified by gender and by term of birth and the information was provided comparatively for the schools set against the EPSI sample using a series of histograms.

Many schools were surprised by the data. Some schools identified clear issues in terms of gender differentials, others found progress from end of Key Stage 1 was not in line with their assumptions, and most found that there was a clear staff development need for moderation and assessment in writing. Some schools felt that the process crystallized their EPSI focus and some even changed their focus as a result. Those who went on to focus on writing were able to use the data to begin to set targets for improvement at the end of the programme in 1998. One school that identified clear under-achievement in writing, set targets, continued with regular subsequent pupil assessments and moderation meetings, involved pupils overtly in the marking process and each term negotiated targets in writing with the cohort of pupils. The cohort attained 90 per cent at level 4 and above in the 1998 English National Curriculum tests, representing progress well above that of the LEA or the EPSI sample. Another school used the data to review its approach to teaching writing. A whole-school approach to the way teaching writing was organized each week was developed following a series of paired classroom observations – initially involving the LEA programme pair and then being taken on by the school. The school also set targets for attainment in writing – dividing the National Curriculum levels into thirds to help show progress within a year. Attainment in writing in the Year 4 tests reached over 80 per cent in 1998 compared with attainment at 29 per cent reaching level 4 and above in 1995.

Pupil Perception Data

The pupil perception data were used in a variety of ways. They were used by programme pairs as a 'way in' to working with schools in many instances and generated a range of interesting and sometimes innovative approaches to collection, analysis and feedback. These are described and examined in detail in Chapter 5. The impacts of the data on evaluation of school improvement and on the programme as a whole are discussed later in this chapter.

Staff Perception Data – the Conditions Rating Scale

Because this was an external instrument used in the very early stages of the programme – often introduced on the programme pair's first or second visit to the school – it provided a useful 'way in' for many programme pairs in working with schools. It also established, very firmly, that the programme was about data collection and analysis. The instrument itself is a small-scale survey of closed items dealing with the specific conditions for improvement set out above. Consequently, its purpose was not felt to be useful or in line with the focus some schools were identifying. Nevertheless, in other schools it identified new issues to consider in planning effective change or, alternatively, confirmed existing issues and added to the picture being formed by those schools who were focusing particularly on issues directly addressed by the survey, such as coordination or enquiry and reflection.

The method of feedback to schools was not prescribed by the pupil data working group. Consequently, a range of methods was devised by programme pairs. These were tailored to suit the culture and nature the feedback required, but also reflected the range of analysis and presentational skills existing among programme pairs early in the programme.

Some heads and programme pairs found the survey – or some of its items – influential in informing improvement and ongoing evaluation, but for many it was merely seen as an externally imposed input and outcome measure. This may be because it was administered at the very outset of the programme, before much activity had taken place and before many skills in data use and effective feedback methods had been developed. It was then not used again until after most of the development activity had finished and opportunities for formative feedback had passed. This limited the formative influence it had. In addition, a significant number of the schools in the programme had teaching staffs of six or fewer. Here, the survey was found more useful as a set of discussion prompts than as a quantitative measure. Some schools administered the survey not only to teaching staff but to *all* staff, which provided interesting and sometimes challenging outcomes.

Reading Data

The reading data were used the most by those schools who had a focus on improving literacy. One school developed a sophisticated approach to using reading data analyses every six months, to gauge the progress pupils were making across the school in reading and to begin to feed this data back to staff and also to pupils. The process was helped by the presence of someone skilled in basic spreadsheet management and presentation of data, which allowed the school to manipulate its own data as well as find the most effective ways of presenting data to provide feedback, which staff and pupils found fair, easy to interpret and formative.

The feedback focused on progress made by pupils. Evidence from this school shows that pupils and staff found this feedback helpful and motivating. The school used the data to set pupil targets for improvement, which became aggregated into school targets. With the careful introduction of a number of reading and organizational strategies, progress in reading rapidly began to increase well ahead of the rate of the LEA.

The development and introduction to schools by the pupil data working group, late in 1996, of a spreadsheet package that would allow schools to interrogate and present a range of their pupil outcome data – including reading ages and standardized reading scores at the push of a button – fuelled greater use of the reading data in schools. It was clear that ICT data management skills, particularly among head teachers, generally were low and this influenced the degree to which data could be analysed and fed into school improvement. The way these are presented, along with skills in analysis and manipulation of data, remain significant issues for schools and the LEA.

Across the programme the reading data were difficult to gather or analyse systematically because they were held in so many forms and formats – reading ages, standardized scores, and all from a range of instruments with varying characteristics. It was, therefore, not possible to gather or analyse reading data comparatively.

The Overall Impact on Schools as Data Users

Use of More Quantitative Data

As has been seen above, by the end of the programme, head teachers certainly viewed themselves and their schools much more as users of a broad range of pupil data than at the outset of the programme. Many of the programme schools reported that jointly analysing the data with their programme pair was a valuable exercise. Some programme pairs took on the analysis and presentation of data as a key feature of their work with the school. The work of one pair in particular has influenced the support offered to all schools in providing simple spreadsheets to manipulate and present data.

This enthusiasm for data is significant in itself, given that EPSI began in a climate where the over-complex assessment requirements of the initial National Curriculum along with suspicions about the data and their use by the government, had led to a national boycott of testing in 1993, and forced a rewrite of the entire curriculum in 1995 to reduce the requirements for record keeping and assessment.

The development, through EPSI, of a 'research culture' where schools build trust with LEA pairs to use data fairly in making joint evaluations with them, has helped in enabling sustained formative use to be made of the data. At the outset, for instance, the value added data were provided to schools using anonymous identification codes for schools. Schools needed time to come to terms with the data and to discuss their implications with programme pairs. This trust and emphasis on fairness has helped both LEA and schools unite around the data as a trigger for change and an important indicator of improvement or decline. It has provided the data with validity of 'consequence' (Messick, 1989, p. 9), because schools are more prepared to act upon the data positively.

How Schools Respond to Data

Taking account of the emotional issues in effective use of data is vital if it is to be used with sustained effect. A study of teachers' responses to pupil survey data (Dudley, 1997) suggested that the management of data presentation and feedback is crucial if it is to be taken on by schools and used for improvement purposes.

The study showed that school teaching staff respond to data as either good news or bad news. The data could produce:

- an action-orientated positive response to improve the issue behind the data;
- a passive 'filing away' of the issue behind the data;
- a passive rejection of the issue behind the data; or
- an active denial or rejection of the issue behind the data.

Interestingly, the first type of response to the data was equally likely to be provoked by either good news or bad news data. The factors that helped promote an action-orientated response were found in the way the data were presented and the feedback managed.

Factors closely associated with positive, action-orientated responses were:

- the availability of comparative data from schools felt to be not dissimilar;
- some prior groundwork done by the discussion leader in identifying possible improvement strategies to feed into the discussion so that people did not feel 'cornered' by the data;
- a climate where speculation and reflection were promoted among staff; and
- a feeling that the process generating the data was valid and could be trusted.

By the end of the programme, schools felt they had sufficient confidence in the value added data to abandon the code of confidentiality – although preferring to keep a code of practice forbidding schools from using the data for promotional purposes or at the expense of other schools. This greater openness contributed to the ability of the LEA to use the data for evaluating improvement among the schools and of the programme. It also enabled firmer challenges to be made in some cases, because of the stronger currency value the data had gained within schools, as well as between schools and LEA. This was against a background in which performance tables of primary Key Stage 2 results were being published for the first time.

These matters combine to suggest that for a formal model (see Chapter 3) of school improvement to be sustained, a strong cultural model needs to be developing alongside – enabling trust, reflection, challenge and risk-taking to occur among schools, within the LEA and between the two.

Use of Mixed Qualitative and Quantitative Data

Both at school level and LEA level, the same data were used for different purposes and with different intentions, depending on the focus and nature of the improvement. If a school succeeds in making an impact on the subject it is aiming to improve, but this is matched by a proportionate decline in another important area, then the evaluation of how or whether the school has improved becomes more complex. Sometimes it was important to confirm that an apparent impact was embedded, by triangulating it against other data – often more qualitative data such as pupil perceptions. Improvements were felt to have taken place most clearly where a range of qualitative and quantitative data were suggesting an improvement and where others were not showing a significant decline.

Data That Triggered Action

Other data were as important in the way they acted as triggers for action as the way they indicated school performance. In addition to learning outcome measures, the pupil perception data was a clear example of formative data.

Figure 4.2 compares the perceived impact of the four EPSI-driven data sets. LEA staff were asked to rate the data sets in terms of:

- the degree to which they helped inform the focus;
- the degree to which they helped the change process itself in school; and
- the degree to which they helped demonstrate improvement.

Interestingly, this identified the pupil perception survey data as having the greatest impact on improvement. It also seems a balanced indicator in that it was perceived equally to impact on the focus, to operate as a trigger for change and to have been a useful outcome indicator of improvement.

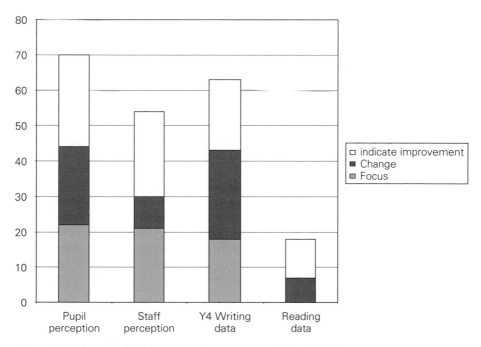

Figure 4.2   The perceived impact on improvement of the EPSI data sets

Nearly all schools commented on the pupil perception data as an important indicator of improvement. For some it also provided the focus, triggers and solutions to problems.

The data generated by the pupil perception interviews were specific to the schools and, as such, the data have important validity. They reflect the views of the intended beneficiaries of the school improvement. They emerge from the experience of learners' lives within the school and, where they are used as triggers or in identifying a focus for improvement, they are clearly valid consequentially – the outcome is of benefit to the user.

It may be that one way to resolve the conflict between imposed external measures and school-determined measures, is through the careful but systematic use of pupil perceptions – not only for identifying the focus and triggering action, but also to capture their judgement of the improvement. Pupils' articulations of the improvement can also be an effective way of disseminating improvement. Pupils' voices speak readily and directly to teachers. Pupil perceptions became an important indicator, which schools and LEA staff placed alongside test and teacher assessment results in judging school improvement.

For this reason, prompts from the EPSI pupil perception interviews have been built into the Essex Quality Framework for Schools – a self-evaluation tool. The prompts are found in 'Dimension 1: Learning and pupil achievement' and offer tangible help to schools and LEA staff in self-evaluation.

Other Issues Important in the Work on Pupil Data

Two issues are important to relate here. The first examines the interrelationship between performance data and primary school self-improvement. The second concerns the measures themselves.

At the time the pupil data group was established, a national debate over the respective virtues of school effectiveness and school improvement was becoming polemical (Elliott, 1996; Stoll and Mortimore, 1995). Stoll and Mortimore (1995) had conceded that 'Both these approaches are important and can, to a certain extent, be combined' (p. 2). Nevertheless, from the perspective of those of us seeking to use research to inform practice on the ground, this debate was beginning to be perceived as a hindrance rather than as a help in efforts to improve pupil learning in schools. In bringing together staff from UCSE, alongside managers of Essex LEA's primary value added project (then in its infancy), the EPSI pupil data group had a clear remit positively to resolve these perspectives for the EPSI programme at least.

As EPSI was attempting to support and study school *self*-improvement, there was a tension in the early debates in attempting to resolve two competing priorities. The need to study school self-improvement in a context of OFSTED key issues and focused LEA support, required sets of data and measures of improvement pertinent to and determined by each school's particular focus. However, there was also a need for some common measure of outcomes, which could be used to make judgements about the comparative improvements of schools, whatever their specific improvement focuses. However, once any one measure was adopted, the programme clearly ran the risk of being perceived to be identifying, in advance, the success criteria for programme schools.

The arguments about 'curriculum backwash' (Gipps, 1990, p. 23) resulting in teachers teaching to the test, are well rehearsed. There is clearly the potential for a parallel effect in the context of any improvement or effectiveness programme. If the EPSI programme, for example, had identified a particular reading test as *the* common measure across schools, it may have failed to register many of the improvements schools subsequently brought about. However, the lack of comparative programme level data on reading reduced the capacity of the programme to evaluate performance in this key area.

Kellner (1997) warns of the more worrying backwash effects of 'measure fixation', which can be brought about when Goodhart's law of economics – 'That perfectly good indicators tend to misbehave once they have become adopted as policy targets' – is applied to education improvement indicators. It was clear from the impact of the writing assessment that some schools did shift their focuses in the light of the measures and a backwash effect was created to some extent, but by no means was this a fixation. The prevailing argument in the adoption of the writing assessment data was that the benefits of collecting the data, whether used as a trigger or in evaluation, outweighed the possible distorting influence upon school self-improvement. William (1996) observed that 'a test is valid to the extent to which one would be happy for teachers to teach towards the test' (p. 134). As such, the writing assessment was a 'test' we felt it appropriate and beneficial 'to teach towards'.

Evidence from the programme now suggests that where schools were confident about their focus and planned actions, the programme-wide measures unsurprisingly were viewed as:

• relevant, if they measured an identified aspect (such as writing, see below); or as
• irrelevant where the school improvement focus was in another area.

It is nevertheless clear that any improvement programme needs to be clear at its outset about its values, focus and intended educational outcomes. Also, in the light of these, participating staff, whether school, LEA or research staff, should monitor whether and how the measures create back-wash effects or fixations, since data collection may predicate outcomes.

Evaluating the Measures Themselves

In evaluating the performance of the EPSI schools, it became clear that different ways of expressing pupil performance needed to be weighed alongside each other. The three measures originally identified proved to be helpful tools. These were the percentage of pupils in Year 6 attaining level 4 and above (% L4+), the average level for the cohort and the school's value added score. It became clear that schools with similar L4+ scores may have different average level scores and that over time the two measures may behave differently.

At its extreme, the % L4+ measure can be affected by the degree to which a group of pupils who may have been on the level 3/4 boundary are coaxed up by the provision of resources potentially at the expense of pupils operating at other levels. This became national policy with the introduction of national targets for literacy and numeracy in 1997, but the backwash may affect the attainment of pupils on the level 4/5 or 2/3 boundaries less.

The average level, however (calculated by dividing the sum of all levels achieved by the total number of pupils assessed), takes account of *all* pupils attaining at *all* levels. It will detect rises or falls in the numbers of pupils attaining low or high levels. The measure was later adopted nation-ally by the DfEE in 1998. Many Essex schools have now begun to use the difference between the average levels for a cohort at Key Stage 1 and the targeted average levels for end of Key Stage 2 to calculate targeted average progress (the difference between the cohort's average level at KS1 and target average level for end of KS2). Because it takes account of starting points and tended to iron out cohort differences, smaller schools in particu-lar favour the 'progress target' over the statutory outcome target for per-centage of pupils targeted to attain level 4 and above.

The 'value added' score gave a further perspective on this. Where a school is making a difference to the learning of all pupils, the measures on all three expressions of the data will improve. It is possible, however, for a positive outcome on the % L4+ measure to be accompanied by a neutral or even a negative average level or value added shift, which questions whether the learning outcome for the *cohort* has, indeed, improved. Table 4.2 shows

Table 4.2 *Contrasting patterns of results for three schools when expressed as percentages at level 4 and above, average levels and value added indicators*

School X	School Y	School Z
L4+ Dramatic improvements KS2 L4+ up 22% Eng, 12% Maths and 35% Science. KS1 Eng up 7%.	*L4+ KS2* Eng up 6% to 30%, Maths down 8% to 30% and Science down 6% to 70%. KS1 reading up 12% to 52%.	*L4+* English down 4% to 78%, Science down 3% to 70% but Maths up 5% to 69%.
Average levels KS2 Up 0.2 Eng/Ma and 0.4 science. Average KS1 reading levels up 0.4 but drop 0.1 in writing. Up 0.2 levels in Maths.	*Average levels KS2* English unchanged at 3.2, Science unchanged at 3.9 and Maths down 0.3 to 3.1. KS1 reading up 0.3 to 2.1 and Maths unchanged at 2.1.	*Average levels* Maths up 0.2 to 4.0, English holds at 3.9 and Science up 0.1 to 3.9.
VA KS2 Dramatic rise in all subjects from below predicted level to above. 8 point rise in English. 10 point rise in Science. 4% in Maths.	*VA KS2* English slightly up at 89.8, Science likewise at 107.1 but Maths 8 points down at 86.	*VA KS2* Maths slightly up by 4% to 105.6, English and Science no significant change – a little above predicted level (103 and 102).
KS1 Dramatic rise in Reading and Mathematics by 10% from 4% below to 6% above in all but writing.	*KS1* Reading up 10 points at 75.5, Writing up 5 points at 89.5. Maths down 1 but still strong at 103.5.	

three contrasting sets of EPSI school data. Interestingly, school Z fell in the published performance table for English and science, but data from the average level and the value added data suggest that the school has at least maintained standards for the cohort.

In each column are working notes made while evaluating the different data sets in order to provide some commentary to the numbers. Comparative judgements are made with anecdotal reference to the typical patterns of school performance at the time to help illustrate what the data represented.

Importantly, the different data sets show how deceptive any one set of numbers can be in isolation. However, as a set of indicators of outcome at a threshold (level 4), outcome of all pupils (average level), and relative outcome taking account of certain 'givens' (value added score), the three indicators provide a better picture of the schools' performance than one alone.

Triangulating a Grounded View of School Improvement

When the harder and softer data are lined up alongside one another, a powerful composite is provided for evaluating changes taking place within

Table 4.3 School data – triangulation of evidence of improvement

School	96–7 test results and value added data	School leadership	LEA staff	Mid KS writing and reading tests	Pupil perceptions from outset and close of programme	Staff perceptions from outset and close of programme
A	strong clear	strong clear	strong clear	little	strong clear	strong clear
B	clear	clear	clear	clear	strong clear	clear
C	strong clear	clear	strong clear	strong clear	strong clear	strong clear
D	little		little	little	little	clear

a school. Table 4.3 shows working notes of a panel of reviewers, summarizing the extent to which data from school management, the LEA pair, and pupils alongside learning outcome measures triangulate to give an indication of improvement. The range of indication of improvement is:

1 strong and clear evidence of improvement;
2 clear evidence of improvement;
3 little evidence of improvement.

The LEA has gone on to develop a primary data profile, providing an annual summary of school and LEA perspectives of a performance for each school in each dimension of the Essex Quality framework (see Chapter 9).

Conclusion: What We Have Learnt as an LEA about Pupil Data Issues

The experience and opportunity to work with EPSI schools in developing and modelling approaches in using pupil data to promote evidence-based school improvement have provided a number of messages for LEA development and improvement. These are that:

* pupil level data are central to any model for evaluating or setting targets for school self-improvement;
* schools – even schools with small cohorts – are more ready to be challenged over *progress* indicators of pupils and cohorts than over simple outcome measures, because they are perceived to be fair, to include all pupils and to take account of context issues. So we need to continue to develop value added measures, average levels and sub-level indicators and to work on the notion of entitlement to progress as well as outcome;

- a mid-key stage assessment is very formative and enhanced by developing teacher moderation of work at school level and by comparative analysis and feedback to schools by the LEA;
- staff in schools and the LEA need further and sustained training in understanding, analysis, presentation and manipulation of performance data;
- we need to work further to strengthen the working links between qualitative classroom or perception data, and more quantitative whole-school data;
- use of data perceived as being fair by schools and LEA will support schools in developing a positive 'cultural' model to promote confident, rigorously challenging and imaginative use of data, to run alongside the formal model (see Chapter 3) in order that school improvement is sustainable in the longer term;
- we need to develop processes for using data across schools to identify effective practice and to create learning networks within which that practice can be replicated.

Many of these points are in line with the new role for LEAs, set out in the DfEE code of practice for LEAs and the 1998 Standards and Frameworks Bill. However, one maxim of government policy is that LEA intervention with schools should be in 'inverse proportion to success' (DfEE, 1997a, p. 8). Government agencies began to provide schools with packages of comparative analyses and benchmark data to use in self-evaluation each year from 1997. The data upon which these are based for Key Stage 2 schools, represent the outcomes of teaching and learning that were going on during the four years before the analysis was carried out. In a sense, then, they contain evidence of 'success' or failure of teaching in previous months and years. The EPSI programme showed that an effectively challenging relationship with schools is dependent on quality, trusted data from a range of sources combined with ongoing knowledge and trust between schools and LEA.

It is impossible to intervene *early* 'in inverse proportion to success', when success is measured using purely outcome, end of key stage and inspection measures. To intervene early, it is necessary to have at hand a range of harder and softer data, a common language and a degree of informed dialogue with schools about the data and their relationship with teaching and learning. In fact, nearly all EPSI schools used lesson observations and many involved LEA staff in the process, in order to make effective connections between the data, judgements and action. It is now important that this be taken forward further, not least because colleagues in school are now aware of these issues, as the following comment demonstrates:

Pete Dudley

to examine how we teach is more complex, and a climate of trust, genuine staff development and teamwork needs to be generated in order that best teaching can be recognized and shared. It is what happens in the classrooms that matters – a model reflecting how we teach, 'Can it be better?', 'What was less successful?', 'Why?' – needs to happen much of the time. The EPSI programme has meant there is more of this on a fixed agenda. (EPSI headteacher reflection)

Chapter 5

Taking Pupil Perspectives Seriously
The Central Place of Pupil Voice in Primary
School Improvement

Michael Fielding, Alan Fuller and Tina Loose

Introduction

There is growing evidence that the voices of pupils in the processes of
school improvement are beginning to be taken more seriously. When an
editorial in the *Times Educational Supplement* (1997) refers approvingly to
research on the views of 6- and 7-year-old pupils about their experience
of schooling and ends by urging that 'adults in general – and schools in
particular – will have to take children's views much more seriously than
they do at present' (p. 20) it is an indicator that attitudes are changing,
however slowly. Such a standpoint, of course, has been gradually gaining
ground in the secondary sector, particularly through the work of Jean Rudduck
(Rudduck, Chaplain and Wallace, 1996) and John MacBeath (MacBeath,
1998a) in the UK, and Gary Goldman and Jay Newman (Goldman and
Newman, 1998) in North America. However, with the exception of the
work of John MacBeath et al. (MacBeath, Boyd, Rand and Bell, 1996) and
the small-scale work of Suzanne SooHoo (SooHoo, 1993) and Patricia
Campbell and her colleagues (Campbell, Edgar and Halsted, 1994) in
middle schools in the USA, similar work with primary school pupils is
virtually unknown.

What is remarkable and unusual about the work reported in this chapter
is, first, that primary pupil perception data was systematically collected as a
key part of a major primary school improvement project; second, that the
data proved to be immensely powerful, perhaps the single most powerful,
agent of change within a sophisticated school improvement programme;
and third, that the approach of involving pupil perceptions, not just the data,
clearly has enormous potential, not just to enhance school effectiveness,
but, at least in some cases, to lead to much more fundamental transformation. Indeed, as we suggest at the end of the chapter, an imaginative, innovative use of pupil perception data within the context of primary school

improvement holds the possibility of placing pupil agency at the heart, both of their own learning, and of schools as educational learning communities that transcend the instrumental and too often narrow pre-occupations of schools as learning organizations (Fielding, 1999).

The chapter is divided into five main parts. We begin by outlining the emergence of pupil perception data within the EPSI programme and the content and rationale of the interview schedule. In the second section we give details of the varied reality of data collection before, in the third section, considering forms and degrees of analysis the EPSI teams under-took prior to feeding back to schools. Section four has a range of examples of action schools took on the basis of their understanding and discussion of the pupil perception data. Finally, in section five, we tease out a number of key points with regard to the gathering and use of pupil perception data before suggesting some future directions that may prove fruitful in taking forward our thinking and our practice in the field of primary school improvement.

EPSI Context and Methods of Data Collection

Why Pupil Data?

The decision to actively seek and make use of pupils' accounts of their schools and any changes that may have taken place during the two-year period of the EPSI initiative was not part of the original plan. It emerged from discussions at steering committee and the data working party level and owed much to the positive experience of some group members' conducting group interviews with pupils as part of the OFSTED inspection process. There was recognition that school improvement can be described in many different ways and that what pupils say about their learning and the culture of their schools has as much to contribute to a rich understanding of school development as the more familiar performance measures. It is important to know what pupils feel about these dimensions of their experience because those feelings and dispositions directly affect their actual learning and the quality of it. Furthermore, it was felt that pupil perception data occasionally provide insights into the need for change that other data mask or miss altogether.

Establishing the Sample and Themes of the Enquiry

Once the decision was made to collect this kind of data across all EPSI schools, a working group was established to advise on methodology. A small group representing the educational psychology, the special needs support, and school development services met with a member of the steering group to explore the type of information it was hoped to collect and therefore the type of questions to ask. The diverse nature of the group turned out to be a real strength, bringing a wide range of very different kinds of expertise in seeking pupils' views through their respective roles and past experiences.

It was agreed that data would be sought from all schools in a consistent way. A sample of Year 4 and Year 6 pupils would be asked questions at the start of the programme and the initial Year 4 pupils would be re-interviewed two years later when they reached Year 6.

Key aspects of pupil experience of schooling were clustered around four areas or themes of enquiry, namely:

- shared values (pupils, staff, parents);
- pupil involvement and responsibility;
- monitoring pupils' work and progress; and
- expectations.

From this it was hoped to discover more about:

- the degree of consistency in the school community;
- what the school hoped to achieve; and
- the degree to which pupils had or could influence factors that affect school improvement.

One of the primary purposes of collecting pupil perception data was to obtain insights into the functioning of schools that may challenge or offer different perspectives from the view of the adults working in them. However, there was an awareness that, however valid, reliable and authentic the data, children's opinions can easily be reinterpreted by adults affected by them or dismissed by third parties if methods of collection are not seen to be rigorous and objective. An agreed approach, which took into account the necessity of a representative sample of views within a school, was therefore seen as important.

Group Interviews

The working group recommended group interviews in order to allow a larger proportion of pupils to be consulted than would be possible through individual interviewing. Additionally, group interviews were considered to provide the further benefit of encouraging interchange between pupils, enabling views and opinions to be developed more fully. Also, the interviewer would be able to check individual views with others in a group and better judge how representative they might be. It was felt that group interviews would provide more information than the sum of individual comments and would encourage greater contribution from children who might find individual interviews threatening. Conversely, the interviewer needed to be aware of potentially negative effects of group dynamics, which could serve to generate a false consensus or 'group think' where individual views are lost through the wish to conform. Perhaps even more so than with individual interviews, the skills of the interviewer are paramount.

Data Collection in Practice

Agreeing the Sample Composition

It was agreed across all schools that data would be collected from Year 4 and Year 6 pupils for later comparison at the end of the programme. Initial data were collected in the Easter Term 1996 with repeated interviews in January/February 1998. For the purpose of comparison, EPSI pairs were asked to re-interview the pupils who were now in Year 6. In many cases these were almost entirely the same children due to stability in the school population. Also, in some cases a further sample of Year 4 pupils was taken in order to contrast perceptions across two equivalent cohorts.

In most schools, group interviews with samples of Year 4 and Year 6 pupils took place with EPSI pairs (two colleagues, each person coming from a different education service, e.g. advisory, educational psychology, special needs) working with the group. For example, in a large junior school with four forms of entry, two representatives from each class were selected, taking into account the need for appropriate gender balance and range of ability and attitude to school. It was considered not helpful to have a skewed sample, for example of pupils who were largely successful and uncritical of the school. In this school's case we also asked to carry out interviews in all four year groups.

Developing Manageable Data-gathering Processes

Using agreed protocols and the interview framework (see Appendix 3), data gathered by EPSI pairs through semi-structured interviews were primarily qualitative, consisting of notes taken by an interviewer or partner. For practical reasons it was decided not to recommend tape-recording of interviews for later transcription. As one of the intended benefits of this exercise was to develop a model of data gathering that schools could use in the future, it would not have been helpful to devise a method that was unrealistically demanding of time or expense. The large volume of data generated by taped transcripts would also make the task of analysis more difficult.

The format for recording responses from children was not standardized, allowing EPSI pairs to determine with school colleagues the most helpful way to note pupils' perceptions. Most pairs used the framework of suggested questions to organize their note-taking, for example, designing record sheets for each of the themes ('shared values and beliefs', etc.) with space under each question to make notes.

Note-taking varied across the programme, depending on individual style and interview context, such as group size and whether a single or pair of interviewers was involved. Data mostly consisted of verbatim quotes and summaries of points raised.

Often the EPSI pair carried out the interviews by alternating as questioner and scribe. Occasionally the scribe intervened to ask a follow-up question or clarify views expressed. The value of working as a pair in this way was significant in enabling the flow of discussion and fully recording ideas.

Modifications

In some schools it was not feasible for the EPSI pair to carry out joint interviews and in a few it was decided that because of the circumstances of the school more valuable data would be obtained through individual interviews with pupils. Thus a range of strategies was used, reflecting the school's needs and, to some extent, differences in professional practice.

Some modifications to the suggested approach led to a few methods that proved to be unsuitable, for example where too much data was collected from every pupil and this was too unwieldy to analyse or where the manner of presentation did not help the pupil make appropriate responses.

In other cases, the modifications proved appropriate and fruitful. For example, in one school a selection of the questions were put to pupils on the basis that these were the most pertinent to their specific school improvement focus. In another case where there was a small number of pupils in the relevant age groups, the interview questions were put into a questionnaire form after the initial interviews and put to the pupils from time to time over the two-year period.

Other modifications proved variable in their success. In one case a selection from the questions was put to the pupils, but the interviewers had found it difficult to establish the programme in the school and this meant that they did not at this stage fully grasp what they really needed to know from the pupils. They were, however, clear at the end of the programme as to the most important questions to ask. By adding in these questions at the final interviews they discovered some useful pointers for the school. On the whole, however, they were unable to make a fair comparison between the two sets of data.

Finally, some of the modifications had more to do with the actual encounter with pupils than with the interview framework itself. Some pupils were badly behaved and much energy had to be expended by the interviewers on managing behaviour. In such cases, the pupils were often very critical of their school and there was indication that they had difficulty in gaining appropriate support from their families. In one such case the school had already decided to have a major focus on behaviour.

Forms of Analysis and Feedback

Forms and Degrees of Analysis

The ways in which EPSI pairs fed back data to schools ranged from the presentation of near-raw data to explicitly worked interpretation. Of course, such a continuum was not utilized evenly, both extremes tending to be infrequently used. Even where data were fed back in an apparently raw form it was likely that some degree of interpretation had taken place, if only in the selection of the words to record. In some cases it was very clear that 'on the spot' analysis occurred during the interviews and summaries took into account other contextual factors such as the number of pupils support- ing a view or the strength of feeling expressed. It is an important message from this research that interviewer interpretations can provide equally valid and sometimes richer data than raw perceptions. However, it is essential that those interpretations are understood and acknowledged as such, and not presented as direct pupil views (cf. Connolly, 1997). In some cases, report- ing of data did not make this distinction clear.

Analysis of data was generally undertaken in two stages. First, EPSI pairs summarized the views expressed by pupils in a write-up for schools. Analysis took the form of grouping perceptions and identifying key themes. Second, following feedback, a further level of analysis took place with school staff. This was not formally reported or, in most cases, articulated as further analysis. However, schools' reactions to feedback clearly con- tributed to further understanding of the data. They also served as a means of triangulation, testing the credibility of data against teachers' knowledge of pupils' views and attitudes.

Year 4 pupils
- It's nice to be given responsibility, but some teachers have favourites.
- Not all teachers are fair. Some get very cross.
  Mrs S always sorts problems out. Sometimes work gets ripped up.
  Not all teachers will help you if you are stuck.
  Not all teachers like to help pupils.
- Not all children work hard.

Year 6 pupils
- There are lots of opportunities to take on jobs and responsibilities.
- Teachers are kind and willing to give up their free time.
  Teachers help with work.
  Pupils help each other with work.
- It's good to work hard and most pupils do.

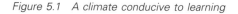

Figure 5.1   A climate conducive to learning

The majority of programme pairs chose to summarize data by cluster-ing key ideas or themes. Many used the headings under which questions were grouped, but in some cases these were re-worked in ways that made better sense of the data. Most schools were provided with a summary of representative responses from the pupils, organized by year group. In the example (Figure 5.1), key perceptions within one of the interview themes were highlighted. In this format the contrast between perceptions of chil-dren in Year 4 and Year 6 about being given responsibility, teacher fairness, and working hard was very clear and needed little interpretation.

In other schools a greater degree of analysis was necessary before feeding back. To encapsulate large amounts of data, some pairs chose to present summaries in a form of diagram with responses grouped thematic-ally. In retrospect, a number of these methods of displaying data took the form of a 'conceptually clustered' matrix (Miles and Huberman, 1984). Another example (Figure 5.2) shows part of a grid presented to one school, in which feedback from pupil interviews was drawn together by theme with suggested pupil perception criteria in one column of the chart. Staff were invited to rate the criteria from 1 (low) to 5 (high) and underline any com-ments they considered particularly significant.

Overall, EPSI pairs undertook more detailed analysis of the data before feeding back after the repeat interviews at the end of the initiative. This is partly explained by the different purposes served by the data at this point. In the initial interviews, pupil perceptions helped to inform a school's decision about its focus and strategy for improvement. It was important for schools to be involved in the analysis and to make decisions about the messages the data offered. The main purpose of data collection at the end of the initiative was to highlight changes or consistencies in pupil perceptions over the two-year period. Thus the role of the external consultant in the analysis process

Pupil perception criteria	Rating (1–5)	Theme
• Learner's clarity about learning purpose, feedback and strategies for improvement in learning		• Girls were positive about pupil commitment to learning and the reactions of peers to achievement were also regarded as important. 'If a teacher shows our work to the class as an example then you feel proud', but the boys were reticent on this. They did not comment.
• Pupil/teacher relationships and perception of teacher as collaborator in learning		• Pupils feel most peers take work seriously – more so now they are in Y6 – though there is a hard core of silly people who don't. There was a strong perception from all that work was about getting through the boring parts to get to the interesting work – 'You rush the boring work' – copying off the board for example – 'to get onto the interesting work'.

Figure 5.2   Feedback format

was initially to prepare data in a digestible form and support the process of interpretation and later to offer an outsider's view of the extent to which the data provided evidence of improvement in the school.

Handling Feedback

As these examples show, pupil perceptions can be openly critical of staff members or school practices. Data can be both powerful and contentious and therefore needs to be handled sensitively. There were instances where a small part of the data was fed back to the headteacher alone in order that the reported matter might be further explored and dealt with confidentially.

Some schools, as in the case of Example A, though welcoming the role of the external interviewers in obtaining valuable data, were surprised and shocked at pupils' views and felt that they needed to take action immediately.

One school where there had been nearly 100 per cent staff changes and a total change of culture was expecting the negative responses. Pupils were angry about the changes and their expressions of this to an outside interviewer helped the staff see the situation from the pupils' point of view and the headteacher to better understand her relationship with the pupils.

Other schools reacted very differently to perceived bad news or implied criticism from pupils. In the case of Example B, the school felt they did not have effective feedback from the EPSI pair, were deeply unhappy

---

Example A

One interviewer was concerned about a number of negative responses of
Y6 in a school where such responses were unexpected. The interviews were
brought to an early close and resumed at a later time so that the interviewer
had time to reflect and change the climate for the interviews so that the
negative cycle could be broken. The school was shocked by the outspoken-
ness of these pupils but wished for the process to continue, as staff felt it
could help the school progress. They felt that had they carried out such
interviews themselves they would not have gotten this valuable feedback.
When interviews were resumed the pupils remained polite but firm in their
unflattering views of some school matters affecting their education. They
were, however, balanced in their responses and readily challenged each other
if they felt a remark was not justified. They also said much in praise of the
school. The responses of Y4 were far more favourable but they had a low
opinion of the previous and the present Y6, some of whom were described as
'muckers'. They also said:
  'Last year's Y6 were big for their boots and were not so nice.'
  'Some were bullies. One boy thought he was smart. So did the others. We
  didn't.'
  'He was funny sometimes.'
  'Some of this year's Y6 don't care. They laugh about things that are wrong.'
  'Hopefully we won't be the same when we are Y6.'
There was total agreement from the group and when re-interviewed as Y6,
two years on, they concluded the interview by asking if they had met their
'target' which they described as being 'a better, more responsible Year 6'.
Their responses indicated a more positive attitude to school than those of the
previous Y6 interviews and their attitudes were consistent with those they
had held as Y4 pupils. Staff agreed with this assessment, but found them to
have less initiative than the previous group. For example, they have a committee for improvement and the first Y6 group would, as individuals, take
responsibility for ringing companies or contractors to get jobs done and made
such suggestions themselves, whereas the most recent Y6 needed much more
support and guidance and did not show such initiative. The recent Y6, however, seemed equally alert as the previously interviewed Y6 to unfair treat-
ment of others, citing inappropriate humour that could be seen as racist and
personal lax behaviour of a teacher.

---

with the messages they were hearing, and were also dismissive of the validity of the data.

Two important messages emerge from Example B (overleaf). First,
when interview data are contentious it is particularly important for recipients
to trust the methods used to gather the data. If fault can be found in the way

---

Example B

One school found the negative messages about staff and the pupils' perception of adult attitudes to the pupils to be unpalatable. It was reported that little note should be taken of this as some of the pupils interviewed were very difficult, negative children and the strong personalities would have influenced other pupils' responses. There was an adult belief that the school was not like the pupils' description of it. They therefore felt that this data was of little use to them: 'We were very sceptical so we ignored it all.' They were concerned about the way the exercise was carried out. However, there is subsequent evidence that the school has developed a number of targets which enabled the pupils to offer their views.

---

interviews were conducted, this may be used to explain away difficult messages. Second, even when the impact of uncomfortable messages is not immediately observable, they may have caused individuals to reappraise their own views. Attitude change is by and large incremental.

Action Arising

One of the most remarkable things to emerge from the EPSI initiative is a fuller realization of the depth and power of pupil perception data as a central, and we would argue, necessary component of school improvement. There were no instances of pupil perception data failing to have an impact on the subsequent work of the schools involved. This is even the case in one school that generally felt it had little benefit from the initiative and where the approach to pupil interviews failed to provide helpful data. Despite these perceptions, this school nonetheless used the technique of interviewing pupils to great effect in a different context. Pupils' views on the helpfulness and effectiveness of the school marking system produced useful data on consistency and what was valuable to the pupils, enabling the school to improve in this area of their work. Further work in the school has produced some impressive results about parental perceptions, which will guide the work of the school in the future.

The overwhelming picture emerging from the use of pupil data is both positive and challenging. There were two instances in which the substantial challenge of pupil data (e.g. pointing to sarcasm by some teachers, teachers seen as being in the job merely to draw the pay cheque, racist use of humour, the frustration of having to do boring work before getting on to something interesting, lack of staff intervention in bullying, low staff expectations, poor teacher/pupil relationships) seemed to lead directly to members of staff moving from the school, but this was unusual. Just as pupil data invariably challenge some aspects of the work of teachers and the school as a learning community, so they are invariably supportive of that work in ways that are enriching and creative.

This can be seen by the range of ways in which schools incorporated pupil perception data into their subsequent ways of working. Some schools, although pleased at the outcome, were keen to see if they had maintained the positive responses over time or made further improvements. Some felt they had useful feedback from the interviewer, which altered their practice, for example explaining outcomes expected of pupils. Another found data useful in helping set targets for improved teacher/pupil interaction. Another school found seeking pupils' views valuable and adapted the method to find out more about pupils' views on mathematics and used the data to influence their development in the maths focus. Finally, in another the impact of pupil perception data had a profound effect on the direction of its ensuing work. In this case the results of the interviews altered the emphasis of the EPSI work by introducing a new area of school improvement relating to pupils' perceptions and attitudes, which had not been identified by the OFSTED inspection. While they managed to also carry on with the work of the two initial areas identified, the school considered this to be more important to the success of its pupils than other agreed focuses.

Pupil Perceptions and Primary School Improvement

One of the key outcomes of the focus on pupil perception data within the EPSI initiative was that schools and LEA staff recognized the value of asking pupils about their experiences of school. Schools' experience of pupil interviews during OFSTED were not overwhelmingly positive, but within this initiative schools reflected that pupil perceptions did add to their understanding of their schools. As with other data collection, this was found to be most influential if schools felt a degree of involvement and active engagement. For example, where data were fully shared and discussions took place about their analysis and use, this data had more impact.

Broadly speaking, there were two different, but related, ways in which pupil perception data shaped and energized the process of school improvement. These were, first, ways in which such data provided evidence of improvement within the schools, and, second, ways in which the data were themselves agents of the improvement process.

With regard to the first of these, in 50 per cent of schools the pupil perception data provided evidence of improvement that was directly related to the school's focus. There were some difficulties in triangulating or sub-stantiating claims for data and there is a need for caution to avoid overstat-ing the case when data rely on comments from a relatively small sample of pupils. Nonetheless, with appropriate regard for these qualifying remarks, our view is that the quality and quantity of evidence that emerged over the two years of the EPSI initiative suggest very strongly that pupil perception data played an important part in establishing the credibility or otherwise of claims by the schools that they had improved in ways they described. It is also important to add that pupil perception data described changes within schools that were not directly related to the area of focus and in some cases this supported the view that a broader-based or cultural change had taken place during the two years of the improvement initiative.

With regard to the second way in which pupil data formed part of the school improvement process – that is how the data were themselves agents of the improvement process – the picture that emerged was more uneven but, where successful, more powerful. Certainly, in a few schools there were dramatic effects in that the reflection on pupil perception data resulted in significant changes within the school. In these schools there was evidence to support Pollard and colleagues' contention that 'children's voices do not necessarily reflect the view of the adults who have power over them. Given voice, they may well criticise the dominant power structures. They may question "how things are" in their worlds and provide alternative interpreta-tions and prescriptions' (Pollard, Thiessen and Filer, 1997:11). There was also some evidence that teachers were prepared to tentatively yet authentic-ally face what Pollard et al. call 'perhaps the biggest challenge of all', namely, 'to allow children a share of the power we, as adults, have in their classrooms and lives' (*ibid.*).

In seeking to locate these findings within a theoretical framework that will help us extend and deepen both our thinking and our practice of seek-ing and using pupil perception data in the developing processes of school improvement, we find the recent complementary work of Dennis Thiessen and Michael Fielding helpful.

In Thiessen's work (Thiessen, 1997) we have an imaginative three-fold typology of engagement with primary school pupil data: learning about / acting on behalf of / working with pupil perspectives. Evidence from the EPSI work pertinent to the first of these, *learning about* primary pupil perspectives, was widespread. Gathering data about the nature and quality of pupils' lived experience of the curriculum and the broader life of the school never failed to have an impact. It invariably underscored the legitim-acy and the insight of children's perspectives on their own experience of the world and their perceptiveness of the role of adults in it. It also sometimes alerted staff to the quite contrary effects of their best intended actions and to pupil misperceptions, as when it transpired that a staff initiative involving new ways of working with physically handicapped pupils led, not to a richer, more expansive equity, but rather to a build-up of resentment among the rest of the pupils in the class.

Because staff often learned more about the pupils' perspectives and came to understand them more deeply, there was also some evidence of Thiessen's second category, *acting on behalf of* primary pupils. Thus, in one school, as a result of the engagement with pupil perception data, staff asked pupils to help them develop aspects of their professional practice that the pupils had identified as causing difficulty. In this case it was the use of questions within teacher pedagogy: pupils had said that some teachers were too abrupt and did not give them time to think; having nearly got the answer or been able to make a response, they were moved on to something else too quickly. Here teachers were not merely learning about pupil perspectives, they were taking those perspectives and acting on behalf of pupils in the furtherance of their learning. Pupil perspectives were driving, not following, the development of professional practice.

With the third category, *working with* primary pupil perspectives, we move from pupils as interesting sources of data to pupils as co-agents of change. Though examples of this category were much more rare, one stands out as particularly interesting. In this school, the headteacher, as part of his way of engaging with his own and other classes that he covered for colleagues, regularly asked pupils about various aspects of their learning. Over time the children engaged in more searching dialogue and, on occasions, began to express their frustration and disappointment that no action seemed to result from these discussions. The headteacher's perception was that action had occurred, but he realized that the pupils had not been made aware of it. Partly as a result of these exchanges and of the influence of pupil data on the professional culture within the school, a school council was formed. In this example we have moved a long way from the raising of teacher awareness (learning about pupils) and some way, too, from advocacy of pupils by committed teachers (acting on behalf of pupils), to pupils and teachers as active partners in the educational process (working with pupils).

Fielding's (1998) work with secondary school student researchers takes Thiessen's third category a stage further. Like Connolly (1997), Fielding challenges the ease with which researchers and others feel able to speak on behalf of pupils and argues for the distinctive insights that pupils themselves bring to researching the present realities and shaping the future possibilities of their schools. Though his advocacy of students as researchers rests on his current work with secondary school students, there is no reason why appropriate equivalents should not be developed within primary schools. It is worth remembering that early work in North America (Campbell et al.,

Michael Fielding, Alan Fuller and Tina Loose

1994; SooHoo, 1993) drew on middle school students and there is a small but growing interest in widening its scope to include elementary schools (Goldman and Newman, 1998).

Fielding's initial work on transformative education (Fielding, 1997, 1999) also suggests an alternative framework for taking forward and widening current approaches to school improvement. As with the 'Students as Researchers' initiative, his advocacy centres on ways in which pupil agency and teacher learning can be brought more explicitly together within a communal, rather than an organizational framework.

Future Directions – School Improvement

From the standpoint of school improvement, we would point to a range of possibilities under the two broad headings of (1) ways of conducting research and (2) ways of using research to inform future development on a regular, systematic basis, which embrace Thiessen's first two levels of engagement.

One of the issues that became clear to us in the course of our work, and which comes through strongly in some of the more recent literature on the difficulties as well as the possibilities of researching pupil perspectives, is the problematic nature of the task itself. Though there are imaginative and interesting new approaches to researching the experience of very young children (e.g. Pryor, 1995), there is a companion awareness that, as Connolly reminds us, research accounts of young children's perspectives 'are all inevitably products of the researcher's own values and assumptions and the influences they have brought to bear through their role in the research process' (Connolly, 1997, p. 163). Furthermore, he reminds us that 'not only will young children offer different voices to different people but those voices will also be documented and re-articulated through the eyes of the researcher' (*ibid.*). These strictures are not, however, intended to immobilize us. Rather, they require us to be more critically reflexive than many contemporary accounts tend to be. If they combine Pryor's imaginative energy with Connolly's positive reflexivity, then LEAs, universities and other providers are well placed to use their expertise and their external standpoint to help schools supplement their internally conducted enquiries into pupil perspectives on a range of school and classroom issues.

With regard to ways of using research to inform future development on a regular systematic basis, the work of Pete Dudley offers some important insights into the difficult and important issue of data presentation and interpretation (Dudley, 1997). What we also need to understand more richly and develop more radically and more imaginatively is how we incorporate both new and old methods of gathering pupil perception data into our daily

120

routines and practices. Pupil perception data only becomes part of the process of school improvement if the school is systematic and rigorous in its collection and equally so in the possibly more important stages in which meaning is made and action agreed.

Future Directions – Transformative Education

From the standpoint of transformative education, (1) new ways of conducting research and (2) new ways of using research to inform future development on a regular systematic basis that both engage with and extend Thiessen's third level of engagement, also need to be developed.

With regard to new ways of conducting research, the fundamental difference between much of the pioneering work developed by people like Jean Rudduck (Rudduck et al., 1996) and John MacBeath (1996, 1998a), and what is being suggested here hangs on the issue of pupil agency. As indicated in our earlier remarks on Fielding's work, the suggestion is that we move away from pupils as interesting and invaluable sources of data to pupils as co-researchers (e.g. SooHoo, 1993) and, ultimately, to students as researchers in their own right (see Fielding, 1998; Steinberg and Kincheloe, 1998; Weatherill, 1998).

With the quantum leap to pupil agency comes the necessity of new ways of using research to inform future development on a regular, systematic basis, and with it a radical transformation in the professional and educational culture of the school. Once you legitimize the responsible agency of pupils as enquirers into and agents of education as a transformative undertaking, you not only begin to change the ways that staff see pupils and pupils see themselves, but also the way staff see themselves as learners. And with cultural transformation comes its structural equivalent. If pupils are to generate questions on their own, with each other, and together with staff; if they are to investigate and gather data pertinent to those questions; if they are to make meaning from that data, how is all this to happen? What kind of support does it need? Who supports it? When do such enquiries take place? When is meaning made from the data and with whom? When, where and to whom are any recommendations for action made? If action follows, who is responsible for carrying it out and how is it then monitored? These and questions like them point to the development of the school as a genuinely dialogic learning community.

Just as pupil perception data are, in our view and our experience, central to school improvement, so pupils as researchers of and agents of their own education is central to a transformative education in and for dialogic democracy in the twenty-first century.

Part 3

LEA Insights

Chapter 6

The LEA and School Improvement

Sue Kerfoot and Gary Nethercott

Introduction

In this chapter, and the next one, we look at how the EPSI programme contributed to building the LEA's capacity to support schools' improvement efforts. The chapter is organized into nine subsections, in which we examine the changing role of LEAs and set out some of the questions that arise from developing the LEA's capacity to support school improvement. The notion of programme teams is explained, their support programme is described and their role with schools outlined. We review the benefits of multi-disciplinary team work, and provide an analysis of the effectiveness of these teams and the implications of multi-disciplinary teams. Lastly we summarize the key points and highlight the main conclusions.

The chapter will be of particular interest to both LEA staff and school staff. For LEA staff we offer insights into a new model of working with schools and portray some of the complexities of supporting school improvement. For staff in schools we imply that working with external agents requires in-school systems and structures to be developed so that sustained critical and productive relations between senior school staff and LEA colleagues can be managed effectively.

The Changing Role of LEAs

Essex LEA, like many others, has had to face unprecedented change in the past ten years. It has affected all aspects of the education service with maximum delegation of financial resources through local management of schools, the potential for schools to opt for grant maintained status under the 1992 Education Schools Act, the introduction of the National Curriculum and the creation of OFSTED. The impact has been significant on advisory and inspection services; from a position where every school had a linked general inspector carrying out LEA reviews and supporting school development planning, many LEAs moved to a position where local authorities seemed 'no longer able to provide a coherent infrastructure of support for schools in respect of advice and in-service training' (MacGilchrist, Myer and Reid, 1997). This period was characterized by the development of advisory services into 'business units', with significant resources delegated to schools where advisory time had to be purchased.

The Essex service, like many others, responded by working hard at establishing high quality purchasable advisory services. The rigours of operating in this way brought about significant cultural change in the service and changed relationships between schools and advisers. Advisers became more client-centred and responsive to a school-led agenda. Such new ways of working tended to develop well with schools that had systematic approaches to planning, clear development plans and an established approach to working with external consultants. However, in the primary sector at least, the more frequently encountered reality was markedly more fragmented, with one-off training events, small-scale developments and little evaluation or follow-up of school development activity. Because of the cost involved, most primary schools had several disconnected inputs and could usually only afford to work with one external consultant for short periods of time. Many schools brought in advisory support to provide specialist subject input or to carry out audit work frequently linked to the inspection structure being introduced at the time.

As the educational agenda has focused increasingly on improving performance, a number of tensions and dilemmas have emerged for the LEA. There has been an increasing need to find ways of marrying together a client-centred approach with the LEA taking a more forceful advocacy role for learners and parents. Second, in relation to the funding base for such work, with the disaggregation of budgets and delegation to schools, there has often been an over-emphasis on notions of entitlement to service providers' time. Understandable though this is in terms of 'fairness' to those who are paying, the need to differentiate support and also ensure focusing of time to enable adequate contribution to the school improvement process is problematic to achieve. If LEAs are to have a significant role in school improvement consistent with current political expectations, there needs to be flexibility in terms of allocating external support. One of the truisms of school improvement must be that the improvement needs of schools vary considerably and the focusing of resources around high need is increasingly the emphasis.

Back in 1995 at the outset of the EPSI programme, we aimed to address the question of how an LEA can best support schools in their improvement efforts. Consideration was given as to how this could be done in a cost-effective and therefore sustainable manner. It was decided to use existing LEA staff and to build on and develop their current skills in school improvement approaches. Here the intention was to develop a pool of staff who could be used both in this project and in the future to support school improvement work. The use of existing LEA staff was also critical in the development of a model of working with schools that could be an integral part of LEA service delivery – 'built in' to the normal range of activities of an LEA and not a 'bolt-on' or a 'one-off'.

Developing the LEA's Capacity to Support School Improvement

This approach is embodied in the research programme's second aim 'to increase the Education Department's capacity to support schools as they seek to improve the quality of the education they provide'. A number of key questions were posed in this regard:

- What models of advisory support are effective in direct work with schools?
- In view of the changing role of the LEA and the sharp focus on how the LEA can add value to such school improvement processes, how can the LEA best use the full range of support staff in supporting effective school improvement?
- If school development advisers, educational psychologists and special needs support staff are central to the LEA strategy for school improvement, how should they be organizing their work?
- What benefits are there in having multi-disciplinary teams contributing to school improvement and what benefits accrue to the separate disciplines from their joint work?
- What are the implications of this approach for the organizational structures of the LEA when the separate disciplines already have prime purposes, which frequently force them to work separately?
- What skills do external consultants need to support school improvement?
- What structure for advisers' continuing professional development is most effective?
- How can LEA advisers reconcile the need to acknowledge improvement as the school's responsibility while sometimes having to work for the LEA with a school in terms of the school's inability to make appropriate improvement?
- How can the benefits be disseminated to all schools through other projects and in the day-to-day work of advisers?

In setting up the multi-disciplinary teams, there was a clear intention to bring together key LEA advisory staff. The teams were comprised of school development advisers, senior educational psychologists and senior managers from the special needs support service. The school development advisers were a newly established group – staff from a background of advisory and inspection work more usually involved in whole-school development, curriculum and management issues; the senior educational psychologists and team leaders from the LEA special needs support service were more usually involved in work relating to individual pupils where existing school organizations are having difficulty in meeting their educational needs. This was seen to be an interesting and important combination of staff for a whole range of reasons, not least of which was the clear focus for the evaluation of the programme in terms of improved learning outcomes for individual pupils and not just changes to school processes.

As well as the contrast in the teams of those more usually dealing with whole-school outcomes and those dealing with outcomes for identified individuals, there was a further contrast of existing remit. Due to the particular client focus of various groups of staff within the LEA, there was also a combination of staff, some of whom are used to focusing on the school as the 'customer' of their services and are reliant on them for income generation, and those who are specifically supporting LEA statutory responsibilities and acting in a regulatory role with schools, and on occasions advocating for individual pupils when schools are focusing on other priorities.

The Programme Teams

In setting up the project teams, the existing roles and responsibilities of LEA staff involved had to be taken into account. The newly created school development advisery team were at the start of establishing their role with schools, and it was decided to involve the entire team in the programme, as it was anticipated this would be a key professional development opportunity for them. Smaller numbers of senior educational psychologists and team leaders from the special needs support service were involved. In planning the support arrangements, it was envisaged that each school would have an identified pair of LEA staff working with them – a school development adviser and a senior educational psychologist or a school development adviser and a team leader or two SDAs.

In identifying the particular pairs to work with particular schools, it was deliberately decided not to assign specific roles to the various professional groups. It was the intention to let the roles develop and it was left to the teams to establish the roles themselves. Some consideration was given to the particular personal attributes and competencies of the individuals, with an intention to ensure some mix or balance in interpersonal skills, for example ensuring that there was a balance of those colleagues who readily assume an 'up front' role in staff meetings with those who are effective in facilitating contributions, those who ensure effective organization and administration and so on. As part of the process of monitoring and evaluating the project, information was collected on the particular roles and areas of specific contributions that individuals and particular professional groups actually made as the project developed.

It should be noted that for some of the programme schools the SDA, or one of the SDAs working with them as a member of the programme team, was also their ongoing link school development adviser. This posed the SDA with a potentially confusing situation at times when it was difficult to see where one role ended and the other began, particularly as both roles were being newly established at the same time. This issue is reflected in the schools' ability to reflect on the contribution of the programme as distinguished from other ongoing school support mechanisms.

Due to a number of staffing changes in the early stages of the project, a number of the SDA programme pair teams became reduced to one. With the increasing recognition of the importance of co-supervision for those working with schools, it was decided early on to 'pair the pairs', thus ensuring that, although each school had an identified key person or key pair that they were working with, there was also access by LEA staff to peers for ongoing support and reflection. This resulted in the six larger team groupings.

Altogether there were 18 school development advisers, 4 senior educational psychologists and 4 special needs support team leaders. The six programme teams quickly established themselves as a major focus for the development of the whole programme. Each of these teams had a member of the university staff attached who acted as a 'researcher-mentor'.

Supporting the Programme Teams

The collaboration with the University of Cambridge School of Education (UCSE) staff was developed as part of the broader thrust within the LEA to develop constructive collaboration with education researchers in higher education. This was but one of several programmes where the LEA has provided a bridge to enable the transition from educational and psychological research to change at school and classroom level that leads to improved outcomes for children and young people. Within the EPSI programme, UCSE staff played a key role in the preparation and training of the multi-disciplinary teams, enabling reflection on how school improvement can be facilitated from the perspectives of research to date and also from the perspective of staff involved in working with schools on a day-to-day basis in advisory and consultancy capacities. The UCSE contribution came from members of the IQEA (Improving the Quality of Education For All) school improvement team. The main thrust of their approach to school improvement centred on a largely processed-based model developed over the past six years (see Hopkins et al., 1994 for the theoretical grounding and Ainscow et al., 1994a for the handbook of staff development activities, which provides ways in which the model can engage with practice in schools). Programme team members undertook a workshop programme (outlined in Appendix 4), which focused on the six 'school conditions' (outlined in Appendix 5), which the model regards as central to successful school improvement. The six school conditions provided the underlying process-based drive that enables the achievement of more overt and specific professional targets and pupil outcomes. The assumption of the IQEA model is that without such a process-based drive, targeted outcomes are likely to flounder or be less effective than expected. Substantial parts of the core programme worked through and developed shared understandings of these process conditions, while at the same time encouraging further exploration of the issues based on a substantial range of experience within the project teams and the UCSE staff.

Another aspect of the IQEA approach to school improvement that informed the programme was the centrality of professional culture as both an inhibitor and an agent of change (Ainscow et al., 1994b). The focus on school culture as a major factor in the development or otherwise of effective change in schools in turn highlighted the need to develop better understandings and experience of process consultancy skills (Southworth and Ainscow, 1996). This formed an ongoing thread in the core programme and is considered in more detail in Chapter 7.

Another key aspect of the support and development programme was that of co-supervision. The need to ensure co-supervision for colleagues working in this taxing and complex area was identified early on and the structure of the multi-disciplinary teams provided the opportunity to ensure ongoing co-supervision and support through the programme. One of the early challenges set to programme managers by one of the senior educational psychologists helped shape this process. He used a clinical counselling analogy to explore the benefits of having some form of case mentoring structure whereby the consultant herself has access to professional debriefing, support and challenge. The opportunities afforded by the structure of the six programme teams for co-supervision were enriched on the programme by the allocation of the linked member of the UCSE staff as researcher-mentor outlined earlier.

An additional key feature of the core programme has been the encouragement and development of a range of processes of reflection. The structure of the programme has been such that programme participants were actively engaged in school improvement processes and could use their experiences to develop their understanding of the process and to contribute to the development of the model in practice. Each team member was encouraged to keep a professional journal to support their own personal self-reflection.

In addition to the input on the processed-based IQEA model, two other key strands were emphasized and explored as the programme progressed. The first of these was to explore how school and LEA staff could be enabled to focus on pupil data to support reflection on the effectiveness of their strategies and approaches and to enable school improvement activity to be evaluated in relation to improved learning outcomes for pupils and pupils' capacity for learning. The second was to focus on developing the ability to identify the characteristics of effective school development plans and the support processes of enabling schools to critically analyse their school development plans and to manage through effective monitoring and review processes.

The Role of the Programme Teams with Schools

The specific role of the multi-disciplinary team developed through the first year of the operation of the project. Key aspects of team operation were as follows:

- to ensure that each school adopted a specific focus for the school development activity;
- to challenge complacency and ensure that the improvement priority/ priorities are not only significant but are likely to make a difference to pupil achievement;
- in the crucial matter of data collection, to ensure that:

    A   the school has decided what data or information to collect to assist in identifying its school improvement focus and to measure progress towards the achievement of the specific school improvement focus;

    B   to help the school make sense of the data and sometimes provide expertise in carrying out the analysis;

    C   to ensure that common data sets are collected across all programme schools to support the overall evaluation of the LEA programme;

- to support the identification of new courses of action as a result of the analysis;
- to act as an external resource for the school and their improvement initiatives, e.g. to contribute with the headteacher or key staff to school staff meetings to provide information on initiatives in other schools in relevant areas, and to undertake specific training activities with staff;
- to support progress in the school's work by prompting the development and review of an action plan and to help the school improvement work keep its focus so that staff maintain their progress in the face of day-to-day school activities, the complexity of the school year and the maintenance pressures that make the efforts required to bring about improvement difficult to sustain. The delicate refocusing on the contract is a valuable role for the adviser and it requires regular and knowledgeable contact with the schools' change leaders; and
- finally, to ensure that the school retains ownership of its problems and solutions and does not become dependent on the external consultant – in this regard appropriate disengagement strategies need to be in place.

In practice, the teams have worked in a variety of ways with varying emphases on these key elements. It should be noted that the key elements were crystallized by the steering group through reflection on the programme as it progressed. The steering group did not impose a particular model for the role of the programme teams at the outset.

The Envisaged Benefits of the Multi-disciplinary Teams

It was envisaged from the outset that the multi-disciplinary teams would have the following benefits:

- LEA staff would have time for enquiry and reflection on both their own roles and the needs of schools;
- operating in supportive teams would provide a rich professional dimension to work that is often isolated;
- teams would be able to challenge their assumptions about successful ways of working by having the detailed response from several schools to compare;
- appreciation of individual strengths and weaknesses would be developed, which would enrich work with schools and also develop a growing respect for each other's work away from the programme;

- teams would develop shared goals;
- there would be increased support for risk-taking; and
- a growing culture of learning and seeking self- and team improvement would develop.

How Effective Were the Multi-disciplinary Teams?

In order to evaluate the effectiveness of the teams, the lead manager of each of the three service areas undertook structured interviews with their staff involved in the project, one year into the project and at its end. All three service areas used the same seven headings to explore perspectives and available evidence. In addition, structured interviews were held with headteachers and where available, the chair of governors, as well as analysis of the final school reports, in order to gain the schools' perceptions of the effectiveness of LEA staff working in this way.

Structured Interviews with LEA Staff

Some of the key issues raised by the interviews are summarized below:

What is your specific input into the project?
- Working with partner and school to identify focus of improvement activity.
- Meeting with headteacher and attendance at staff meetings to progress activities.
- Meeting with partner to develop plans.
- Data analysis / pupil interviews.

What is the input of the others in the team?
- Providing specific input, e.g. INSET.
- Secondary perspective on analysing data.
- Providing moral support in the teeth of resistance.
- It was negotiated based on individual strengths.

Why have roles worked out like this?
- Through discussion and in relation to the complementary skills and aptitudes of the individuals.
- An emphasis on the use of respective skills and expertise.

Are there any distinct advantages in working in a multi-disciplinary team – and why?
- Cross-checking of perceptions and meaning.
- Effective use of a wide range of skills.
- Cross-service collaboration built mutual confidence and respect.

- Shared consistent messages being given by key LEA staff.
- Support and advice for schools from a range of areas of expertise within the LEA that the school may not normally have access to or benefit from.
- Effective challenge to perspectives and sharing of different approaches to problem-solving.
- Helped develop a more reflective process for problem-solving.

Has the process of working together enhanced your professional skills – and those of others in the team?
- Improved data analysis.
- Placed special educational needs issues within a general schools context.
- Negotiation and team-building skills.

From your experience so far, is this way of working with schools increasing the likelihood of improving outcomes for pupils? Why?
- Increased likelihood of improving learning outcomes because of the effects of increasing professional dialogue within the school in reflecting on features that support effective teaching.
- Has provided a common agenda for school improvement for LEA and school staff.
- Shared input has increased the school's ability to review its own procedures and teaching and learning strategies.
- The programme has provided schools with a focus of collecting, collating and reviewing data, which informs future developments and identifies where improvements have been, or need to be made.
- Staff within the schools are better able to share their views and have their views considered within a context of collective responsibility for school improvement.

What support or additional support do you need to contribute effectively to this project? What would be your developmental needs to contribute to this form of work on an ongoing basis?
- Consensus on key developmental issues.
- Joint training on specific issues.
- Time.

From the headteachers' perspective through the interview process, a number of themes emerged in relation to the teams supporting the school improvement process. Among the key issues identified were the following:

- effective use of complementary skills of the team;
- helpful in keeping the school on target and pushing for necessary clarification;

- external perspective, which was honestly and supportively delivered;
- it has supported the process of teachers evaluating each others' and their own work;
- it has supported a culture of feeling positive about progress; and
- the very nature of coordinated support from outside helped keep up the momentum.

From the teams' perspective, the interdisciplinary nature of the work made certain kinds of learning possible. For example, educational psychologists felt they were now taking a broader view in relation to teaching and learning issues, special needs support staff were relating whole school approaches to individual pupil development, and school development advisers were developing an increased focus on the individual pupil perspective. Clearly, groups of staff within the LEA with distinct functions have benefited from the shared experience of working in multi-disciplinary teams, and this appears to have had a significant impact both in relation to common issues surrounding their work with schools, and in relating transferable skills back to their core functions within the LEA. This has significant potential impact on the quality of input to schools and has implications for how LEAs organize to maximize benefits of their staff's input into school improvement processes.

Implications for Working Practice

Analysis of the data available highlights a number of key themes that have implications for the working practices of multi-disciplinary teams within LEAs. The most important of these were:

- **Time for teams to develop mutual respect and confidence in each other**
  This is important in the early stages of the teams' operation and there is evidence that if this early stage was left out, then the multi-disciplinary team had less impact on the school improvement process. It appears to be cost-effective for the LEA to invest time through planned training opportunities and time for individual members of the team to discuss core values and perceptions around key professional issues.
- **Secure knowledge**
  All members of the multi-disciplinary team value the contribution of others being underpinned by a secure individual knowledge base. This was seen as particularly crucial by headteachers.

- **To have or obtain the professional confidence of a range of school staff**

  This factor is important both to individual team members as well as to the schools themselves. Without professional confidence, there is evidence to suggest that barriers occur to effective working that inhibit the investment of time and application by a range of key staff.

- **Complementary skills with clearly defined roles, negotiated and accepted by all**

  The issue here both for individuals within teams and for schools is that there is more effective working for all concerned if individuals are clear about the contribution they are making to the process and that this is explicitly discussed and shared in order that each individual can see their contribution and responsibility to the school improvement process. The role and skills that individuals took up within the team were not predicated by their core job purpose within the LEA. This meant that individuals negotiated clear roles that were fit for purpose, rather than constrained by their primary focus of work.

- **Ability to network and provide perspectives on an issue**

  Schools felt this added significant value to the school improvement process. The multi-disciplinary team's experience across a wide range of school settings meant that helpful perspectives could be offered on issues and solutions that had already been tried in similar contexts. This ability to bring clarity and meaning to individual school issues based on a wide base of experience was valued by the schools, as was the network of exchanges arising from schools being put in touch with each other in order to address similar issues.

- **Clear team focus**

  Where the most effective multi-disciplinary teamwork occurred, there is evidence to suggest that not only were the teams effectively focused on the issues of improvement, but that they also had the ability to galvanize and focus individuals and teams within the school itself. This meant that finite energy and time was used effectively and widely for maximum gain by all concerned.

- **Supportive to school context**

  An important feature of effective working was the ability of teams to analyse the complexity of the school context and support the key players within the school to address the agreed issues in an appropriate way and at a pace through support and challenge that was relevant to the school. There is evidence to suggest that the more focused the teams were on the individual school context, the more likely progress on issues became.

- **Schools having the primary responsibility for school effectiveness and improvement**
  It is important that the LEA team of staff and the school are clear
  about this. The role of the multi-disciplinary team was to support
  and enhance the process of school improvement, not to take it over.
  It is a significant skill for LEA staff to orchestrate and support
  effective practice while encouraging and developing the school's
  own capacity for solutions. The most effective teams achieved this
  through sensitive partnership and knowledge of the school.
- **The team bringing in 'added' value that is clearly defined, supports, complements and, when appropriate, challenges**
  Effective teams have a way of analysing what conditions are appropriate for support or challenge. Though an environment of mutual
  trust and support is a necessity, there is the maturity of approach that
  allows appropriate professional challenge and the clear application
  of complementing skills and analysis brought to a common issue.
- **A 'mature' approach to problem solving, based on a recognition
  and confidence from each individual in their own knowledge,
  skills and contribution, which is shared with others as well as
  received**
  This approach is important if effective collaborative teams are to
  develop. If an individual within a team finds this approach difficult,
  it provides an environment in which competition for recognition
  and contribution may be developed at the expense of focusing on
  the key issues for the school. It is therefore important that it is
  recognized and acknowledged that there may be differences in
  approach, but that these are valued and incorporated to develop a
  shared responsibility. This in effect provides a template for a cultural change within an LEA, which supports effective working with
  schools on school improvement processes.

Conclusion

The evidence from the interviews with both the LEA staff and the schools
points clearly to the advantages of bringing together LEA staff in multi-
disciplinary teams to work with schools on their improvement efforts. Such
an approach within an LEA is still comparatively rare. The norm is for staff
to keep to their own professional territory, but in the process to miss out on
the richness and integration that results from working together in this multi-
disciplinary approach. For Essex LEA it established a way of working
together that has been further developed, as described in Chapter 9.

An important concluding point needs to be emphasized in relation to the LEA's capacity to support school improvement. The resource and time devoted to this role must be realistic. The LEA must have sufficient capacity and expertise to be able to add value to the work of the school through its challenge and support, but not so much as to make the school dependent on that support, as this would undermine the principle described in Chapter 9 that the school is the main agent for improvement, not the LEA. A delicate balance needs to be found here, particularly in the context of the current national debate about the role of the LEA in school improvement. At one extreme are those who take the principle of 'LEA intervention in inverse proportion to success' to its logical conclusion and argue that for most schools an annual analysis of its performance data is sufficient. At the other extreme are those who argue that LEAs need to retain considerable capacity to be able to exercise the role effectively.

The evidence from EPSI highlights two key ingredients which need to be held in balance:

1   LEA staff need to know their schools well enough to know when and how to intervene. Those that had this knowledge added most value, regardless of whether the school was starting from a position of strength or relative weakness. This is because school improvement is not a simple but a complex process involving many different interactions as described in Chapter 3.

2   LEA staff who are skilled in the analysis of performance data as well as in the culture of the school are the most efficient in the performance of this role and need less time to do it than those who are less skilled. There is, therefore, a strong argument for a concerted local and national programme to develop these skills.

Chapter 7

Process Consultancy
The Role of LEA Consultants in Supporting School Improvement

Alan Fuller and Sue Fisher

Introduction

In this chapter we are concerned with the second broad aim of the EPSI programme, to increase the LEA's capacity to support schools in the improvement process. Anticipating the changing relationship between LEAs and schools, recently embodied in the Draft Code of Practice on LEA–school relations (DfEE, 1998a), with the emphasis on school self-improvement, one of the key aims of this programme was to investigate new ways of working with schools that helped to build their capacity to improve outcomes for children. The EPSI framework, outlined in Chapter 1, placed schools at the centre of the process, with a variety of external systems made available to support them in their improvement activities. Central to this were LEA advisers who made regular visits to schools over the two years of the programme. Pairs of school development advisers (SDAs), senior educational psychologists (SEPs) and special needs support service team leaders (SNSSTLs) provided consultancy to schools and were themselves supported by a professional development programme. Our aim in this chapter is to examine the roles they undertook at various stages of their engagement with schools and to pinpoint key lessons for the LEA about the training and deployment of advisers in this future role.

The following questions were posed at the outset of the programme:

- What skills do external consultants need to support school improvement?
- How can LEA advisers reconcile the need to acknowledge improvement as the schools' responsibility while sometimes having to work for the LEA with a school in terms of the schools' inability to make appropriate improvement?
- What structure for advisers' continuing professional development is most effective? (Corbett, Fielding and Kerfoot, 1996)

At the beginning of the EPSI programme the LEA faced a number of tensions and dilemmas in attempting to refocus attention on school improvement. For example, the restricted resource base limited the number of advisers and their ability to take into account schools' individual improvement needs. Second, the LEA needed to manage the tension between a client-centred approach, providing services that locally managed schools wished to receive, with a more forceful advocacy role for learners and parents (Corbett et al., 1996). EPSI enabled the LEA to explore models of advisory services to suit schools at different phases of development and which provided a balance of support and challenge. Coinciding with the programme, a new role of school development adviser was created. Supporting school improvement was a key function and the programme, therefore, served as a test-bed for both different models of support and professional development for staff. Before describing the detail of their work in schools, models of consultancy that have influenced the practice of EPSI teams and which help to conceptualize the nature of their role with schools will be examined.

Models of Consultancy

Consultancy in various forms is long established but little researched, perhaps because of the highly competitive and secretive nature of the field. Lundberg (1997) describes the literature as fragmented and discursive because in his view consultancy is under-conceptualized, even atheoretical. Most models, for example, attempt to describe roles and activities of consultants through the use of metaphor. In the field of school improvement, external advisers have been variously described as change agents (Miles, Saxl and Lieberman, 1988), consultants (Fullan, 1991), critical friends (MacBeath, 1998b) and trouble-shooters (Learmonth and Lowers, 1998). Although these terms reflect differences in the adviser–school relationship, each emphasizes the adviser's key role as supporting schools in the process of change. The external adviser is increasingly viewed as a consultant on the change process as well as a technical expert in, for example, curriculum or management issues (Fullan, 1991). This shift from providing expert advice towards helping a school develop its 'internal capacity' to improve the quality of education for their children (Southworth and Ainscow, 1996) mirrors changing views of the roles of consultants, over a longer period, in other sectors. In this sense, advising schools on improvement strategies can be considered to fall within Schein's (1969, reprinted in 1988) model of 'process consultation' described below.

Schein distinguished between three models of consultancy: the purchase of information or expertise, doctor–patient, and process consultation.

In the first, a client decides what problem they have that needs resolving and who to go to for help. The consultant is the expert with the required skills or knowledge. Success relies on the client's ability to accurately diagnose the problem and choose the consultant wisely. The doctor–patient model is a variant of the first, in which the consultant is also required to make a diagnosis; thus the client delegates responsibility for locating the problem as well as proposing action to resolve it. Essentially process consultation differs from these two models in its central premise that the 'client owns the problem and continues to own it throughout the consultation process' (Schein, 1987, p. 29). The model assumes that organizations can become more effective if they learn to diagnose and manage their own strengths and weaknesses and that external consultants are unlikely to learn enough about the culture of an organization to suggest workable solutions on their own. Diagnosis and intervention are not separable in practice and need to be joint enterprises. Process consultation is defined as a set of activities that 'help the client to perceive, understand and act upon the process events that occur in the client's environment in order to improve the situation as defined by the client' (Schein, 1988, p. 11).

Schein's three models of consultancy can be readily applied to an analysis of the relationships between external advisers and schools. The increasing impact of the market and local management of schools have led to LEA and other providers responding to schools as customers for their services. Schools often seek advisory support for needs they have themselves identified, following in Schein's terms the purchase of expertise model. With the advent of OFSTED inspection there has also been increasing demand for advisers to provide diagnosis as well as remedy when weaknesses are identified. Pre-OFSTED reviews, for example, can be seen as examples of the doctor–patient model in practice. Although both trends represent a shift in the balance of power towards schools, these models of consultancy, in Schein's view, do not encourage the degree of ownership necessary for an organization to learn how to diagnose and solve its own future problems. If the aim is for each school to be able 'to take the lead in working out for itself what needs to be done to raise standards' (Code of Practice on LEA–School Relations, 1998, p. 6), the job of LEA consultants must be to help build their capacity to do so. Process consultation provides a model for this that encourages partnership with the external adviser rather than dependency.

In the business world there are parallel debates about the importance of consultants offering process skills in addition to specialist knowledge. Kubr (1983) plots the relationship between client and consultant on a continuum of dependency. Process consultant and observer-reflector strategies are viewed as encouraging least dependence whereas information/skills specialist and advocate roles lead to ownership being handed over to the consultant. Turner (1988) supports the view that the outcome of intervention should be measured not only through the content of changes, but also in terms of the competence development in the client system. He states, 'Increasingly management consultants are worth their fees not only because of their ability to analyse client problems and provide sound recommendations, but also because of their skill in conducting a human process that facilitates needed learning and change' (Turner, 1988, p. 12).

There have been a handful of studies into the role of consultants in school improvement programmes. Miles, Saxl and Lieberman (1988) report a two-year evaluation of the skills required of educational change agents, known as assistors, in three New York City improvement programmes. A synthesis of the findings based on semi-structured interviews and observations of assistors' work with schools highlighted 19 key skills. Many of these were considered to be trainable regardless of the background of the consultant and formed the basis of a training programme. Skills were combined in six clusters: Trust/rapport building; organizational diagnosis; dealing with the process; resource utilization; managing the work; building skill and confidence in people to continue. Each cluster subsumes several skills, for example dealing with the process includes the skills of collaboration, conflict mediation and confrontation.

Ainscow and Southworth (1996) investigated clients' perceptions of the roles of consultants in a project titled 'Improving the Quality of Education for All' (IQEA). Semi-structured interviews were undertaken with teachers in four schools where clear signs of development had occurred. The teachers had all taken on leadership roles in their schools as members of a 'cadre' group with whom the external consultants (Cambridge University tutors) engaged. Analysis of their responses revealed five categories of activity that had impact on their leadership roles: pushing thinking forward; framing the issues; encouraging partnership; providing incentives; modelling ways of working. The first two categories suggest that a key function of the consultants was to stimulate discussion and reflection among teachers. Through the encouragement of evidence-based enquiry, consultants could be seen as fostering a climate of organizational learning. The aim was to help teachers develop as 'teacher researchers' and 'use the data from their research to plan and implement actions' (Southworth and Ainscow, 1996, p. 12). Hence the notion of consultants as capacity builders rather than experts.

In the model of school improvement adopted by the EPSI programme, the expectation was that consultants would support schools in their self-improvement activity. It was not the intention to drive schools in directions they did not want or need to go in. However, this did not mean that LEA involvement was entirely client-centred. Consultants operated as part of a team (project-wide and area) within a framework for improvement developed centrally, with guidelines provided for both consultants and schools. For example, it was expected that a school's focus for improvement would relate to the findings of their recent OFSTED report, emphasis would be placed on teaching and learning rather than organizational structures and pupil data would be used in the selection of focuses and targets. Though there was considerable scope for individual differences in terms of consulting style or school needs, the professional development programme emphasized these messages and promoted discussion of the consultant's role at the outset in order to achieve a degree of consistency across the programme.

Consultancy in Action – the Work of EPSI Advisers

Data Sources and Analysis

In the next section we describe the work of advisers in the EPSI programme. Substantial evidence about this was gathered from three main sources. First, written reports were requested from advisers and schools at the end of the programme. Both were asked to comment on the process and outcomes of their improvement activities. The following questions directly related to the roles of advisers:

- What effective support and challenge has been provided through EPSI programme pairs, your SDA and other related LEA services during the period of the EPSI programme?
- What evidence does the school have of effective support and challenge from programme pair and other related LEA services?
- Has the contact with these staff (programme pairs, unit managers and Cambridge University tutors) supported the school in understanding school improvement?

Second, LEA unit managers and Cambridge University tutors undertook semi-structured interviews with schools (combinations of headteachers, senior staff and governors) and advisers during and at the end of the programme. Interviews with schools asked for their observations about the LEA's support received and their views about the kinds of external support schools most need. Where a senior educational psychologist or special needs support service team leader was one of the pair, schools were asked about their particular contribution.

Tutor interviews with programme pairs asked open questions about what contributed to or hindered a school's progress and specifically what support the pair had provided for action planning, working with data and staff development. Managers' interviews asked advisers about their specific input, the input of their partner, why roles had worked out like this and whether working in this way had increased the likelihood of improving learning outcomes for pupils.

A third source of data was a collection of artefacts including interim programme pair reports, notes of meetings (e.g. discussions at professional development sessions) and journals kept by programme pairs.

It is worth reiterating that this programme took the form of a 'real-life' action research project with a large number of participants. As might be expected, there were some gaps in data coverage, mostly as a result of staff changes. However, the size of the programme and the variety of work undertaken have led to a rich gathering of qualitative data, on which the following summary is based. Analysis of the data took place throughout the programme at a number of levels. Robson's (1993) helpful summary of 'basic rules for dealing with qualitative data' reminds us that analysis should consist of the generation of themes, categories or codes as the data is collected. In EPSI this took place, initially, at the individual school level with advisers, schools and LEA managers building explanations of what was taking place. A further iterative process took place through discussion in teams and across the programme through two multi-disciplinary groups – the pupil data working group and the EPSI steering group. Following the final collection of data, joint meetings of these two groups have developed revised explanations, which are summarized below.

Stages of Involvement with Schools

One of the strongest patterns to emerge from the data indicates that the roles of advisers, across the range of schools, changed in similar ways during the course of the programme. Four distinct stages of involvement have been identified, although the significance of each stage (e.g. in terms of the time spent) differed between schools:

- Preparation
- Entry ˙
- Action
- Exit

Preparation

This stage began before contact was made with schools and refers to both the preparation of advisers and the schools themselves. Four elements to this stage were identified:

- building a theoretical framework and knowledge about school effectiveness and school improvement;
- team development;
- examining evidence provided by the schools; and
- the school's introduction to the programme (not dealt with here).

The first two were closely interlinked. In the interviews, a number of advisers remarked that the early professional development days served a broader agenda, to encourage partnerships between staff in different units working with schools. The initial weekend of professional development was the first occasion that the three professional groups, SDAs, SEPs and SNSSTLs, had been brought together to work with a common focus for an extended period of time. As well as receiving input, it was, therefore, an opportunity to examine a range of issues from three different professional perspectives in an atmosphere of enquiry and reflection.

During the first term of the programme, before the LEA staff went into schools, UCIE tutors provided input to the team of advisers on recent research and theories of school effectiveness and school improvement. This staff development continued throughout the programme and included a pre-sentation by Geoff Southworth on the role of consultants, describing his earlier research referred to above (Ainscow and Southworth, 1996).

A further important element to preparation was the time given for programme pairs (PPs) to examine information provided by the schools. This included the OFSTED report, the post-OFSTED Action Plan, the School Development Plan and in some cases additional information such as school prospectus and Governors' Annual Report to parents. This created an oppor-tunity for the PPs to begin to hypothesize about the issues in schools and to frame questions to raise with them. Additional data for collection across all schools in the programme were also identified at this time.

Entry

During this stage programme pairs made initial contact with schools and a working relationship was established. Five elements to the entry phase were identified:

- collection of data for the programme;
- analysis of data;
- determining the focus;
- developing an action plan; and
- agreeing a way of working for the advisers and the school.

Early contact with schools in this programme was unusual for most LEA staff, in that the agenda was largely externally driven, focusing primarily on data collection. As described in earlier chapters, at the beginning of EPSI it was decided to collect a range of data across all schools. Programme pairs were directly involved in collecting two of these data sets, pupil perceptions and the conditions rating scale, and undertook much of the analysis and feedback of findings to schools. The writing data were also collected at this time and some analysis was conducted centrally but then given to PPs for sharing with schools. The method of analysing the data was negotiated between PPs and schools and contributed to the exploration of issues arising. In all cases data were returned to the school to support the notion that the data belonged to them and that the focus of improvement was owned by the school rather than imposed by the LEA or the EPSI programme.

Data analysis was an area about which many headteachers felt uncertain and some schools reported that PPs had been helpful in the process of analysing data and using the evidence to develop targets for action strategies to meet those targets. Programme pairs themselves reported that assisting schools with collecting and analysing data was a key function during the programme. Also, having an externally determined role in the early stages supported advisers in establishing a relationship with schools. It gave a purpose to their engagement with schools, helping them to get beyond the headteachers' office and to get to know the school better. Interviews with pupils and in some cases with staff were most helpful in providing an additional dimension to advisers' understanding of schools' contexts and needs.

Though analysis of the data sometimes confirmed issues or concerns that schools were aware of, in a number of cases it provided a new avenue for enquiry and reflection. Sometimes the data analysis surprised schools and jolted them into action. Although some schools already had a clear focus prior to engagement in the programme, for many others analysis of the data informed discussions that led to setting a focus. Programme pairs helped schools explore issues raised by asking questions, extending the scope of the questioning beyond headteachers and senior management teams and challenging accepted notions about issues, for example through the use of data analysis or other available evidence. Programme pair and school reports indicated that the advisers' key functions during this phase were to provide an external perspective, help schools frame issues in ways that led to action and push towards the selection of a focus for improvement.

All schools had school development plans or action plans before joining the programme. However, the improvement focus within EPSI usually differed from targets set in existing school plans. In most cases targets for improvement were tighter. Programme pairs supported schools in developing specific, measurable targets related to pupil outcomes or performance in the classroom. At this stage PPs were providing direction for schools by giving specific advice and providing a framework for target-setting. This could be seen as more directive than the process consultancy model suggests, even though the schools maintained responsibility for determining their focus for improvement. The aim of a more directive approach at this stage was to support the development of a school's capacity to instigate and implement school improvement strategies in the future. It is also important to register the value schools placed on the support and challenge provided by advisers. Some made direct reference to this in the interviews or referred to PPs keeping them on track. The role of external agent in providing a push to action, or providing incentives (Southworth and Ainscow, 1996), comes across strongly here.

In order to meet improvement targets, schools developed action plans with support from PPs. The action plan laid out the strategies by which the targets could be met, by specifying what was to be done, by whom and by when. At this stage there was some variation in the degree and nature of involvement of advisers, described in the next section.

Action

During this stage, schools' improvement action plans were implemented. In most cases this meant a significant change in the involvement of the LEA advisers, who had been more prominent during the earlier stages. During the entry stage PPs were often driving the process, bringing with them a model from the EPSI programme. However, once schools reached the stage of implementing their improvement plans, there was more diversity of activity across the programme and a greater sense of ownership among the schools themselves.

In some cases PPs were written into schools' improvement plans because of their specific knowledge or expertise. For example, PPs provided advice or support to individual staff members, led staff discussions and delivered INSET on teaching and learning issues. In other cases they helped schools to find suitable expertise from adviser colleagues or other contacts. Though familiar to LEA staff, these roles of expert adviser or resource broker were qualitatively different within the EPSI programme in comparison to most contacts with schools. Prior involvement in the process of enquiry, prioritizing and target-setting led to more highly informed decisions about the nature of expert support required. The fact that in many cases the PPs did not take on a lead role in training or providing expertise supports the notion that advisers were adopting the role of process consultant rather than the more common role of provider of expertise.

In most schools implementation of the action plans took place independently of the PPs. In fact some schools reported that they felt the LEA support waned in the latter half of the programme. This reflects the reduced involvement of most PPs during the action phase and the increased responsibility placed on schools for carrying out agreed actions. Most PPs took on a monitoring and evaluation role during this phase. This involved visits to discuss progress with key staff members, to carry out observations and to provide feedback and challenge about changes made. In addition, the programme of visits provided schools with deadlines, which one school described as a 'timed framework for action in school'. At meetings of LEA staff during the programme there was much discussion about the need to support schools in maintaining and, sometimes, increasing the pace of their improvement activities.

The EPSI programme provided opportunities for LEA staff and schools to develop contacts with others working in similar circumstances. Programme pairs were brought together throughout the programme. This gave an opportunity for information-sharing and problem-solving. The programme also supported schools in forming networks both within area teams and across the EPSI group. The gathering of schools together provided a further incentive for action, by virtue of having a deadline at which to report back. It also enabled a number of schools to develop partnerships. In one case an area team developed a common focus. In the action phase there was some reduction in contact between schools, which was apparently more valuable in the early stages.

Exit

In this final phase the programme pairs undertook three main functions, contributing to the evaluation of the programme, writing final reports and supporting schools in planning next steps.

In all schools PPs were asked to revisit data collection in ways similar to the start of the programme to enable comparison and hence evaluation of improvements. As in the entry stage, PPs provided a valuable external perspective and expertise in data analysis and interpretation. There are fewer references to the role of advisers in data analysis at this stage in reports from schools. This may reflect schools' increasing confidence in handling data.

In most cases both members of the programme pair ceased their involvement with the schools at the end of the programme. There was therefore a need to plan disengagement. Generally this took the form of meetings with school staff or senior management teams where final data analyses and evaluation of the outcomes of the programme were aired. These meetings also gave the opportunity to discuss the EPSI programme itself and helped to crystallize schools' views, on which they later reported.

Conclusions and Key Lessons for the LEA

One of the primary aims of the EPSI programme, stated at the beginning of this chapter, was to investigate new ways of working with schools that helped to build their capacity to improve outcomes for children. The summary of the roles and activities of LEA consultants highlights some differences from their usual contacts with schools. For school development advisers this was an important period for trialling new models of working. For other LEA staff, senior educational psychologists and special needs support service team leaders, the programme gave an opportunity to utilize consultancy skills and specialist knowledge beyond their usual remit. For all LEA staff it is clear that there was a shift in the direction described by commentators on adviser–school relationships outlined earlier (e.g. Fullan, 1991; Southworth and Ainscow, 1996), from providing expert advice towards helping schools develop their 'internal capacity' to improve. In broad terms process consultation does provide a helpful model of the intended role of advisers in this programme and there is evidence that some of the consultants' skills and functions described fit the model proposed by Schein (1988).

One main area of divergence in practice from the espoused model of process consultation centres on the issue of ownership. Though there was a degree of autonomy for PPs and research schools, there was also significant external direction which, according to a number of reports, resulted in overdependence on outside support and in some cases a sense of rejection when this was not available or was withdrawn. This was also the case for LEA staff who were at times unclear about their role and looked to the programme to provide direction. However, there is evidence that schools and advisers became more independent as the programme progressed. It is possible that the lack of ownership initially may have resulted from the change process that the programme itself represented. In one school, for example, the adviser reports that support was initially quite intensive, with pathways mapped. When support was eased off, the school began to misconstrue the point of the project and it was necessary to revisit why the school had become involved. However, towards the end of the programme the adviser reports that the school had 'embraced learning about school improvement and happily and effectively worked on targets they had set themselves, attaining many of the success criteria'.

The issue of ownership is not simply resolved by adopting a client-centred approach in which consultants respond to clients' wishes. One of the key messages from the EPSI programme was that schools vary considerably in their capacity to instigate effective change. At times, some schools will require a high level of direction or pressure before they are able to take full control of the change process. Two examples demonstrate the range of schools' readiness for this. In one, school adviser support was considered not effective because of 'a lack of driving and prompting from the LEA'. The headteacher thought this was necessary to gain staff commitment. By contrast, another school reported initial hostility towards the support offered until they felt in control. From this point the programme took off and the school valued the external input. Working with schools to support their improvement certainly requires adherence to the underlying assumption that organizations can become more effective if they learn to diagnose and manage their own strengths and weaknesses, but it is also essential to recognize what stage schools are at in being able to achieve this.

The following points summarize the key lessons for the LEA in considering the future role and deployment of staff working to support schools' self improvement:

- The relationship between LEA advisers and schools followed a number of distinct stages, during which the roles of the consultants varied considerably. In most cases input was more intensive in the early stages, with a tailing off during the action or implementation phase. This has clear implications for the allocation of time to support schools at different stages.
- The role of the consultant also changed during the course of the programme. For example, during the entry stage key functions were to support data collection, analysis and interpretation; organizational diagnosis; clarifying and framing issues; prioritizing and target-setting. During the action stage some advisers provided an 'expert' role and all focused on monitoring; keeping schools on track; supporting the process of change. Future training of advisers for school improvement work will need to prepare staff for the changes in role at different stages of the process.
- Individual differences between schools are considerable and influence the type of support that is appropriate at a given time. Schools have been characterized as being at various stages of development along a continuum, such as 'stuck' to 'moving'. Awareness of a school's stage of development and receptivity to particular types of support will increase the likelihood of positive outcomes. However, there is no simple formula for matching school type with consultancy style. It is not always the case, for example, that schools with serious weaknesses respond to highly directive approaches, which may unintentionally encourage dependency.

- One of the key dilemmas for staff operating as consultants is to provide necessary support to schools without encouraging dependency. To enable this, there needs to be greater emphasis in training for consultants on understanding change and the process skills needed to instigate and support change.
- Expertise or specialist knowledge in areas relevant to a school's improvement needs is highly valuable when schools are most able to take advantage of it. An important function of the improvement consultant was not necessarily to provide this expertise, but to help schools identify knowledge and skills required and how best to develop them. This involved making most use of internal expertise and seeking contacts outside the school via school and LEA networks.
- The benefit of advisers working in pairs and multi-disciplinary teams was reported by many programme pairs and schools. The different knowledge and experience of SDAs, SEPs and SNSSTLs added to the breadth of the external perspective provided. The partnerships were considered supportive by PPs and were particularly helpful when there was a need for greater challenge to a school. A fringe benefit arising from the programme has been an increased awareness of each others' roles and expertise and more effective joint working.
- The need to agree the involvement of advisers with schools was not sufficiently recognized. Reports from schools indicate that there was not always clarity about the contact with advisers. When this tailed off in the action stage, some schools attributed this to a change in priority or interest rather than a planned reduction. Similarly, disengagement was expected at the end of the project, but there was little scope to take into account individual schools' needs. Involving schools in the negotiation of the consultant's role is essential if the aim is to encourage ownership of the improvement process.
- The programme provided a significant opportunity for professional development of LEA staff. Many report that they have transferred the skills and knowledge developed to their work in other schools. Also, the data summarized here have contributed to a greater understanding among staff and managers of the complexity of the adviser's role in supporting school improvement. Given the applicability of the models described earlier to the work of LEA consultants, there is a need for the development of training in the skills and knowledge required of process consultants as part of the preparation for advisers engaging in school improvement work.

Part 4

Wider Issues and Conclusions

Chapter 8

Evaluating School Improvement

Tina Loose and Judy Sebba

Introduction

The research literature on school effectiveness and, more recently, on school improvement is prolific. Yet, relatively little attention has been given to the measurement of improvement and the time-scale that is needed for improvements to become evident. The EPSI programme adopted a definition of school improvement that focused upon increased pupils' learning. Hence, measurements that provided evidence of pupil outcomes were central.

The school improvement literature suggests that innovation is more likely to occur and be sustained when it builds on teachers' current practice. A review of current assessment procedures used by the schools at the outset of the programme revealed the use of seven different reading tests, and in a few schools, no tests at all. It was decided that schools should continue using their test or adopt one of those most commonly used by the other schools. A writing task was specifically devised for all the schools in order to provide a basis for tracking improvement across the programme (see also Chapter 4).

It was recognized that improvement may take longer to be reflected in test or task scores in some schools or some aspects within a school, than in others. A broad range of data collection was adopted to ensure that conflicting findings could be thoroughly explored and a greater understanding of the process of school improvement developed. In addition to the data from the inspection reports and analysis of the post-inspection action plans, perceptions of pupils, teachers, governors, senior managers and LEA staff supporting the school were collected and analysed. Ten of the schools were also visited by an inspector who reapplied relevant inspection criteria at the end of the programme.

At an early stage it was recognized that there was a need to establish a pupil data working party that could manage and coordinate the data. Data collection has been carried out by school staff, the programme pairs from the LEA, and through school visits undertaken by the university lecturers from University of Cambridge School of Education (UCSE) and senior managers from the LEA.

Inspection Reports and Post-inspection Action Plans

Most of the schools had been inspected before the start of the programme and the rest were inspected shortly after. These inspections served as the baseline for the programme. The assumption made at the outset of the programme was that action planning is a central mechanism by which schools can use their inspection findings to enhance their own improvement. As a result, the starting point for their data collection was their inspection report, as few schools had been collecting data previously. Schools used the report as a source of data, analysing the judgements made and drawing up post-inspection action plans near to the start of the programme.

An analysis of the first 21 reports and action plans produced (Sebba and Loose, 1996) showed that the key issues, in many cases, did not address teaching and learning, with the result that few schools set specific targets addressing pupil outcomes. In many cases it was felt that this difficulty had arisen because of the lack of clarity and precision in the key issues, which often focused on administrative and managerial matters. Their links to teaching and learning could not always be clarified from the text of the report, which resulted in a dearth of reference within targets to pupil outcomes. Most success criteria related to completion of tasks rather than to improvements in pupil's learning. This finding has been noted in other analyses of post-inspection action plans (Sebba, Clarke and Emery, 1996; Thomas et al., 1998). A few schools had managed to translate some key issues that did not explicitly address pupils' learning into targets and success criteria that did so. Where they had not, programme pairs provided support in setting targets and defining success criteria that were expressed in terms of pupil outcomes, because the EPSI programme required schools to define targets and success criteria that did so.

Some of those critical of the current model of inspection (e.g. Hargreaves, 1995) argue that school improvement would be more likely to occur if greater emphasis were placed on quality assurance and less on quality control. This would require schools to continually improve by establishing procedures for monitoring their practices and designing and implementing change. In order to do this, it would seem that staff in schools will need to be confident in approaches to monitoring and the analysis and evaluation of the information collected. Effective planning processes will be needed to identify priorities, set targets, develop success criteria and allocate tasks and responsibilities to ensure these targets are met. This should occur through the initial post-inspection action planning and subsequent merging of this with the school development plan.

In the initial analysis of inspection reports, development planning was a key issue for almost half. Monitoring and evaluation were identified as key issues in most of the schools. This confirmed the findings of previous studies. It is therefore not surprising that the schools encountered some difficulties in producing an effective action plan with suitably planned monitoring and evaluation procedures. As a consequence, many programme pairs supported schools in creating a more detailed plan of action relating to a focus for the EPSI programme developed from at least one of their key issues.

Clearly, data collection would go beyond that provided by the inspection report and it would be necessary to analyse and evaluate the information collected. The Essex programme set out to determine what data were likely to be most helpful. The action plans provided one way of prioritizing data collection for individual schools. The initial versions of the action plans frequently confused tasks with targets, leading to schools defining data sets intended to provide evaluative information that merely reflected task completion. Many schools had to clarify the difference between monitoring the tasks to be done and collecting the data to evaluate the effectiveness of the pupil outcomes. For example, in one school a key issue was: *to raise the attainment of pupils in English*; the target given was: *to produce a policy document in English*; the success criterion was defined as: *the policy has been produced*. The potential for this process to lead to school improvement in terms of pupils' learning remained guesswork.

Gray and Wilcox (1995) have noted the tendency for greater attention to managerialism with consequent lack of emphasis on the quality of teaching and learning during the post-inspection process. The more detailed plan for the chosen EPSI focus generally made this clearer. Schools noted the need to gather specific data relating to their individual priorities and reflecting their chosen focus from the post-inspection action plan. For example, the school collected data through classroom observations or pupils' perceptions of issues relating to the focus.

Defining Success Criteria for School Improvement

At the outset the EPSI programme laid out success indicators for its targets within its three aims. Aim 1 and its targets and success criteria related specifically to schools.

Aim 1: *To enable schools to develop strategies to improve the quality of teaching and learning provided for all pupils.*
Target 1.1: *All schools within the programme will show improvement in teaching and learning in KS2 classrooms.*
Target 1.2: *All schools will have strategies for improving teaching and learning.*

These aims and targets required the development of a range of measures or adoption of existing measures, which could be used by all the programme schools to inform their development and help them monitor and evaluate their improvement. Additionally, LEA-based data common across all schools in the LEA, and in some cases linked to other initiatives, were to be collected for the individual schools.

The success criteria and data sources used for measuring school improvement relating to each of these targets can be found in Appendix 1.

Data Collection and Analysis

The data to be used to evaluate the degree of success against the criteria were identified by the data working party. The analysis of some individual school data was carried out by programme pairs, whereas the LEA external team and members from UCSE analysed the full data sets.

Many schools carried out their own evaluation as they progressed. This took a variety of forms depending on the school's focus and its internal development of the programme. They used available materials or created their own data-gathering instruments. Some of these were collected as potential material for a 'tool kit' of suitable materials for supporting school improvement. Information about this was summarized and supplemented with other detail in a written final report.

At the outset, the IQEA conditions rating scale (see Ainscow et al., 1994a) was used and reapplied towards the conclusion of the programme. Likewise the perceptions of pupils were sought at the start and end through a series of questions relating to their attitudes about school, learning and achievement. Writing tasks were set early on for selected age groups and some repeated these towards the end. Reading test results were collected and Key Stage 2 test results were analysed.

In some cases, outside professionals from the team aided the school in its evaluation by carrying out classroom observations. In a few cases additional information was gleaned as a result of HMI revisits following OFSTED inspections. Headteachers, some staff and a few governors were interviewed at regular intervals by UCSE staff and senior managers of the LEA. Members of the programme pair teams were interviewed by their senior managers and the UCSE staff.

Finally, ten schools were revisited by an experienced registered inspector who was supported in five schools by the LEA development adviser linked to that school. In each case a range of OFSTED criteria was reapplied in relation to the school's chosen improvement focuses. During this visit, information was gathered through interviews with adults and pupils, classroom observations and scrutiny of documentation.

These data sets were supported by the regular reports from programme pairs and their final report, which used the success criteria as a framework for reporting. The schools produced their final self-analysis report to the same framework.

The Effectiveness of Data in Measuring Improvement

The quantity of data generated for evaluation purposes for the whole programme was huge. This has in some instances created difficulties of management and control. Some data sets for a number of schools have not been submitted, although the revisits generally helped fill in important gaps. In all cases there were at least two and often more sets of data, which could provide evidence of the level of achievement in relation to the success criteria. As a result, the lack of some sets was not a hindrance to judging the degree of school improvement.

The team managing data for evaluation was of necessity large and individuals took responsibility for various aspects of the work. Although much of the data was summarized in a methodical way, it was still sometimes difficult to get a clear overview as to the precise level of improvement in some schools.

Where one person has been involved over the two years with an individual school and in particular with its ongoing evaluation, a clearer picture emerged. It was much easier to evaluate progress during the revisit in relation to the individual focus where the evaluator had been part of the original inspection team and had therefore studied the school very closely at the outset. It was almost as trouble-free where there had been an ongoing link with the school throughout the process. It was generally far more difficult where the evaluation revisit was the first contact with the school. There is, therefore, a case for individual schools being monitored closely by a consistent person throughout the process so that a clearer, more holistic overview can be gained. The reasons why certain methods and use of data are more effective in one school than another might then emerge more clearly. However, previous involvement with the school may create problems of 'bias' in the form of 'preconceived views'. This level of support may be more difficult for LEAs to provide in the future, given the definition of their role and contact with schools in the LEA Code of Practice and Fair Funding policies.

Management and control of data were, on the whole, easier in individual schools, as they were able to concentrate on those elements that seemed to have the most relevance to their development and that would most effectively help them measure their success. The review visits to ten schools at the close of the programme clearly showed this was true for most of them. A number of schools felt they had learned the importance of using data of all kinds for guiding school improvement and felt more confident about analysis and drawing judgements. This helped them plan more precisely for the future. However, there are still some schools who feel insecure about analysing quantitative data, while successfully drawing conclusions from qualitative data upon which they confidently act.

Some schools reported difficulty in isolating what had brought about the changes and improvements and sometimes felt that they would have come about without the support of EPSI, but at a slower rate. In some cases the programme had helped clarify more precisely than stated in their action plan what they needed to be doing in relation to their key issues. The resulting planning for the EPSI targets greatly enhanced the possibility that the change referred to in their action plan would become a reality. These new plans for improvement became an extension of the original action plan.

In many cases schools felt that the additional time spent with educationalists from outside helped them clarify their thinking and was a significant professional boost. Some felt, however, that it was difficult to disentangle support funded by EPSI and support provided through other entitlements where the personnel was the same. This made it difficult for them to evaluate the impact of EPSI on their school.

In some cases evaluation was difficult because of the change of staff and it was felt that these changes may have resulted in improvement in any case. However, where the programme had directly influenced the decision of a member of staff to depart, for example as a result of pupil perceptions, the school was in no doubt that EPSI had helped bring about improvement in an unexpected manner.

How far did the data reflect school improvement?

As stated earlier, one of the major aims of the programme was to enable schools to develop strategies for improving the quality of teaching and learning provided for all pupils. This generated two targets with their own success criteria and range of data sets. Examples follow of some of the judgements and evidence gathered from the identified data sets in relation to the success criteria.

*Target 1.1: All schools within the programme will show
improvement in teaching and learning in KS2 classrooms.*

All schools showed some improvement in teaching and learning in Key
Stage 2. The degree of improvement, however, was variable. In most cases
it related to specific aspects of teaching or learning and the same was not
always true for all in a school. There were cases of outstanding and secure
improvement, while in some contexts the state of change and improvement
was still fragile.

*Success criterion 1.1.1: Evidence from the school's EPSI focus
areas will indicate improvement in teaching and learning in KS2.*

In some cases the improvements were very marked and some outstanding
teaching and learning was recorded at the revisits. In one school the teachers
had hoped to improve the pupil's independent learning. This had required
some radical rethinking of teaching approaches and a total change of culture. Although pupils and parents had not initially responded well to the
changes, the pupils were now enthusiastic, confident learners responding to
very skilful teaching.

In another school the coordinator's involvement in classroom observations had intended to lead to higher-quality teaching. The pupils' perception
was that they had improved their attitudes and that teaching had become
more interesting. However, monitoring of lessons by coordinators and at the
review visit suggested that overall there had been a decline in quality. It did
not appear that involving middle managers in classroom monitoring had
been of overall benefit in raising quality and standards. By contrast, there
had been a significant impact on classroom teaching in a third school as a
result of training them for classroom monitoring. This had been supported
by clearly identified criteria followed by developmental feedback and was
recognized in an HMI follow-up of the OFSTED inspection as a strong
feature in supporting improvement.

*Success criterion 1.1.2: Evidence from the writing tasks, reading
tests, value added and other standardized measures used by the
schools will indicate improvement in achievement in KS2.*

For many schools the standardized measures showed improvement over
time, though not in all cases for all measures.

Data from 1996 and 1997 end of Key Stage 2 Test scores show the
increase in attainment in EPSI schools as a net rise of 50 per cent above the

rise in all Essex schools over the same period. The major gains were made in English and to a lesser extent in mathematics, while there was a much smaller rise in science (less than the rise in Essex schools as a whole). When compared with the Essex Primary School Improvement and Added Value Project (SIVA), which included 272 schools with Key Stage 2 pupils, the EPSI schools outstripped the improvements in the SIVA schools between two and six times.

The writing tasks included narrative and non-narrative writing and generally any improvement over the two years was in the narrative style, though many schools did not reapply the non-narrative writing task. One school aimed at improving attainment in writing. Eighteen months into the programme the improvements were clear, but no later gains were evident. Matters such as the loss of key figures in the senior management team, changes to teaching and levelling arrangements were being considered as reasons why progress appeared to have halted. As in a number of cases, consistency of personnel appears to be important in carrying specific school improvement forward smoothly. In some cases a staff change has been beneficial, while in others it has not.

Not all schools submitted reading test data, as many felt it had little bearing on their particular focus. Of those returning reading data, almost all showed improvement over the two years.

Success criterion 1.1.3: Teacher assessment, teachers' records, samples of pupils' work, IEPs indicate improvement in learning at KS2.

Many pupils reported improvements in learning. They were becoming more perceptive about the requirements of learning and about standards. Many pupils had become more reflective and independent. Some could talk fluently about research skills, collaborative work and how individuals function in teams. Overall, teachers appeared to know their pupils better, made better provision for them as individuals and were developing increasingly higher expectations of them. For example, in one school Key Stage 2 test scores were considerably higher than teacher assessments at the outset, but drew much closer together at the close. Samples of work and interaction in problem-solving showed many pupils to be achieving at an above-average level.

The school working on meeting individual needs identified that targets were almost always met term by term and that broader areas were now included in IEPs. The observations showed an improvement in learning for these pupils. Parents endorsed this and teacher evaluations were additional evidence of improved learning.

Success criterion 1.1.4: Pupil perception data indicates improvement in teaching and learning in KS2, including use of wider and more flexible range of teaching strategies.

In one school the pupil perception data had identified an anti-achievement culture, among Year 6 boys, that was not present in Year 4. It also revealed negative attitudes to the schools' reading material. Pupils' advice was sought and the reading material extended to include magazines and more information books. The Pupil Individual Reading Profile was introduced for assessing, target-setting, monitoring and evaluation of reading across the school. The number of assistants supporting reading was increased. Reading outcomes improved on both the test used by the school and in the key stage tests. Pupil perception data had identified a specific barrier to learning, which, once addressed, appeared to enable a rise in standards.

In many schools pupils were experiencing a wider range of teaching strategies and some were able to identify this improvement and link it to their improved study skills. In a few cases staff reported the pupils' views of their teaching to be professionally bruising at the outset and were pleased at the later responses, which indicated improvements. In some of the schools pupils referred to the increased range of teaching strategies used in their lessons.

In one case the pupils' perceptions were used to develop targets for the teacher's interaction with pupils within the lesson. In another they helped staff appreciate the pupils' grievances in relation to change and helped staff manage the changes to teaching approaches.

Success criterion 1.1.5: Pupil perception data indicates an improvement in attitudes, motivation to learning and commitment to achievement.

Many pupils voiced improved positive attitudes to learning, high levels of motivation and clear views on the value of education in relation to future success and status. This was confirmed by classroom observations midway and at the close of the programme.

One group of Year 6 pupils wanted to know if they had met their target from Year 4 to be better Year 6 classes with more responsible attitudes than their predecessors. The school had worked hard at reducing factors that demotivated earlier pupils and built on the determination of this group to do well.

In another large school the complaints of Year 4 had been dealt with by the time they reached Year 6. They demonstrated more confidence and a very high level of motivation.

One group of pupils saw the teachers as more approachable and having higher expectations. They had a greater understanding of their own learning and personal responsibility for it. They referred to achievement in reading and writing as a whole-school goal and were all aware of their reading levels and the degree of improvement they had individually made during the two-year period. Other data showed they had improved confidence about asking for help, had learned from their mistakes and had appreciated the improved reward systems.

Many pupils now rated success highly, recognized that teachers were consulting them more about their work, felt better understood and were more aware of their achievements and those of others. They had an improved understanding of the importance of learning and appreciated the improved marking of their work and increased teacher help. One group had, however, developed a more negative view of the successful or very able pupils and another group resented the positive discrimination for a child with a disability.

Some recognized an increased challenge and felt they had to be responsible for how hard they worked. Overall, pupils showed considerable improvement in their ability to express their views clearly.

> *Success criterion 1.1.6: Pupil perception and/or EPSI focus data indicate improved 'study' skills such as problem-solving, investigation, research, communication.*

In many schools pupils were able to identify their improved study skills. Some pupils identified an increased awareness of their own strengths and weaknesses through evaluating their own work. Others referred to greater peer support being helpful.

In one case pupils noted that work was now harder and they re-called the days when it was more fun and involved them in 'doing things'. One child referred to the fact that doing something active meant 'it stays in my mind better'. However, they recognized that there was more collaborative work. At one school they said that collaborative working meant 'You get the work done easier, share ideas and make the work better overall.'

In another small village school where the target had related to improv-ing collaborative work, all Key Stage 2 pupils talked impressively about their increased skills and could identify the key features and benefits for their learning while discussing the collaborative work on display. Similar evidence of marked improvement was found in a number of schools.

Success criterion 1.1.7: Staff, governors, parents and others'
perceptions are that teaching and learning in KS2 has improved.

Those most closely associated with the pupils usually reported that teaching and learning had improved, with pupils sometimes saying their parents agreed. A few schools sought parents' views. There were fewer negative comments and those relating to curriculum had declined.

There were few examples of significant school-based involvement by governors, though in a few cases they were making more classroom visits, which were sometimes more sharply focused. These visits reported improvements. In one case there had been significant classroom involvement of a governor and her data clearly indicated improvement in pupils' independence in learning and increased competence in research and library skills.

Only one school demonstrated that all parties had evidence to back their belief that there had been improvements. They conclude, 'We have a culture of working together for school improvement.'

In many cases the reports suggest that teachers feel there have been significant improvements, though some feel this is because of staff changes. Some recognized that they have a much better understanding of school improvement and are therefore in a stronger position to bring it about.

Success criterion 1.1.8: Reports (termly, personal log, etc.)
from programme pairs suggest improvement in teaching and
learning at KS2.

Programme pair reports generally indicated improvement. There were also cases of deterioration in the same school where other teachers had progressed, for example in one school a Key Stage 2 teacher had made significant progress in improving teaching and learning while another had deteriorated markedly over the two years. In a few cases the reports from the schools and those working with the school could not be reconciled, as they had quite differing views as to the degree of improvement. In these instances more reliance had to be placed on the quantitative data.

In a few cases it was recognized that after one year the Key Stage 2 test results had not improved, but other evidence showed improvement for younger pupils and there was confidence that improvements in test results would eventually be seen.

The improvements reported, sometimes hesitantly, by programme pairs could be clearly seen in most of the review visits.

> *Target 1.2: All schools will have strategies for improving*
> *teaching and learning.*

All schools had developed strategies for improving teaching and learning, though some were to a modest degree while others had forged forward. Most had tried to improve the teachers' understanding of school improvement, the importance of high-quality teaching that would lead to better-quality learning and how these features can influence achievement.

Some had tried using new ideas and outside support to build up their own capacity for developing and sustaining improvement. Many used the pupils' views to help modify practice and some developed models of effective practice, systems, research materials and detailed success criteria to aid and focus on their improvement efforts.

> *Success criterion 1.2.1: Schools use their inspection report to*
> *identify key issues in teaching and learning (whether or not the*
> *report itself identifies them as key issues).*

In the majority of the schools, there was a very good match between the key issues identified in the OFSTED reports and the EPSI indicators. There is evidence of EPSI pairs helping the schools make the focus of the programme explicit through detailed analysis of the school report.

At an interview with one of the LEA senior managers, one headteacher felt that reviewing the post-OFSTED action plan with support from the programme team had refined staff thoughts and helped clarify and broaden how a coordinator could influence improvements in teaching and learning.

Not all schools were so happy about the process of identifying the focus, with one final report stating:

> Because we were slightly unhappy with the focus we were forced to take due to the nature of the criteria imposed on us we have had less benefit from the EPSI programme . . . the LEA did not seem to be geared up to our particular focus.

Other schools felt they had been encouraged to choose the wrong focus or, having chosen the focus, suitable support was not immediately forthcoming. Sometimes the pairs found difficulties at this early stage too, with one reporting that getting the action plan from the school was like 'tooth extraction'.

In some cases the EPSI focus came from within the report rather than as a key issue, as the key issues did not, in the way they were expressed, appear to focus on improving teaching or learning. In one case participation in the programme had led to refocusing of the OFSTED action plan.

In general, the programme illustrated a constructive means of taking the action planning process forward in a way that was developmentally useful for many of the schools.

Success criterion 1.2.2: Post-inspection action plan/school development plan identifies clear targets and success criteria in teaching and learning.

At the outset a sample of eight of the schools were interviewed about their OFSTED action plan and the teaching and learning elements within it. Five of the schools felt that there was some distortion in the key issues (often in their favour), which subsequently led to distortion in the action plan. The opportunity to review the teaching and learning elements in the action plan and the full report at the start of the EPSI programme helped them to be more detailed in their developmental plans for their specific focus. Clear targets and success criteria were set for the focus.

It remains to be seen whether schools transfer what they have learned about focusing on teaching and learning when incorporating remaining elements of their OFSTED action plans into their new school development plans.

Success criterion 1.2.3: Resources are allocated realistically to the improvement of teaching and learning (as identified in the plan).

Each school's focus was realistically resourced through the use of school, action plan and EPSI funding. Some schools also used their EPSI programme pair to enhance in-service and monitoring.

One school reported that it had greatly appreciated the opportunity to target an area with existing resources and additional LEA support. However, they said they would have great difficulty in completing the work to its natural conclusion, as they had a severely constrained budget in the forthcoming year.

Success criterion 1.2.4: Responsibilities for monitoring and evaluating teaching and learning are clearly allocated and costed.

This was well managed in all but four cases, but two of these corrected this early on. Some expressed problems relating to their small budget, with one school having to discontinue monitoring in classrooms because governors could no longer maintain the fund. Others would not be able to fund it in the future and in some cases it was costed in terms of headteacher non-contact time rather than monetary costs.

Not all forms of monitoring of teaching and learning included class-room observations. In many cases there appears to be a narrow view of monitoring and evaluating teaching and learning.

> *Success criterion 1.2.5: Teamwork and coordination by staff within the school support the improvement of teaching and learning.*

Views about school improvements through teamwork and coordination by staff were variable. In many cases there was a sense of EPSI being part of a whole-school programme, but in others teachers felt they had been insufficiently involved, they could not talk about its effect and they felt information of interest and help to them had not been shared.

The conditions ratings scale generally indicated that schools had at least maintained their capacity for school improvement or improved it over time. This was supported by observations of staff in some meetings and their comments about the value of the EPSI experience for them.

> *Success criterion 1.2.6: There were perceptions of increased levels of staff dialogue about teaching (e.g. pedagogy).*

Many schools reported an increased dialogue within the school about teach-ing. This is illustrated by one headteacher's comment:

> Participation in the project has helped change the culture of the staff to one where teachers are learners. Teachers are open to debates about improving and accepting responsibility for change and development . . . and being given the opportunity to try and take control of this.

In another school a coordinator said:

> There is beginning to be a staff culture change but you cannot do it overnight. They are all very experienced so you have to nibble away at them. They include things in their teaching and in their vocabulary that they would not have done before.

Reports and the review visit, which identified much improved coordina-tion and educational dialogue, did not always agree with the conditions rating scale at the end of the programme. This may be because as teachers develop, their expectations rise and they become more critical and demanding of themselves as a team. In other cases the staff had changed and incoming staff may have had higher expectations.

> *Success criterion 1.2.7: Data relating to teaching and learning are collected systematically and regularly (e.g. through the use of a tool kit).*

There were many ways in which programme participants had worked co-operatively to bring about improvements in the collecting and use of data. Those included, for example, programme pairs helping to bring about a greater understanding of the OFSTED report and the involvement of the whole staff in learning about collecting and interpreting data. Some schools with a similar focus were linked and, as a result, they were able to compare the data-collecting instruments they had developed.

Many interesting instruments were developed by programme participants in order to research more deeply into their chosen focus. The intention is to bring the best of these together as a tool kit for supporting schools in their school improvement activities.

Many schools responded positively by suggesting that the project had given them the skill and confidence to manage data, interpret it and use it to help bring about improvement.

> *Success criterion 1.2.8: Data relating to teaching and learning are analysed and interpreted appropriately.*

There were numerous examples of schools using data effectively and appropriately to influence and make judgements about improvements in teaching and learning. One report suggested that:

> The school has had a great deal of success meeting the targets set; the main sources of evidence come from the pupil attitude survey, class observation of teaching and learning, the conditions rating scale, observation of pupils' behaviour, the ethos of the school and teacher attitudes and practice.

This report also indicated that:

> There are higher standards at the end of KS2. Observations during the two years of EPSI have shown that the teaching and learning from an independent focus has improved measurably.

A detailed description of the strengths of this higher-quality teaching and learning followed and concluded:

> they delight in sharing and receiving ideas, work with enjoyment and satisfaction because they own more of their learning and attain more consistent standards.

These views were entirely supported by the findings of the continuous monitoring and review visit.

Careful consideration of findings and a willingness to accept and use unfavourable data constructively is a hallmark of many of the schools who made greatest improvements.

> *Success criterion 1.2.9: The analysis and interpretation of data relating to teaching and learning inform subsequent improvement.*

The school described earlier in 1.2.8 is a good example of improvement being based on analysis and interpretation of teaching and learning data. However, not all schools were as open as this school. In one school it was suggested that the school felt their OFSTED report had done little more than tell them what they already knew and that from the perspective of the pair working with the school the difficulty had been one of 'opening up minds to the idea that critical reflection and observation is not a criticism of the person'.

In other schools there has been a realization that monitoring and collecting and analysing data can give a clearer picture of where to go next in their search for improvement. A substantial number felt they had moved faster by using data on teaching and learning more critically as a basis for determining what they did next to support improvement.

> *Success criterion 1.2.10: There are perceptions of increased staff awareness and confidence in using these strategies.*

In a number of the final reports, experience of participation in the project is thought to have affected teachers' perceptions about the value of standardized testing and the need for careful analysis of the quantitative information this provides. Individuals, groups of children, teachers and improvements to the curriculum were regularly cited as benefiting from a growth of staff awareness and confidence in the use of data. There was evidence in many of the reports of the developing skills of analysis, which were beginning to be used to identify appropriate targets for action. As one report commented:

> Collecting, analysing and using data have been central to the project over the past two years.

The recognition that the use of data is encroaching on schools is illustrated from another school report:

> Research data plays an increased role in the way the LEA operates for school improvement than was necessarily the case in 1996.

One third of the schools had used the analysis of the conditions rating scale to help focus their improvement efforts, with one school saying:

> We continue to use this to influence our planning.

For some, the data of greatest value were good-quality observations and feedback from their lessons.

The range of data for some schools offered qualitative data on the process of school improvement, which, along with the quantitative evidence of cognitive gains made, provides evidence of the benefits of involvement in the programme. The importance of all data was recognized and endorsed by many.

Conclusion

Evaluating school improvement is messy. Real schools and pupils are affected by many influences that are difficult to isolate. There was evidence in the schools of the impact of other school improvement initiatives, which in one school was perceived as having made as much or more impact as the programme itself. The need to ensure that any relevant area of development was monitored and evaluated led to a wide range of data being collected. This created difficulties of management, analysis and feedback. Analysis and interpretation of data were areas in which many staff reported an increase in confidence during the programme, but others still felt they needed more support for these activities. Some schools were unable to collect all the data requested, resulting in gaps, although at least several sources were available for each school, enabling findings to be verified.

It was possible to demonstrate school improvement in terms of pupil outcomes over the period of the programme. The key stage test results improved substantially more for the schools in the project than for the whole LEA. On the reading tests and writing tasks, most schools showed improvement over time, although not all schools and not in all measures. The pupil perception data revealed improved attitudes, motivation and commitment and pupils reported positively on their experience of improvements in the quality of teaching, which they linked to improvement in their study skills. There was considerable evidence that pupil perceptions fed back to staff were a most powerful catalyst for school improvement.

Improvement is strongly influenced in primary schools by the quality of class teaching and the headteacher, and therefore changes in staffing can have a marked influence on the outcomes. Changes in staffing in some cases can bring about rapid improvement, while in others a gradual withering of the earlier progress can occur. The perceived reason for a headteacher choosing to be involved in the programme was also a significant factor in the degree of success experienced by a school. The school staff turbulence experienced midway in the programme, caused by the rush for early retirement before August 1997, influenced the progress towards improvement in different ways. In all cases it disrupted the continuity of the programme but brought in new, valuable staff in some cases, while creating an unwelcome loss in others.

While the programme helped improve aspects of teaching, learning, pupil progress and attainment in many ways, it also helped develop and challenge all participants in a manner that will influence their approach to and understanding of school improvement in the future. It identified and clarified the various roles and ways in which professionals with very different backgrounds can work together to influence school improvement.

Conditions for school improvement are difficult to trace in situations where there are staff changes, and the culture changes brought about by the programme were even elusive in some of the stable schools. However, participation in the programme appeared to help change the culture of a number of the schools, so that they spent more time on careful reflection on their practice. In such contexts, teachers were more open to debate about improvement and accepted responsibility for change and development as well as making sure it came about. These influences on culture change need studying more deeply at a later time.

In the majority of cases the regular contact with their key workers from the programme had a significant impact on the school's improvement and its evaluation. Unfortunately the new LEA arrangements are unlikely to provide for this kind of support in the future, so the schools need to develop their own strategies for evaluating school improvement. It is important to continue to develop a more secure technology for evaluating school improvement than that which presently exists. The success criteria that this chapter sets out may provide a starting point in the future for all those engaged in school development and its evaluation.

Though not wishing to compromise the independence of OFSTED inspection teams, our experience indicates a helpful role for them in revisiting schools engaged on major school improvement activities. The perspective of a third party at final evaluation from someone with detailed knowledge of the school's starting point proved a most valuable evaluation measure in the schools where it was applied. This may offer a signpost for the future, especially if LEAs have a reduced capacity for this kind of work.

It is clear that tracking school improvement through a wide range of measures is possible. More problematic is attributing changes to any one initiative. Schools and LEAs are becoming much more data-focused as a result of the requirements of national and local policies. Handling these data competently and confidently is one positive outcome of the EPSI programme, but recognizing the continuing need for support on data handling needs to be addressed. It is unclear how the national policies defining the role of the LEA in school improvement will enable this support to be provided. In the long term, with or without this support, schools will need to develop their use of data to identify priorities and monitor and evaluate school improvement.

Chapter 9

Improvement Policies and LEA Strategies in Light of the EPSI Programme Findings

Paul Lincoln

Introduction

The EPSI programme started when the Conservative government's attitude to LEAs' role in school improvement was at best ambiguous. Much of the rhetoric from ministers asserted that central government can, with the assistance of its 'quangos', set the framework through legislation and motivate schools to improve through local management, the National Curriculum, the OFSTED inspection cycle, competition between schools, and the publication of results and league tables. The inference, often explicitly stated, was that there is no need for LEA interference in this field apart from providing a last resort, a safety net. The Labour government has given LEAs a clearer role, but with much sharper accountability. LEAs are tasked with monitoring and raising levels of achievement, with 'intervention in inverse proportion to success'. They will be held accountable for their effectiveness in relation to school improvement through the Education Development Plan and the OFSTED inspection of LEAs.

The ambiguity of central government's expectations of LEAs remains. If a school is successful, that is down to the school, but if it fails, then the LEA is to blame. This ambivalence becomes apparent when the LEA is asked to respond to the DfEE and OFSTED in relation to one of its schools that is deemed through the inspection process to require special measures. Searching questions are asked about when the LEA first realized that the school was in difficulty, why the LEA had not found out earlier, and what action had been taken to rectify the problem. Here the expectation is not of an LEA of 'last resort', adopting a light touch at a strategic level, but of an LEA that closely and regularly monitors the performance of its schools and actively intervenes at an early stage.

The new Code of Practice on LEA/school relations has put increased emphasis on the LEA acting as a safety net in a context of largely autonomous schools. This requires a differential use of resources to meet the greatest needs and moves away from the concept of an entitlement for all schools to support from the LEA.

The EPSI programme enabled us to grapple with some of the issues around how, as an LEA, we could work most effectively with schools on their improvement strategies within the national context described above. It has been a very powerful learning process, which has been timely in preparing the LEA for its new role in raising achievement levels. Above all else, the programme process has highlighted the necessity of having a clear focus, rigorous action plans, and effective use of performance data at both LEA and school level, alongside a culture and way of working that brings together multiple perspectives and encourages continuous learning.

Impact of EPSI on Essex LEA

'Improving learning for all' was the first of my three breakthrough object-ives when I took over as director early in 1995. EPSI was initiated by me, partly to give expression to this overriding objective. The programme, with its successes and failures, has had a major influence on the way we work. Indeed, we have probably learned most from our mistakes.

The programme directly informed the principles that underpinned our 'improving learning for all' strategy, which, in turn, prepared the way for our education development plan. Ten key principles have been identified to inform and challenge our work:

- *Success for all learners is the primary purpose.*
  Recent government attention to driving up levels of achievement has resulted in schools focusing on particular cohorts. For example, by targeting the group of children currently just below level 4 at Key Stage 2, a school can improve its performance. Experience has shown that this can be at a cost for other groups of children, such as those in the lowest 20 per cent of the achievement range. The principle adopted is that real school improvement has taken place when the achievement of *all* learners has been raised.
- *Raising the learner's self-esteem and motivation is fundamental to success.*
  The use of pupil perception data in EPSI highlighted the import-ance of engaging children in their learning and developing their self-confidence, which in turn leads to improved learning outcomes.
- *All schools have the potential for continuous improvement.*
  The programme revealed that schools were at very different stages of development, but that all had the potential to improve and that potential was realized to a greater or lesser extent.

- *Schools are the main agents for improvement, with challenge and support from the LEA or an external agency.*
  This principle underpinned the role of LEA staff with schools as described in Chapters 6 and 7, and helped in turn to prepare the LEA for the government's recent reinforcement of this approach.
- *Attention to both processes and outcomes is vital.*
  From the initial planning of the programme through to drafting this publication, these two key ingredients have been held in tension and balance. Too much of the early research on school improvement focused on processes and too much of recent government approaches have focused on outcomes. Attention to both is necessary.
- *Enquiry and reflection, and the use of performance information, are essential.*
  The EPSI programme was based on the assumption that asking hard questions about performance data and acting on the answers will stimulate school improvement at both LEA and school level. Chapters 4 and 8 reveal that the analysis and use of performance data is not without its problems but that, with the right sort of support, it is a powerful motivator.
- *Research evidence should be disseminated to inform practice.*
  The director has emphasized, through the establishment of a variety of research and development initiatives, the importance for both policy and practice of good educational research. EPSI was one such initiative.
- *Activity should be supported by collaborative learning networks.*
  There is evidence from EPSI of the benefit of networking for learning, both across the LEA's service areas and between schools. The School Improvement Value Added Project was an extension of EPSI, from which many more primary schools in Essex have benefited.
- *A focus should be maintained on teaching and learning, and leadership.*
  Chapters 3, 4 and 5 in particular highlight the emphasis in the programme on these key ingredients.
- *Innovative approaches to school organization and learning must be encouraged.*
  Those schools in the programme showing the most confidence and progress were best placed to develop more innovative and challenging approaches to learning.

Multi-disciplinary working, building on the EPSI experience as described in Chapter 6, has become a normal way of working within the LEA.

In a sample of schools, a senior educational psychologist, a planning and admissions adviser and a school development adviser have together represented the LEA in discussions with the headteacher and chairman of governors about the school's targets for the following year.

Special educational needs staff and school development advisers together engage annually with a sample of schools in reviewing their SEN practice, deliberately building on the coherence gained from the EPSI experiences of bringing together the perspectives of the whole school and that of individual pupils' learning. This has also developed a common awareness and understanding of the issues, as the LEA embarks on meeting the government's challenge of including more children with SEN in mainstream schools. Essex is possibly the only LEA where the lead officer for the literacy strategy is also the head of the psychology and assessment service. This is just another example of the LEA bringing a different perspective and focus from the norm to a particular issue. The Essex Quality Framework, a set of tools to support schools practically in self-evaluation and review, developed out of the learning that took place within the LEA during the EPSI programme. The overview was published in autumn 1998 and has been developed collaboratively across service areas and schools.

The EPSI programme was extended into the School Improvement Value Added Project, with well over 250 primary schools involved. Much of the work done by the pupil data group was quickly extended to this much larger group of schools, who were supported in using pupil data effectively to inform their improvement efforts. The pupil data technology that was developed through the EPSI programme is now in widespread use as part of target-setting processes.

One strategy that schools in the programme began to adopt was target-setting. The focus on learning outcomes, pupil data and comparative analyses, combined with the need to be clear about how school improvement could be measured in relation to a school's focus, brought this about. The target-setting process was also developing at a national level. The EPSI experience contributed to the LEA's successful bid for GEST 1B funding to develop target-setting with an additional 90 schools in 1996. The headteacher seconded to lead this project became a valuable member of the EPSI pupil data working group.

Where EPSI schools had made effective use of targets in improving pupil attainment, there were clear links between individual pupil targets and school targets. The process also led to improved consistency in teacher assessment across the school and a re-evaluation of teaching programmes in light of pupil needs and target demands. Schools in the wider GEST 1B project were finding quantitative target-setting a difficult process initially: 'Schools came to the process of target setting from very different starting

points. Difficulties were encountered by schools . . . to varying [degrees]'
(Essex County Council, 1997, p. 9).

Evidence from the EPSI programme suggests that inputs from a range
of perspectives help schools identify targets and strategies to achieve those
targets, where the targets are based not merely on statistical 'gauntlets'
thrown down as national challenges, but, importantly, on an analysis of the
needs of individual pupils and cohorts, by teachers, senior staff and external
LEA personnel. This is made clear in the first conclusion of the DfEE's
evaluation of the same GEST 1B project: 'Target setting benefits from
attention to individual pupil assessment data, teacher forecasts, and LEA
perceptions and analyses' (DfEE, 1998, unpublished evaluation).

Essex's response to the challenge in 'Excellence in Schools' (DfEE,
1997a) to LEAs to work with schools in agreeing and monitoring schools'
quantitative targets for pupil attainment, was set out initially in the booklet
Setting and Achieving Challenging Targets (Essex County Council, 1997).
This builds very closely on models for target-setting developed through
EPSI. Schools are taken through a process of analysis of expected and
potential attainment and progress for individual pupils using subdivisions
of National Curriculum levels as a prerequisite to target-setting at school
level. Challenging targets both for individual pupils and for the cohort are
identified by the school. These are then discussed with LEA advisers in
terms of the degree to which the targets are:

- relevant and appropriate to cohort;
- rigorously well informed;
- high in expectation;
- demonstrating commitment to LEA and national targets;
- representing significant underlying improvement in progress; and
- achievable through identified strategies and improvement planning.

The last point is achieved through an analysis by the school of what needs
to change within the school if the targets are to be met. This question can be
considered against each of the 12 dimensions of the Essex Quality Framework (Figure 9.1) in relation to current practice at the school.

In order to provide opportunities for 'joined up' multiple LEA perspectives to inform school improvement, a multi-disciplinary approach to target-
setting is currently being trialled in Essex. School development advisers, the
LEA representatives whose role it is to 'agree' a school's statutory targets, are
being joined by colleagues from the Psychology and Assessment Service
and the Planning and Admissions Service. School targets are discussed with
the headteacher and the chairman of governors. In one set of trials, both LEA
staff and the school leadership are asked, in advance of the target-setting

CURRICULUM	SPECIAL EDUCATIONAL NEEDS	ASSESSMENT, RECORDING AND REPORTING	PUPIL SUPPORT AND WELFARE
EQUAL OPPORTUNITIES	LEARNING AND PUPIL ACHIEVEMENT	TEACHING	SCHOOL IN THE COMMUNITY
STAFFING	FINANCIAL MANAGEMENT	PREMISES AND RESOURCE MANAGEMENT	STRATEGIC MANAGEMENT

Figure 9.1   The Essex Quality Framework – the 12 quality dimensions

meeting, to review and rate the school against the 12 dimensions of the quality framework in response to these questions (Figure 9.2).

The resulting targets become a mutual expression of LEA and school expectations. The steps agreed by the school leadership and LEA services involved, form the basis of a coherent contract for improvement

In addition to the statutory minimum requirement for primary and junior schools to publish targets for the percentages of pupils to attain level 4 and above in English and mathematics tests at the end of Year 6, Essex is encouraging schools to re-express these as progress rates for the cohort and to identify qualitative 'learning targets', which describe strategic improvements that will contribute to the processes. These may relate to specific groups of pupils. They also relate to actions and developments the school needs to take in relation to teaching and learning, curriculum or other quality dimensions. The multi-disciplinary target-setting meetings jointly agree these learning targets. The multi-disciplinary perspective is intended to smarten the LEA's capacity for consistency in expectation and coherent support as well as appropriate challenge for schools.

The research and development model on which the programme was based has been further developed through our Early Reading Research in collaboration with Warwick University. Essex LEA has demonstrated its ability to act as a bridge between research and practice, and facilitated effective collaboration between higher education, LEA and schools. We contributed to the DfEE-commissioned review of educational research by the Institute of Employment Studies (IES) at the University of Sussex. The final report from the IES said:

Our overall conclusion is that the actions and decisions of policy-makers and practitioners are insufficiently informed by research ... To support

1 Learning and pupil achievement	2 Teaching	3 Assessment recording and reporting	4 People management
Is pupil progress in line with identified potential?	Is the teaching effective and does it contribute to pupil attainment and progress, and are teacher expectations appropriate?	Are there procedures for measuring pupil progress and attainment, and do they inform planning for the next stage in learning?	Are there strategies in the school for attracting, retaining and developing all staff to meet the needs of the school and pupils?
5 Premises and resource management	6 Financial management	7 Pupil support and welfare	8 Special educational needs
Does the school maintain and develop a safe and secure environment along with sufficient resources to ensure effective delivery of the planned curriculum?	Does the school ensure efficient and effective management of its financial resources to support pupils' learning?	Has the school developed a climate in which pupils are safe, secure and feel valued?	Does the provision meet the needs of all pupils?
9 Curriculum	10 Strategic management	11 Equal opportunities	12 School in the community
Is the curriculum designed to meet the needs of all pupils?	Does the school promote systematic and collaborative planning to ensure it meets present and future requirements focused on improving pupils' learning and achievement?	Does the school ensure equal access to all pupils?	How does the school contribute to and reflect the aspirations of the community?

Figure 9.2 The Essex Quality Framework – the 12 questions

policy formation and practice the research community has to have both a thriving theoretical and applied base which are fit for the purposes they seek to serve . . . Mediation needs to be built in at the start of research and we would encourage researchers and research funders to identify strategies for maximising the impact of research from the outset. (DfEE, 1998b)

The EPSI research model provides a way forward for the educational community in that the outcomes have informed both policy makers and practitioners and mediation and dissemination were built into our plans from the beginning, when we designed the programme.

In all of these ways, the lessons learned from EPSI have made us more effective in adding value to the work of schools in school improvement and to understanding the processes of school improvement.

Research Questions Relating to the LEA's Role

In Chapter 1, we outlined the questions relating to the LEA's role that the research programme was hoping to answer. The remainder of this chapter will attempt to summarize what the research evidence has identified in response to each question.

How can an LEA best support schools in their
improvement efforts?

Schools often need help in clarifying their focus and priorities for improvement from the data and evidence available to them. Without such help or challenge from an external perspective, a school can easily focus on a priority that is interesting but marginal to making a real difference to pupil achievement. The LEA/HE perspective needs to rigorously question the clarity of focus early on if valuable time and energy is not to be lost by the school.

The LEA must help the school to focus on outcomes for children, not just processes, and hold the two in tension and balance. There was an ongoing healthy dialogue, sometimes developing into heated argument, on this key issue within the steering group throughout the programme. Through this debate we have learned that targets and tasks need to be expressed as pupil outcomes. This is both a significant shift in teachers' and headteachers' thinking and in LEA staff thinking, but it is one we are now embarked upon.

LEA staff must be skilled in the use of pupil data, at individual pupil, class, and whole-school level. They must also be able to empower school staff to question the data and act on the answers. The lack of confidence in some schools in the analysis of data is described in Chapter 4. This makes it even more important that the consultancy skills of LEA staff, particularly with the use of data, are well developed.

The quality of a school's action plan is crucial to success, and the more concrete, specific and related to what teachers do in their classrooms, the better. Inevitably, we found that the weaker the school, the more external help was needed in action planning, but in a way that developed the school's capacity to do it better in the future.

Schools valued the external monitoring perspective. The more confident schools enjoyed having their assumptions challenged, but those less confident had to be handled more sensitively.

The role of the person challenging and supporting the school from outside has to be clearly focused, so that the school knows what its role is and what the purpose of each visit is.

Clear protocols and expectations around visits are necessary to enable schools and the external agent to be in agreement about the added value. There is often a danger, particularly for advisory services, to operate on the basis of individual personalities rather than consistency of practice. Training and skills development are essential for this kind of consistency to be widely available.

> *How can the focus on an individual pupil's learning and the focus on whole-school development processes complement each other?*

The focus on pupil data from assessments and pupil perception surveys enables the two processes to complement each other for the first time and to be held in balance. Too often in the past, whole-school planning has been uninformed by the data on individual pupils' progress.

The LEA can assist in bringing these focuses together. The programme powerfully illustrated the value of special educational needs professionals with their focus on outcomes for those with learning difficulties, and advisers with their focus on whole-school development working together to challenge and complement their different perspectives.

> *Can an LEA engage all schools in a systematic and cumulative programme of improvement?*

Yes, it can, but only on the basis that different amounts and types of involvement are required for schools at different stages of development. This statement presumes, however, that an LEA knows where each school is on its improvement journey. Better use of performance data and benchmarking by the LEA will enable it to make more informed judgements about which schools will need more support than others. The EPSI programme was based on an entitlement for all schools involved rather than on the differentiated approach that is increasingly being adopted. The government may want LEAs to go further down this route, but their expectations are often at odds with those of successful schools, many of whom feel denied if they do not have access to the external perspective of the LEA. The differentiated model, if taken to an extreme, could lead to dangers of isolation for schools and an inability on the part of the LEA to identify and disseminate best practice.

> *What sort of capacity and skills does an LEA require to achieve this?*

In terms of capacity, the accepted wisdom nationally is for one adviser to 30 primary schools. The EPSI research, as described in Chapter 7, has helped us to focus more importantly on what LEA staff do that is effective rather than on how many are needed. There is sometimes too much emphasis on the uniqueness of individual schools, when the reality is that they have much in common. This debate relates back to the 'formal' and 'cultural' models of school improvement described in Chapter 3. The Essex quality framework highlights the systems and processes that *all* schools need to have in place to be successful. The emphasis on each school being different carries with it the danger of LEAs retaining a large capacity in order to be able to respond to such diversity.

The EPSI evidence reinforces the need for consistent minimum quality, systems and ways of working in and with all schools, and that differences can blossom on top of that. For example, the LEA's approach to target-setting and reviewing progress on an annual cycle, as described earlier in this chapter, may provide the minimum level necessary. This would not, of course, rule out more in-depth work with schools that either requested it or needed it on the basis of an analysis of current performance compared with other similar schools. As LEAs and schools become more effective with data handling, then we may find that what is needed is better systems and fewer, more effective external people who more clearly add value.

The skills required of LEA staff have already been touched on in answer to the first question, particularly concerning the use of data. Not all staff have these skills currently, nor are some of them willing to admit it.

The most valuable skills for LEA staff to have from a school's perspective are the ability to analyse clearly what issues the school needs to address as priorities, how to enable the school to problem-solve, create capacity to manage change and implement solutions, and how to keep pressure and support in balance.

The development of school improvement 'tool kits', which might be accessed through distance learning, may in the longer term be more cost-effective than investing in people.

The EPSI programme revealed that there is certainly a training and development need if LEA staff are to have the skills necessary to work effectively and efficiently with schools in a manner that adds value to the work of the schools. The kinds of training on the job that were provided by EPSI ought to be available regionally or nationally for LEA staff if LEAs are to meet the government's expectations of them in school improvement.

How can this work be 'built into' the normal activities of
a school and an LEA rather than be seen as a 'bolt-on'?

From the outset, a conscious decision was made for the programme not to be resource rich, on the basis that, if we did not build it into our normal work, we would not be able to make it available to all schools without an unrealistic increase in resources. It was built in to some staff's normal programme, but added on for SEN staff as a pilot exercise. We are now building it into the target-setting process with schools.

The data indicate that some of the schools that made least progress often saw the programme as an add-on. Interestingly, there seemed to be an attitude in some schools that, if they could not identify EPSI as something separate, then it had not happened. This points perhaps to a need for the LEA to be clearer about what LEA staff are doing with the school.

How can LEA staff from different professional backgrounds
combine to support school improvement?

This question has been answered fully in Chapter 6. Multi-disciplinary teams break down the barriers of compartmentalized agencies and provide multiple perspectives on common problems.

How can pace and a sense of urgency be maintained at the same
time as recognizing that school improvement takes time?

The programme gave no easy answers to this question, except to reinforce that all involved need to hang on to and hold in balance both concepts simultaneously, as with the emphasis on both processes and outcomes.

A regular external monitoring perspective helped to focus the mind and give a momentum to activities. This was as true in terms of the impact of the steering group on the programme pairs as it was of the programme pairs on the schools. Whenever the external monitoring lagged or lacked rigour, the momentum of the programme slowed. It simply reinforces the fact that an element of accountability is essential at each level of activity.

With the benefit of hindsight, the programme would have had greater impact had the steering group insisted on greater rigour and consistency from the outset, for example in relation to the collection of data by schools or consistency of practice among the programme pairs. When the programme started in 1995, neither the schools nor LEA staff were at the point they are now. EPSI enabled us to learn these lessons together and, in that sense, has probably been stronger on development than it has been on research. Certainly, without EPSI, we would not be as well placed as we are now to fulfil our current role in school improvement. To that extent, the investment has paid dividends.

The jury is out on whether or not LEAs can rise successfully to the challenge laid down by the Labour government in relation to their role in school improvement. What is clear is the need for an agency or agencies to operate at a local or regional level with schools that are at varying stages of development, to both support and challenge them in their improvement efforts. The EPSI programme provides evidence that schools require and value such an external perspective, regardless of the provider, which helps them to focus and to review their progress on a regular basis.

At present, it is also clear that LEAs, warts and all, have the potential to provide such an external perspective with comprehensive coverage. However, the OFSTED inspection of LEAs is revealing that some are better placed, with the relevant expertise, to perform this role than others.

The EPSI programme was specifically initiated by the director four years ago to prepare Essex LEA for its current role and to enable us to understand better the nature of primary school improvement. In that respect, it definitely served its purpose and has helped us to develop as a learning organization, along with our schools. In turn, it has stimulated a range of other developments that have equipped us to meet the challenges of the future with greater skill and confidence.

Chapter 10

Key Points and Conclusions

Geoff Southworth and Paul Lincoln

Introduction

In this chapter we draw together the findings, lessons and insights that have emerged from the EPSI programme. The discussion is organized into four sections. In the first section we draw upon the programme teams' perspectives collected at the end of the programme. This section reviews what those colleagues who worked most closely with the schools had to say about improvement and working with the schools. In essence, these comments represent their conclusions about the EPSI programme.

The second section outlines the key points we have identified about improving primary schools and discusses them. In the third section we consider the implications of the EPSI programme for educational research. In the fourth section we set out the main conclusions from our work on the EPSI programme.

The Programme Teams' Views and Conclusions

Towards the close of the programme, time was set aside to capture and record what the programme teams thought about the programme. These colleagues had worked in multi-disciplinary teams and had, in part, been a focus for development themselves, as well as being required to play a key role in supporting the schools' improvement efforts.

Staff from the UCSE, along with a member of the steering group, took responsibility for collecting these data. Group interviews were conducted, with the interviewers working in pairs and using a common schedule of questions. The interviews were semi-structured to allow scope for unanticipated issues to be explored and to give respondents the opportunity to identify their concerns as well as to respond to those of the interviewers. The interviews were conducted one month before the schools and the programme pairs undertook the end-of-programme assessments and produced their detailed reports on the schools. These reports and end-of-programme data provided a school-by-school view and enabled us to examine whether and how each school had made progress. These interviews, by contrast, aimed to provide a more over-arching perspective and offered the programme teams the chance to note issues they had identified from their work in the field. Overall, 11 main points emerged. The first six relate to their observations about the schools' efforts and progress. The latter five points relate to the role the programme teams played and to what they found beneficial or not.

First, the dominant picture emerging from the programme teams was one in which progress had undoubtedly been made in the EPSI schools. However, as one might expect, in a very small number of cases progress had taken time (18 months) to manifest itself, was uneven in its development and fragile in its sustainability.

The programme teams cited a range of indicators of progress. They had seen improvement inside classrooms, such as improvements in pupils' reading and writing, as well as in pupils' attitudes to learning. The pupil perception data had proved especially helpful here, as discussed in Chapter 5. Changes in teachers' understandings and attitudes to learning were also mentioned. Some respondents reported a more sophisticated understanding of formative assessment, and others reported a rise in teachers' expectations of pupils.

The teams also reported improvements in planning in the schools. Teachers' lesson plans had developed, as had schemes of work, which now included key indicators for each subject area. The teams said that benchmarking and target-setting strategies had become common in the EPSI schools. More monitoring was taking place in the schools than formerly, with subject coordinators and leaders generally taking a more active role than previously. There was also evidence in several schools of staff formally tracking pupils' progress.

Communication between teachers in their respective schools had generally improved and was seen as a sign of progress. For example, in a number of schools there was better liaison between teachers in Years 3, 4, 5 and 6 than there had been before the EPSI programme began.

Second, these examples led the teams to generally conclude that there had been changes in the schools' professional cultures throughout the time of the programme. The changes in the teacher culture described movement towards ones that were more collegial. Also, in these cultures, staff were more focused on the processes and evidence of learning and teaching. The programme team responses included examples of:

- lively discussions in the staffroom;
- some acceptance now of the need by staff to look inward, e.g. at reading results, rather than simply look for external reasons for pupils' levels of progress;

- staff meetings focused on teaching and learning;
- teachers being more reflective;
- much more attention to research, recording, analysing and acting upon data;
- more professional openness;
- a greater sense of cohesion in the school as an organization; and
- willingness in many schools to use expertise within the staff group.

Third, the most frequently cited factors that were seen to have helped in the schools' progress were associated with becoming clear about what the focus of the improvement work was to be and how it might best be translated into action. The range of factors included: establishing a clear focus and sense of priority; action planning; bench-marking; target-setting – particularly what you do with individual pupils, as opposed to a whole-school approach; using data – particularly pupil perception data.

Alongside these were developments the teams also noted about factors that enabled a change in the professional culture to take place. For example, classroom observation by pairs of teachers was seen as an effective way to influence teacher collaboration, especially when it was followed up by whole-staff discussion and when the emerging data were used with all staff to focus on practice and to change it. The observation data sometimes showed inconsistencies in teachers' practice (e.g. how they started lessons) and led to staff setting agreed expectations in all classrooms. Policies for teaching and learning were also seen as very helpful tools for staff to develop and use.

The impact of particular members of staff emerged as a strong influence on progress in the schools. Apart from the influence of the headteacher, which is discussed separately below, other key players were identified. These were often deputy heads, although not always. These individuals kept driving the schools' projects forward and without their persistence the programme would not have moved ahead.

A number of respondents also recognized the value of their own work as external change agents. Their external support enabled the schools to keep focused and the work they did alongside school staff proved beneficial. Indeed, in one school there was for a period of time no senior management team and the EPSI programme pair kept the staff together.

Fourth, progress was limited by a number of factors. In some schools difficult conditions confronted the staff. These included large classes of 36 pupils, professional fatigue and unforeseen incidents and events blocking progress. Staff turbulence was another factor. If there was a change in personnel, particularly the loss of a valued and leading colleague, this was a setback to progress. Other factors were more amenable to professional intervention and included: an initial lack of understanding about the EPSI programme; a failure in some schools to grasp some of the basics of educational change (e.g. lack of involvement, lack of time dedicated to the school's priorities); a culture of blame or division. Such a culture involved a tendency to blame the infant school, fragmentation between Key Stages 1 and 2 in the same school, or a general lack of cohesion among the staff.

Fifth, the involvement of the headteacher emerged as a crucial factor. It was a positive feature when progress was made and a negative factor when progress was less apparent. Examples of positive headteacher involvement were when a new headteacher had used the EPSI programme to develop the professional culture and when new heads had been very supportive of the programme's aims and objectives. Experienced heads who used the programme productively were those who kept their schools working towards their improvement targets, refined their schools' development plans and developed the roles of senior management teams.

Negative involvement was associated with heads who chose to be involved in the programme and did not consult with others, heads who subsequently kept things to themselves or those who tried to control too much in the school. The programme teams also noted heads who were not able managers of staff, poor communicators and those who were unable to become or remain focused, as examples of weak leadership.

Sixth, it was acknowledged that the programme was characterized by a lack of governor involvement. There were only a small number of examples of proactive, positive governor involvement. Typically, governors were informed about the programme, but not directly involved.

Seventh, the programme pairs and teams were involved in a range of tasks and activities. Their role was wide-ranging, but was summarized by most as involving them in being a critical friend to the schools they worked with. More specifically, they played a part in collecting, analysing and interpreting performance data with their schools and in assisting senior staff and key players to develop action plans. The comments of the programme teams also showed, in line with the findings in Chapters 3 and 5, that the pupil perception data were enormously powerful. However, the teams also reported that data were sometimes flawed and difficult to interpret. Changes in the composition of the staff sometimes made the data less trustworthy, as did changes in pupil groups or when pupil numbers were very small. Some respondents acknowledged that they had developed a greater appreciation of the importance of data as a result of the programme and now felt it should play a more significant role in the future.

The programme teams undoubtedly played an important staff development role with the schools to which they were attached. A range of development activities and engagements were cited, including:

- working with coordinators to run INSET sessions;
- leading staff meetings;
- re-clarifying the school's improvement focus;
- classroom observation;
- modelling teaching and being open and vulnerable to develop staff discussions;
- interviewing pupils;
- providing examples of papers to aid schools' document and policy production;
- bringing internal groups of teachers together;
- supporting leading players in the schools who were driving EPSI forward;
- evaluating aspects of work undertaken in the schools; and
- creating new networks for information exchange between schools.

Eighth, the respondents believed they had benefited and developed through several aspects of the programme. Many spoke very positively about working in pairs. The sharing of perspectives and the opportunity to learn from the other person were highly valued, as was the chance to talk things over with a trusted colleague and the opportunity to analyse data together and work out a strategy for supporting their schools. Some difficulties were also reported, such as finding the time to liaise and the need to coordinate the work more carefully, but these were not seen as major impediments and did not detract from the benefits.

The core programme days were viewed as positive and helpful. The overall quality of them was reported as good, although some variation was noted. The enquiry and reflection sessions, when teams shared progress and reported on their activities, were valued greatly. It was felt that the steering group might have used the expertise within the programme teams more than they did.

Ninth, the introduction of multi-disciplinary teams was seen as a very positive initiative. Though at the beginning of the programme there had been some mutual suspicion, this had soon evaporated. Respondents spoke of how they had gained from working with other colleagues from other service groups and how broader perspectives and a wider frame of reference had developed.

Tenth, as a result of the EPSI experience, the programme teams believed that the LEA now needs to consider three particular, but inter-related issues:

- The LEA needs actively to support rigorous self-evaluation in each school.

- All schools would benefit from similar levels of support, time and rigour as the EPSI schools had.
- A delicate balance needs to be established between schools taking control of their improvement efforts, with support from the LEA, and the LEA creating a dependency culture.

The eleventh finding centres on one of the themes emerging from these observations and insights about the programme. In line with discussions and points in other chapters in this book, and in common with other research into organizational development, the management of educational change, and school improvement studies, it is clear that:

- cultural renewal lies at the heart of school improvement; and
- such renewal applies as much to LEAs as it does to schools.

Though it is clear from several data sources that within the schools their professional cultures were transforming and being transformed by many factors, it was also true that the culture of the LEA was changing. Both types of change had things in common, most notably the shift to an evidence-based approach to school improvement in general, and within primary schools in particular. It is also important to emphasize that the two occurred side by side. Indeed, recognition that the two took place simultaneously suggests that not only do staff in schools need to develop an awareness of cultural renewal, but that so too do staff in LEAs. Moreover, just as the work of senior staff in schools has a strong influence on the teacher cultures inside their schools, so too does the work of senior colleagues in LEAs impinge on the professional culture of their organizations.

Key Points about Improving Primary Schools

There are six sets of points we want to highlight and discuss. It is important to note that they interrelate and are not presented in any priority order.

Focus Matters

The first point concerns the idea that for primary school improvement to have any chance of success, efforts must be focused. As we have noted on a number of occasions in the previous chapters, focus was a key issue raised by the heads and programme teams and pairs. Typically, focus was used with reference to the priorities the schools selected. To be focused on something was regarded as a vital part of making things happen in the schools.

How schools developed their focuses varied considerably. In some, the OFSTED inspection had helped staff to see more clearly than otherwise what needed attention. Yet, in some other schools, the inspection process had hindered them because the reports lacked clarity. There were also instances of staff in school determining their own focus, or of the LEA support staff helping them.

However the focus was identified, the main point is that for schools to improve they need to be clear about what they are going to concentrate their resources, energies and efforts on. It is plain that staff in primary schools cannot attend to everything, all at once. There has to be a prioritized approach that, over time, allows staff to attend to some things before moving to look at others. This is well understood by headteachers and teachers who often use the juggler or 'plate spinner' metaphors to portray an image of trying to deal with many things at once. Yet, what emerged from listening to the headteachers in this programme, was their belief that while they had to keep lots of things going, to improve aspects of the school they needed to concentrate their efforts to ensure that improvements reached deep into the school, rather than remained at a surface level.

Auditing, Monitoring and Self-evaluation

Second, establishing a focus and checking progress towards it required that a variety of systems and processes be put in place and used. Essentially these systems were those of self-evaluation. An initial audit was necessary to identify needs and targets. Action plans then had to be devised and systems for monitoring progress and performance developed. Feedback processes were used to ensure that colleagues were aware of matters arising, successes and revisions to plans. This broad framework was generally adopted in the schools and all appeared to find it useful.

At the same time, however, it emerged that the framework for self-evaluation is rather more difficult in practice than in theory. Handling the data collected from audits and monitoring exercises was a challenge for teachers and headteachers (see Chapter 4). Too much data could overwhelm some staff groups, while too little provided only a partial picture of what was happening in the school. The pupil perception information proved to be an important set of data for two reasons. For one thing, it supplemented the assessment-based, quantitative view of pupils' learning outcomes and gains. For another, it challenged teachers' assumptions about the learning process and the school as a learning environment for the children.

Teacher involvement in data handling tended not to be as high as the headteachers' and senior staffs' levels of participation. Governors did not appear to be involved very much at all. It seems, therefore, that school improvement may rest, in substantial part, on the headteachers' and senior staff's capacity to establish and sustain systems of auditing and monitoring and their ability to analyse the quantitative and qualitative data that emanate from them.

Moreover, to avoid too limited a view of learning developing, because a staff group might hold a narrow set of expectations about pupils' potential, some external input appears to be necessary. OFSTED sometimes provided this, but not always. Also, their contact with the staff is too infrequent and, being judgmental rather than discursive, may be too easily denied or rejected, especially when the headteacher shares the same low expectations as the staff. Despite the fact that the EPSI schools had all been recently inspected around the start of the programme, not everyone found the inspectors' audit insightful.

Two other tactics were necessary to puncture some staffs' assumptions, when relevant to do so: the LEA's value-added data, which enabled schools to bench-mark the pupils' achievements against other similar schools; engagement with the SDAs and programme pairs. These, along with inspection reports, provided a reasonable degree of external challenge to long established teacher and headteacher expectations.

Recognizing that school self-evaluation is an important feature of the improvement process, the LEA has now developed as part of its quality framework a 'tool kit', which schools can use to support their monitoring and evaluation.

School Improvement is Differentiated

The third set of findings centres on the fact that improvement in these primary schools was variegated. Certainly there were many common strands, but these should not submerge the fact that there are many subtle, and not so subtle, differences in how staff in each school went about trying to enhance the pupils' learning.

Some of the differences relate to the variety of improvement targets the schools adopted. As can be seen in Chapter 2, the content of improvement varied by school. Yet this is not the only basis for schools' differences in development. Each also had a particular starting point for their specific efforts. Some schools were starting from a relatively low point because their performance levels were characterized by under-achievement. Others were places where there was a lack of consistency in approach among the teaching staff. Some were schools with high levels of attainment, but with areas of learning that nevertheless needed attention.

In other words, the EPSI schools could not be described as places that needed a 'save and rescue' approach to their improvement. They were not schools that necessarily needed an injection of strong leadership. Nor did the schools fall neatly into the 'stuck' or 'moving' categories (Rosenholtz, 1989), or Stoll and Fink's (1998) classification of moving, cruising, strolling, struggling and sinking schools. These classifications are too simplistic and fail to demonstrate the differentiated nature of primary school improvement. The EPSI programme schools were differentiated by their improvement focuses, their starting points, school contexts, professional cultures and pace of progress. These differences should be recognized so that their improvement efforts and strategies can be examined to see if they are suitable for their needs and plans.

Another reason why differentiation in the improvement processes is important is because of the way staffing impinges so strongly upon primary school development. The quality of individual staff, be they headteachers, deputy heads or teachers, is of paramount importance in primary schools. This statement is true in all schools, but in relatively small organizations the influence of individuals proportionally increases their impact.

The loss of an able and experienced subject coordinator is always significant for at least two reasons. First, their value as a skilful class teacher is high. In schools with one form entry, or less, their impact as a class teacher will be considerable. Second, their subject knowledge and experience as a curriculum leader are important resources and strengths. Indeed, in many primary schools when an able subject leader, say in mathematics, leaves, it is akin in a secondary school to the departure of the whole maths department! The loss of both class teaching and curricular skills and knowledge will, at the very least, temporarily inhibit the school's performance. Of course, the reverse is also true. When a weak teacher leaves, the headteacher and governors can strengthen the quality of the teaching if they can attract, identify and appoint an able successor.

In all the EPSI schools, the headteachers were acutely aware of staff strengths and weaknesses and were sensitive to staff leaving the school, or being absent for some length of time. Indeed, with the unusually large number of early retirements over the summer of 1997, this feature became very prominent. While this spate of staff turnover helped some schools move forward, it undoubtedly hindered others. This was because it created discontinuity in the schools' teaching arrangements, unsettled staffing structures and may have threatened the stability of the organization for a period. This was particularly true in schools where more than one colleague left simultaneously.

Staff recruitment and retention is a major feature in improving primary schools. This is not by any means a new insight, but it is something that is often underplayed in school improvement studies. Furthermore, it is often underestimated in its power and impact on primary school improvement efforts, for reasons discussed in the introduction to this book.

Consequently, primary school improvement needs to be considered and conceptualized in more detailed and sensitive ways than at present. Each school's contextual circumstances need to be carefully analysed, as do staff strengths and weaknesses. As improvement efforts unfold over time, the constraints and opportunities posed by the staff's skills, development needs and turnover rates also need to be kept in view, since these will modulate the school's capacity to improve and the pace at which progress can be made.

Emphasis on Learning and Teaching

A common characteristic of the EPSI schools was the attention they gave to pupils' learning. As has been made clear in previous chapters, the schools became more committed to looking into learning and to analysing outcome data (see Chapter 4). Without doubt, this was one of the major developments within the EPSI programme.

Yet it was not accompanied, to any great extent, except in a couple of schools, with a concerted emphasis on teaching. Attention to learning took precedence over reviews of pedagogy. In Chapter 3 several reasons were offered as to why this pattern existed and it is not necessary to rehearse them again here. Rather, what needs to be noted here is the fact that in schools that had established (or were establishing) systems for monitoring, collating and analysing information and had developed an evidence-based approach to improvement, this did not generally include the examination of the quality of teaching. Thus, those who call for greater attention to be paid to teaching, cannot assume that school self-evaluation alone will create the conditions for staff to introduce explicit and formal reviews of teaching.

The Formal Model of School Improvement

Many changes occurred in the schools during the EPSI programme. Yet, overall, three major shifts took place:

- An evidence-based approach to improvement was established.
- Headteachers and teachers looked in some depth at pupils' learning and progress.
- The teacher cultures in many schools altered.

Two of these three changes form part of what we have called the 'formal' model of school improvement (see Chapter 3). This model originates from central government, although it is based on work in numerous schools around the country. It has been articulated and prescribed in a number of publications from the DfEE and OFSTED (OFSTED and DfEE, 1996; DfEE, 1997b; OFSTED, 1998). The findings from EPSI show that the model is sound.

However, though the model is undoubtedly helpful, it is not as straightforward to implement as it might appear or as some might like to believe. Some reasons for making this statement have been presented in the earlier discussion on self-evaluation. Here we want to elaborate on this theme a little more.

Two sets of interrelated reasons can be offered to defend our claim that the formal model of improvement is too plain and austere. First, it fails to say anything about the need for staff to establish and sustain the internal conditions to support improvement efforts. This has long been recognized in the school improvement literature (e.g. Fullan, 1991; Hopkins et al., 1994). Yet its relevance for improving primary schools is possibly even greater than in secondary schools, for reasons outlined earlier (i.e. staffing constraints). It is also true, as noted in some of the headteacher data reported in Chapter 3, that the general lack of organizational 'slack' in primary schools, importantly the lack of release time for coordinators and deputy heads to monitor across the school, inhibits the development of an organizational capacity to improve. In some ways this is another variant of the argument we have developed about the differentiated nature of school improvement. Greater recognition of the differences (as well as the similarities) between secondary and primary schools is needed, as it also is within the primary phase, since small schools do not enjoy the same organizational conditions as large primary schools. Nevertheless, the main point here is that schools need to adapt their internal conditions to meet the demands of the improvement process.

Second, improving primary schools involves cultural transformation. In some cases this will mean relatively small-scale changes, in others it may require more drastic, even wholesale shifts in the ways teachers relate to one another.

Primary school improvement today looks like a set of processes that include auditing and evaluating pupils' learning from a variety of standpoints and over protracted periods of time. This includes teachers conducting a number of investigations into curriculum policies and their implementation and success, analyses of the received curriculum, the development of new policies and schemes of work, as well as action plans, school, year cohort and pupil targets, lesson plans and changes in teaching strategies.

Typically all of these have led to teachers working together in new ways. Professional collaboration has become more of a norm in primary education than ever before, even though such cooperation is still something that cannot be taken for granted in every primary school, as we saw or heard about in a number of the EPSI schools.

However, it also seems that although professional collaboration may be a necessary condition in an improving primary school and a characteristic of the teacher culture in such schools, it is not sufficient. It is necessary to enable staff to plan together, to develop agreed policies and priorities, to develop continuous and consistent approaches to the curriculum. But it now seems that heads and teachers need to go beyond these levels of interaction.

As we saw in a number of the EPSI schools, there is also a need for the teaching staff to observe one another's teaching. There is a clear case for schools to put in place regular, frequent sessions when staff visit one another's classrooms, during the school day, to look in detail at each other's teaching and the pupils' learning in action. These observations need to be followed up by time for feedback and discussion between observer and the observed. Later, staff discussions will be needed to develop a bigger picture of teaching and learning across the school and where deep and sustained professional dialogues about what is actually happening in the school can be developed. Staff should create and share knowledge about their teaching practice, their respective strengths and development needs and how these relate to the pupils' learning. Also, pupil learning data should be examined in terms of what it may suggest about the teaching in the school.

These are challenging issues that dig deep inside teachers' views about themselves and may challenge their professional assumptions. Yet it is precisely because these are sensitive matters, which may threaten teachers' confidence and undermine their self-esteem, that their professional cultures need to change. There may need to be greater professional openness, so that colleagues can speak honestly and candidly, without individuals feeling they are being attacked, or without them becoming defensive or taking up a position of denial.

In Chapter 4 we show how teachers responded to pupil data. It is likely that when they move to examining pedagogy, similar reactions and, perhaps, even more acute ones will occur unless such self-evaluation takes place in a culture of challenge and support and in circumstances where successes, as well as teachers' development needs, are recognized and valued.

To move beyond the current levels of teacher collaboration in primary schools is to make another important and big step. Those who prescribe school self-evaluation do not always appear to acknowledge or appreciate what it involves for teachers and headteachers in terms of their professional relationships, meetings and micro-politics. The EPSI programme showed what it may require and provided us with valuable glimpses of it happening in some schools. Certainly there is more to explore and study here.

Tracking School Improvement

In Chapters 2 and 8 we showed how we attempted to track improvements in the EPSI schools. Following on from the above points, it now seems that efforts inside and outside schools to monitor and record their improvement efforts need to adopt a twin-track approach. This twin-track approach involves focusing on the school's progress towards the targets staff have set themselves, and attention to the processes by which they are moving along.

Monitoring progress will involve the use of baseline data, school, year group, cohort and pupil outcome data, as well as the school's action plans. The Essex LEA 'tool kit' has been designed to support schools in these areas. It is a new and emerging methodology that enables staff in schools to track their efforts using a variety of measures. The EPSI programme played an important role in clarifying what the tool kit needed to contain.

Staff should also consider, from time to time, whether they are creating the internal conditions for their schools to improve. They should review their capacities as a staff group, senior management team and individuals to lead, coordinate, enquire, plan, develop and involve one another and pupils, parents and governors. By attending to these capacities, they will also be simultaneously attending to the school's culture and whether and how it might be changing.

The IQEA project (Ainscow et al., 1994b) developed a condition rating scale to help staff to focus on these conditions, and this scale was used in many EPSI schools. However, it now seems that such a scale needs to be refined and supplemented by other instruments. Some LEAs have produced checklists, which help schools examine leadership or parental involvement. Others have tried to set out questions primary heads and deputies might address to help them concentrate on leading their schools' improvement efforts (Southworth, 1998). Yet, generally, it seems that little work has been done in this area.

There is a strong case for staff looking at the cultural conditions in their schools and there is an equally strong case for the development of resources and materials to assist them in their reviews.

EPSI and Educational Research

In the recent past educational research has been the subject of some criticism and debate. One criticism levelled at educational enquiry is that it involves lone researchers tackling 'big issues'. Individuals who work in isolation are unlikely, it is believed, to have very much impact on these issues, let alone resolve them. Another criticism is that educational research has not had adequate influence on the improvement of practice. Researchers are regarded as being too interested in theory and not enough in practice. A third complaint is that researchers do not involve 'user communities' in their research. At best, they only work with LEAs and schools in order to obtain access to the research sites that they need to conduct 'their' research in other people's setting. These are important criticisms and there is a considerable basis for them.

The EPSI programme, however, adopted a stance that we believe counters these criticisms. We did so because, from the very beginning, we were unequivocal in seeking to illuminate educational practice in order to provide information for those who make policy and practical decisions that lead to changes and improvements in practice.

We did this in four ways. First, the research was inclusive, in that colleagues from schools, the LEA and higher education worked together to forge new understandings, share insights and puzzles, and consulted with one another about what to do. In other words, the criticism that educational researchers work in isolation was not a problem in this programme because of the collaborative nature of the study. The principle of working in partnership was built into our planning and practice from the outset.

The inclusive nature of the programme also provided multiple perspectives on school improvement. This seems to be particularly important, given that school improvement is not a single event, but a complex, multi-faceted set of interrelated processes. Moreover, the multiple perspectives overcome the problem of researchers tackling a topic that is too ambitious for any lone investigator. Numerous opportunities to share issues were built into the programme, notably at the pupil data working party and the steering group, and when the university staff reported back emerging findings and ideas to the programme teams and to the schools during sessions dedicated to such formative feedback. This process of sharing was enhanced when staff from the schools and colleagues from the LEA led sessions and offered their insights into how elements of the programme were developing.

In effect, these seminars and 'briefings' became dialogues where ideas and assumptions could be articulated, reflected upon and challenged. In several senses, the programme provided many opportunities for ideas to be critiqued, debated and defended. The research was thus a reciprocal process of conceptual refinement in terms of both the breadth of perspective and depth of understandings. Indeed, the debate continued and became more focused during the process of drafting and redrafting the manuscript for this book.

Second, the research was grounded in the experience and actions of a range of practitioners and it was relevant to their work, professional interests and institutional needs. It was therefore highly practical, but also enquiring and reflective. Indeed, it was similar to Elliott's belief that educational research is practical enquiry that fuses enquiry with practice. Educational research involves teachers playing an important part in the process of articulating, analysing and hypothesizing solutions to complex educational problems (Elliott, 1990).

Third, because of the inclusive and grounded nature of the research, there was a relatively high degree of involvement of 'user communities'. We implicitly agreed with Hargreaves' (1996) argument that educational research should take as its primary purpose the involvement of user communities, especially policy-makers and practitioners, in all aspects of the research process, from the creation of strategic research plans, the selection of research priorities and the funding of projects, through to the dissemination and implementation of policies and practices arising from or influenced by the research activities and findings.

The Director of Education for Essex LEA, Paul Lincoln, and his senior colleagues were central players in designing the programme along with staff from UCSE. As a leading policy maker in Essex LEA, Lincoln's leadership and direct participation in the programme ensured that 'users' were involved in all aspects of the research process and throughout the life of the project.

Nor should it be overlooked that this was an Essex project. Such a strong local investment meant that many staff in the participating schools looked favourably upon the programme because they saw it as addressing their particular needs and concerns and saw the LEA as doing something about them and for them. The programme was close to them because they saw it as 'home-grown' and a local product.

Fifth, the EPSI programme was a research and development project. The programme sought to explore and develop a number of ways of working in schools and in the LEA, as we have described in the previous chapters. Through these multiple and simultaneous developments the programme was educative for many participants, albeit in different ways. All who were involved in the programme wanted to deepen their understanding of the processes and outcomes of managed improvement efforts. Also, the development strand of the programme showed to those inside and outside the programme that it had a practical intent. This was an important issue for the user communities and for the research sponsors as well. Not only did the LEA directorate want this, but so too did elected members.

For too long there has been an unfortunate division between theory and practice, which has created and sustained an implicit hierarchy, with theory somehow being seen to be superior to – more intellectual, more clever, better than – practice. Not only is this kind of outlook wrong, because of the interactive and symbiotic nature of theory and practice, but it is also wholly inappropriate.

Educational research should explore the relationship between theory and practice. Given that our professional work is theory-laden, it is import-ant to understand the theories that heads, teachers and LEA staff have of their work. In the case of the EPSI programme, this meant exploring what a group of primary headteachers and teachers believed about improving their schools and what LEA staff believed their role to be. What were their subjective constructs, values and explanations of the strategies they used to improve their schools; in short, what were their 'folk theories'? Unless we know these things, the subjective meaning of school improvement may be misconstrued, and attempts to change schools could run foul of practitioners' assumptions, interests and beliefs.

Furthermore, in areas such as teaching and learning, curriculum design and innovation, school improvement, leadership and management, organ-izational development and so on, research and development are essential. Research needs to be developmental and developments need to be researched.

Indeed, the idea of enquiry being R & D seems crucial at a time when there is growing interest in teachers being researchers. We are committed to this ideal, but believe either the notion of research should explicitly convey development, or that we now actively advocate teaching being a research and development-led profession. Professional action research has much to offer teachers, pupils, parents and governors. Where enquiry leads to pro-fessional developments that enhance teachers' practice and the pupils' learn-ing, it has a very valuable contribution to make to educational practice. But sometimes individual action research by teachers can be too isolated or idiosyncratic to be anything more than interesting to their colleagues. The EPSI programme provided a framework within which teachers, schools and LEA staffs' enquiries and reflections could influence the policies and practices of others. In short, alongside classroom enquiry and reflection should go professional developments that improve professional practices and outcomes. Development is therefore not an adjunct to research, it should be deeply embedded and implicated within it and vice versa.

However, it seems to be a feature of the past ten years or so that there has been too much educational change and not enough research and develop-ment. Too many initiatives were mandated with much too little develop-ment work. The introduction of the National Curriculum is the most obvious example of this pattern, but other changes such as the pupil assessment arrangements at the end of Key Stages 1, 2 and 3 have not stood the test of time and, at best, appeared to be underdeveloped or, at worst, ill-conceived. Even when pilot studies were conducted, they were declared successful before they were completed (Barber, 1996, p. 59). Given the lack of R & D and the absence of 'rigorous' trialling and testing of proposals, it is no surprise that the process of implementing government reforms was 'slipshod' (Barber, 1996, p. 57). While it may be no surprise, it is nevertheless deeply disappointing and seems to have left many who lived and worked through these times of change with a strong sense of professional dissatisfaction with centralized reforms.

In other words, the absence of R & D may have contributed to a lack of belief in government's initiatives, which was then confirmed, first-hand, when the new initiatives did not work. In turn, this meant that educational change developed a poor reputation and, because dealing with the reforms was so uncomfortable and the experience of coping with them was so alienating, the subjective meaning of change was negative. While government demanded change, the very process they adopted of managing the changes was counter-productive. Indeed, given all the revisions and adjustments needed to make some policies work in practice, it could be argued that it took longer to implement some reforms than if a more gradualist, R & D approach had been used. Certainly the resources involved in implementing these changes might have been used more productively.

Over the past decade or so we have seen policy-makers and politicians reach for structural solutions and top-down regulations to deal with perceived problems in education. Though experience in this country confirms the clumsiness of centralized reforms, what should not be overlooked is the fact that these reforms are, for politicians, high-stakes solutions. One of the lessons of the recent past is surely that we need to move forward through educational R & D programmes. Such programmes permit all participants to learn their way forward, provided there are sufficient feedback loops. Change and improvement in learning seem more suited to contemporary aspirations for schools to become learning organizations and for LEAs, universities and schools to contribute to the establishment of a learning society.

Conclusions

The EPSI programme has developed a range of insights and highlighted many issues, as we have shown throughout the book. We do not claim that all of these findings are necessarily original or revelatory, since some are plainly confirmatory. However, educational research and thinking are not always concerned with new discoveries; it is also important to validate other work and ideas and to see if they translate into different settings. Our findings in summary form include the following.

We have found evidence of:

- the benefits to schools' developing and sustaining a clear focus for their improvement efforts;
- the need for schools to articulate their improvement targets in terms of pupils' learning outcomes, as well as experiences and processes;
- the need for school inspection reports to be very clear about the key issues each school needs to consider and for the inspectors to ensure senior staff understand these issues;
- the advantages and challenges of using an evidence-based approach to school improvement;
- the power of pupils' perspective data in capturing teachers' attention;
- recognition that while the principle of using an evidence-based approach to improvement is now reasonably established, at least among senior staff, the skills primary teachers need to conduct such analyses are not yet well developed;
- the need for primary school leaders to develop the organizational capacity to improve the school is an important task for some, especially with regard to monitoring pupils' learning and the quality of teaching and to enabling teachers to respond positively to data;
- school leaders who work towards creating the conditions for school improvement also develop an awareness that they are transforming the teacher cultures in their schools and implicitly recognize that cultural renewal lies at the heart of school improvement;
- advances taking place in the schools in analysing pupil learning data, but fewer signs of these analyses being related to pedagogy, or of teachers focusing strongly on their teaching styles and skills;
- teaching staff in self-managing schools wanting to learn with and from colleagues in other schools;
- staff in self-managing schools acknowledging and appreciating that they need external support and challenge, and for headteachers and others to create the conditions for this advice to be received, rather than rejected out of hand;
- the advantages of LEA staff providing a third-party perspective on issues of quality and school performance, particularly through monitoring activities and the analysis of school data;
- the challenge for LEA staff to provide, over time, a judicious blend of support and pressure to schools with whom they work;
- the challenge for an LEA and its staff and agencies to meet the expectations that staff in school hold of them;
- the need for LEAs to transform their professional cultures to meet better the needs of schools and teachers;

- the value of educational research underpinning and driving developments; and
- the value of educational enquiry, which is essentially research and development.

Taken together, it is possible to distil all that we have learned into seven points:

Point 1

The 'formal' strategy for school improvement does appear to enhance primary schools' performance levels, certainly in Key Stage 2. In this sense the now official strategy for school improvement, as prescribed by the DfEE and OFSTED, makes a positive difference. This strategy, incorporating such tactics as:

- school self-evaluation, supplemented by inspection audits and evidence;
- action planning and target setting; and
- examining pupils' achievements, monitoring pupil progress and provision.

leads to the development of an evidence-based approach to school improvement that uses both process and product indicators. Furthermore, this approach has relevance and validity in a range of primary school types and settings and works when tracked over two to three years and examined in depth.

In making these claims, it is necessary to add that we did not set out to show whether the formal model worked or not, because when we embarked on the EPSI programme little of this was then government policy. As the EPSI programme and government policy converged, we felt it was appropriate to use our work in a local, albeit large LEA context to comment on national policy. However, there are a number of important riders to add to this initial observation, which are presented in points 2 to 7.

Point 2

In saying that the formal model works, we believe such a strategy to school improvement needs to be seen in a fuller light. It 'works' when there is effective leadership in the school. This leadership takes two forms. Headteachers have to be active participants, valuing the strategy, using it systematically and ensuring that it is supported in the school by their actions and by the careful use of resources. The involvement of other leaders is also important. Deputy heads, senior teachers, key stage coordinators or a subject/assessment coordinator should also play a leading role in moving the school's improvement focus and efforts along.

The establishment and sustenance of an evidence-based approach has to be led, led effectively and usually by more than one colleague.

Point 3

Linked to leadership is the fact that developing self-evaluation and using evidence in schools requires changing the teacher culture in many primary schools. Monitoring pupils' learning outcomes and progress, observing classroom practice, working with external agents from the LEA who offer critical and sometimes challenging insights, means that teachers and headteachers need to create new or stronger workplace norms and patterns that enable them to deal with such professional and peer analysis and debate.

These new forms of teacher culture require further detailed research. Whatever forms they may take, they should assist staff to deal positively with collegial and external investigations into aspects of their practice. They will require some teachers to move beyond existing patterns of collaboration and to engage in concrete, factual, practical discussions of their work. Such conversations involve them in creating the vocabulary and its meanings to identify the strengths and weaknesses of their classroom and school-wide practice, as shown by pupils' learning data, assessment data, pupils' comments, external perspectives provided by LEA and national data, benchmarking and LEA staff assessments from visiting the school. Also, staff need to take action on the basis of what the data are telling them, which will, almost inevitably, involve making changes to present practice.

Moreover, as schools work towards using their monitoring and evaluation activities to focus on the quality of teaching and the development of pedagogy, staff discussions on occasions are likely to become more pointed and uncomfortable for some. If defensiveness, denial and resistance are to be avoided, such discussions will need to be carefully managed and led so that a culture characterized by professional openness develops.

Point 4

We believe an evidence-based approach to school improvement needs to include primary pupils' perceptions. The programme showed that school and LEA staff recognized the value of asking pupils about their experiences of school. Pupils' perception data shaped and energized the process of school improvement in a number of the EPSI schools.

Also, while we are aware that the inclusion of pupil perceptions can be argued from a number of standpoints, including moral ones as suggested in Chapter 5, we support the stance adopted by Pollard, Thiessen and Filer (1997) that:

> The grounded, pragmatic reality is that pupils' educational attainments are likely to rise most effectively if teachers are able to leaven any necessary, systematic curricular requirements with adequate recognition of pupil experience. Effective teaching must recognise the concerns, interests and motivations of learners. (p. 11)

At the close of the programme we are even more committed to including pupil perceptions than at the outset. Initially we were influenced by colleagues whose OFSTED inspection work involved them in talking to pupils about their learning. We developed this approach and assembled the interview schedules reported in Chapter 5. The data emanating from this method was of such power and influence that we are now convinced that all primary schools should use it from time to time.

Moreover, these data provide an important counterbalance to the otherwise assessment-orientated data that the formal model of school improvement rests on. Pupil perception data offer a very different and sometimes strikingly alternative picture of classrooms and schools. It should not be excluded from the evidence-base that staff in schools and LEAs use to inform and evaluate school improvement efforts.

Point 5

From the very beginning, we accepted what has now become explicit government policy, namely that schools have the responsibility for their own improvement. Throughout the programme we have advocated school self-improvement. However, we did not see this as meaning that schools were entirely on their own. Much school improvement is plainly DIY, but these efforts often need to be supported by external agents who have important roles to play. External assistance is a blend of support and challenge and the latter is especially important to combat professional parochialism, insularity and conservatism.

External support also seems to be especially useful when it is not narrow but multi-disciplinary, and when it is not static but developing.

Part of the EPSI programme involved development days for the programme teams so that they could learn about and reflect on school improvement, as well as learn from each other's experiences. It now seems to us that such work is a vital part of enhancing the role of LEAs. For one thing, these development activities increased LEA staff's awareness of and sensitivity *to primary school* improvement. For another, they better equipped those working with schools to do their work more effectively. Third, during development days senior LEA managers explicitly embarked on creating the conditions necessary to support improving schools and to transform professional culture in the LEA as an organization.

There may now also be a case for further development of LEA support. At present most development work is conducted by individual LEAs themselves, or by LEA staff undertaking further professional development opportunities on an individual basis. Government agencies sometimes also provide briefings for senior colleagues and inspectors. However, given the national crusade to raise levels of achievement, the time may now be right to develop national training programmes for LEA inspectors/advisers, who play such important roles in supporting schools' improvement efforts. Such a national programme would benefit from the insights and skills developed through the EPSI programme.

Point 6

An evidenced-based approach to school improvement needs to be infused by the very principles and procedures that underscore its *raison d'être*. That is, school improvement activities should themselves be monitored, evaluated and developed in schools and LEAs as time goes by.

Important lessons were learned during the course of the programme and revisions were subsequently made in schools and in the LEA. In other words, school improvement must be a reflexive activity, where flexibility, adjustment and refinement are characteristics of the process. School improvement efforts are evolutionary and too important to become frozen inside an unyielding or fixed framework.

The formal model of school improvement seems to work at present. It is successful in enhancing pupils' learning as measured by end of key stage assessments and other test data the schools used. Yet, these gains may in the future only establish new baselines for further improvement. These 'second phase' improvements may, for example, incorporate developing pedagogy more directly than at present. The EPSI programme, though concerned to influence teaching, has less to say about this because these developments were underway in only a limited number of schools. Therefore, in the near future we can anticipate needing to explore in detail how staff in some schools improve the quality of their teaching. When this is better understood and examples of successful practices are identified, these will need to be incorporated into the formal framework for improvement.

If school improvement relies on moving schools, then the advances they make must be incorporated into the school improvement movement. If school improvement is to be guided by self-evaluation, improvement strategies themselves should be monitored and evaluated so that subsequent actions can be informed and directed by enquiry and reflection.

Point 7

The previous point relates to this one. The EPSI programme played a part in enabling LEA staff to learn their way forward in supporting primary schools and it assisted staff in primary schools to reflect on their improvement efforts and to act on their insights. The idea that educational change is a learning process has been persuasively argued by Fullan (1991, 1993). Given this understanding, it follows that we need to use the improvement process as a learning opportunity. To do this we need to enquire, reflect and act on our reflections. These three steps need to be taken in any research and development exercise. EPSI was an R & D programme and, as such, it was a learning process and programme for all of us involved in it. The official model of school improvement is broadly helpful, but it needs to be researched and developed inside schools and LEAs and knowledge about it shared so that all may benefit. This we tried to do in Essex, but it now seems important to do this nationally as well.

The formal, official model of school improvement must be rigorously researched in primary, secondary and special schools, so that it can be tested, refined, developed and improved. Also, this process is a cyclical one, since subsequent refinements will need to be monitored and tested. We now need longitudinal studies of improving schools in order to detect any patterns and rhythms over time. If schools are to improve on their previous best, so too must we improve our 'best' strategies for school development. We must continue to learn with and from staff in schools, to share this knowledge and to develop more sophisticated and richer understandings of the school improvement processes and outcomes.

If we are serious as a nation about school improvement, central government, as well as LEAs and schools, must use the lessons of the present to inform the developments of the future and we must use research, as well as experience and inspection data, to guide us on this journey.

Programme Aims, Targets and Success Criteria

Key:

IR: Inspection Report	AP: Action Plan	MAP: Modified action plan
SDP: School Development	TK: Tool Kit	(EPSI plan)
Plan	SSA: School Self Analysis	CRS: Conditions Rating
CO: Classroom Observation	UCIE: MF/GS/JS/TL	Scale
R: Reports from prog. pairs	interviews	RI: Review by Inspection
PP: Pupil Perception	WT: Writing Task	Team
		SM: Snr Mgt Interview
		RT: Reading Tests

AIM 1: To enable schools to develop strategies for improving the quality of teaching and learning provided for all pupils

Target 1.1   All schools within the programme will show improvement in teaching and learning in KS2 classrooms

Success criteria	*Data sources include*
1.1.1 Evidence from the schools' EPSI focus areas will indicate improvement in teaching and learning in KS2	PP, CO, RI, SSA, WT, RT
1.1.2 Evidence from the writing tasks, reading tests, value-added and other standardized measures used by the schools will indicate improvement in achievement in KS2	WT, RT, R
1.1.3 Teacher assessment, teachers' records, samples of pupils' work, IEPs indicate improvement in learning at KS2	PP, SSA, WT, R, RT
1.1.4 Pupil perception data indicates improvement in teaching and learning in KS2, including use of a wider and more flexible range of teaching strategies	PP, CO, RI, SSA
1.1.5 Pupil perception data indicates an improvement in attitudes, motivation to learning and commitment to achievement	PP, SSA, CO, RI
1.1.6 Pupil perception and/or EPSI focus data indicate improved 'study' skills such as problem-solving, investigation, research, communication	PP, RI, SSA, CO, R
1.1.7 Staff, governors, parents and others' perceptions are that teaching and learning in KS2 have improved	SSA, R, Governors' reports
1.1.8 Reports (termly, personal log, etc.) from programme pairs suggest improvement in teaching and learning at KS2	R (as result of analysis of all other data)

Target 1.2   All schools will have strategies for improving teaching and learning

Success criteria		Data sources include
1.2.1	Schools use their inspection report to identify key issues in teaching and learning (whether or not the report itself identifies them in the key issues)	IR
1.2.2	Post-inspection action plan/school development plan identifies clear targets and success criteria in teaching and learning	AP, MAP
1.2.3	Resources are allocated realistically to the improvement of teaching and learning (as identified in the plan)	AP, SDP
1.2.4	Responsibilities for monitoring and evaluating teaching and learning are clearly allocated and costed	AP, SDP Governing body minutes
1.2.5	Teamwork and coordination by staff within the school support the improvement of teaching and learning	CRS (reapplied)
1.2.6	Perceptions of increased levels of staff dialogue about teaching (e.g. pedagogy)	CRS (reapplied)
1.2.7	Data relating to teaching and learning are collected systematically and regularly (e.g. through the use of a toolkit)	All data systems listed
1.2.8	Data relating to teaching and learning are analysed and interpreted appropriately	IR, MAP, PP, WT, RT, AP, SDP, RI, CO, SSA
1.2.9	The analysis and interpretation of data relating to teaching and learning inform subsequent improvement strategies	TK
1.2.10	Perceptions of increased staff awareness and confidence in using these strategies	CRS (reapplied), SSA, RI, R, later SDPs

AIM 2:   To increase the LEA's capacity to support schools as they seek to improve the quality of education they provide

Target 2.1   The LEA provides effective support and challenge to schools in relation to improvement for pupils in KS2

Success criteria		Data sources include
2.1.1	Staff in schools report effective support and challenge is provided through programme pairs and other related LEA services	R – Other LEA Questionnaire related to this (they send them out periodically), SM, UCIE
2.1.2	Evidence in schools (e.g. notes of meetings, planning, etc.) of effective support and challenge from programme pairs and other related LEA services	UCIE, SM and collection of hard evidence as here described
2.1.3	Appropriate support materials are developed by the LEA to assist schools to improve	UCIE, SM
2.1.4	The LEA creates opportunities for schools to support and challenge one another (e.g. through networks, value-added group, other projects)	UCIE, SM, Records of opportunities provided
2.1.5	Effective dissemination of the EPSI work is used to enhance the improvement efforts of schools other than those in EPSI	Analysis of support offered by prog. pairs. Working independently with other schools

Target 2.1   (cont'd)

Success criteria	Data sources include
2.1.6 Teams across the programme collaborate effectively to provide support and challenge to schools	R, Logs
2.1.7 Programme members report increasing competence and confidence in their own skills in school improvement	R, Logs
2.1.8 The LEA uses an overview of the outcomes from inspection to determine priorities for staff development and resources	IR across LEA annually and comparison with previous reports
2.1.9 The LEA uses the data from the EPSI programme (e.g. personal diaries, monitoring by unit managers, research data from UCIE tutors, etc.) to improve the quality of support and challenge provided	All data, TK especially

Target 2.2   *There is greater clarity about the preparation and support that LEA staff need in order to carry out their role in school improvement*

Success criteria	Data sources include
2.2.1 LEA staff are clear about their role and responsibilities within school improvement	Personal interviews with line managers. R, UCIE, SM
2.2.2 The LEA systematically interprets relevant data to identify staff development needs for the support of school improvement	All data, M, AP, UCIE. 3M Interviews, SSA, Diaries/logs
2.2.3 Staff development provided for LEA staff involved in school improvement is monitored and evaluated and the outcomes inform future planning	SM, UCIE, LEA staff interviews with line managers

AIM 3:   To increase understanding of the process and outcomes of school improvement across the LEA and beyond

Target 3.1   *Staff within the schools, LEA units, elected members and the wider community have an increased understanding of the process and outcomes of school improvement*

Success criteria	Data sources include
3.1.1 Monitoring by the programme pairs, unit managers and UCIE tutors enhances understanding of school improvement	R, UCIE, SM, RI, CO
3.1.2 Discussions and decision-making in other areas of the LEA's work reflect a greater understanding of school improvement	Consideration of all data
3.1.3 The findings of the EPSI programme are disseminated widely to practitioners, governors, politicians, administrators and academics	Any/all data used
3.1.4 The wider educational community demonstrates an interest in the EPSI findings	All data available

Target 3.2   The outcomes from the EPSI programme make a major contribution to the shaping of the LEA improvement strategy

Success criteria	*Data sources include*
3.2.1 The LEA improvement strategy builds on the outcomes of the EPSI programme	Final report and any data as appropriate
3.2.2 Resource allocation is influenced by the outcomes of the EPSI programme	Analysis of what made a difference in the improving/achieving schools
3.2.3 The LEA improvement strategy has built in monitoring and evaluation procedures to test out whether the EPSI outcomes are reflected in other programmes and whether other areas of understanding about school improvement emerge	All data

Pupil Data Working Party – January 1997

Common Measures Agreed Across All EPSI Programme Schools

Measure/data	Rationale for use across EPSI programme	Collection method	Indicator of . . .	Comment
1. National Curriculum measures				
% of pupils attaining L4 and above in English, Mathematics and Science KS2 NC tests and Y6 Teacher Assessment	L4 is viewed nationally as the 'expected' level. There was a strong likelihood of this becoming the public accountability measure in performance tables (subsequently first published in March 1997).	National Data Collection Agency.	Attainment of a group of *typical* pupils in norm referenced grouping.	This was a measure being used in the wider group of schools participating in the first Essex primary 'value added' analysis.
Average level attained by the cohort in the above subjects at end of Key Stage	The average (mean) level is a measure which includes the performance of *all* pupils – not only those attaining at or above a particular level. As such it can be used to derive a notional measure of progress. Average levels given here are the mean of all those assessed. See below.	As above.	The attainment of pupils operating at all levels – not only the *typical* or *expected* levels.	
Essex 'value added' score	This was a comparative score based on the construction of a model from a wider group of schools to which all EPSI schools belonged. From the individual pupils data a calculation was made of the effect of: • affluence (free school meal entitlement) • term of birth • gender	Essex Primary School Effectiveness and Added Value Project.	Relative performance of school compared with schools with similar intakes.	Although there was no prior attainment data available upon which to calculate a progress measure, the value added score provided a useful means of exploding myths around the relative performance of, for instance, cohorts of pupils in schools in deprived areas where wide differences existed.

Appendices

Measure/data	Rationale for use across EPSI programme	Collection method	Indicator of . . .	Comment
2. Other curriculum measures				
Year 4 writing test scores	1. A number of schools were focusing on literacy and writing. Most schools were using a reading test, and many standardized reading tests were commercially available. There was no such measure for writing. 2. Furthermore, KS2 is the longest key stage. At no other point in public education until post-graduate level study, are people required to study over so long a period with no summative public assessment or examination. 3. The Y4 writing measure provided a means of capturing pupils' attainment at the outset of the programme which was common across the schools. This would be captured again subsequently after the close of the programme as the cohort were assessed and tested in writing at the end of the key stage in summer 1998.	A specially devised mark scheme was applied to a controlled conditions writing task for Y4 pupils based on SCAA Y6 English test stimulae. Y4 teachers were given training in administering the tests and using the mark scheme. They were also involved in a cross programme school moderation agreement trial of marked scripts.	The attainment of the 1996 Y4 cohort in a basic skill area which would be tested again through NC tests in 1998 – the outcome year for the programme.	Many of the Y4 teachers had never been involved in formal assessment of marking of pupils' work against National Curriculum criteria. The process of the assessment revealed and began to address wide discrepancies in Y4 teachers' interpretation of NC levels in writing. Data was fed back to the schools giving a comparative analysis of attainment in relation to other EPSI schools with a further comparative analysis of attainment by boys and girls.
Reading test data	In the interest of continuity of data at school level, schools were requested to continue with whichever reading test they used. (The LEA had dropped the expectation for all schools to use a common test some years earlier.)	At school level.	Impact of focus where reading or literacy was an intended outcome. Also – a background safety net indicator of any negative 'mattress' effects of the programme.	As a result of the diverse sets of data schools were holding but not using, the programme devised an Excel spreadsheet which was widely used by schools to review a range of performance data.

Pupil Perception Interview

A Shared Attitudes and Beliefs
1 Why do you come to school?
2 What is the most important reason for coming to school?
3 Do you think your teacher thinks the same way?
4 What are the best things about this school?
5 What do you like least?
6 If you had a wish and could change one thing, what would it be?
7 What do you do when you are working hard and how would you describe it?
8 How do you know when you have done something well? Does this happen to other children in the school?
9 Who would be interested if you had done a good piece of work?
10 Do you like telling others when you have done a good piece of work?

B Student Involvement and Responsibility
1 What are you best at?
2 What are you least good at?
3 Do you have any jobs or special responsibilities in the school?
4 How do you get these responsibilities?
5 Are you encouraged to ask questions?
6 What happens when you ask questions?
7 What happens when you get things wrong?
8 How do you know what you are supposed to do? (day, session, next)
9 Can you use other pupils' thoughts and ideas?
10 What happens when you disagree? (with teachers, others?)

C Recognition and Incentives
1 How do you know when you have done well?
 Is it because
 • you're praised?
 • work is marked regularly?
 • how do you like it marked?

2   Is it only you who knows you are pleased/disappointed?

3   How do teachers help you?

4   What happens if you get stuck?

D   **Parental Involvement**

1   Do your family know how you learn in school?

2   Does anyone come to school?

3   Do you take work home? (why or when?)

4   How do your family know what is going on at school?

E   **Frequent Monitoring of Pupil Progress**

1   How do you know how well you're doing? (Progress day to day, week to week, term to term)

2   Does the teacher talk to you on your own / group / class?

3   Are you grouped for your learning?

4   Why in this way?

5   Do you have tests and tasks to see how well you are doing?

F   **High Expectations**

1   Let's talk about you and the work you do at school

      (a)   Is the work usually easy or do you have to try hard?

      (b)   Does your teacher think you work hard enough?

      (c)   What do your family expect of you at school?

      (d)   What are you aiming for?

      (e)   How will you get there?

      (f)   What makes you anxious in class?

      (g)   What do you feel really confident about in class?

2   Do you know what is expected of you as a Year 3/4/5?

Appendix 4

EPSI Workshop Programmes

Core Workshop Programme for LEA Staff

Days 1 and 2
6–7 October 1995
Residential

Introductory workshop:
Background to the Programme
Improving Primary Schools – setting the scene
Six conditions for school improvement –
an overview
School conditions 1:   Enquiry and reflection

Days 3 and 4
3–4 November 1995
Non-residential

Theory and practice of school improvement
School conditions 2:   Planning

Days 5 and 6
18–19 December 1995
Non-residential

Review of progress
School conditions 3:   Involvement
School conditions 4:   Leadership

Days 7 and 8
25–26 March 1996
Non-residential

Feedback from Working Group on Pupil Data
Feedback from Programme Pairs on their work
in schools
Action planning – preparing for further work
with Research Partner schools

Days 9 and 10
18–19 April 1996
Non-residential

Learning schools
School conditions 5:   Coordination
School conditions 6:   Staff development

Days 11 and 12
10–11 June 1996
Non-residential

Reviewing progress
Emerging issues

Days 13 and 14
18–19 July 1996
Residential

Collaborative planning
Looking ahead to Year 2

Workshops for Programme Pairs

There were further workshops for the programme pairs – a very broad outline of programmes as follows:

21 October 1996	Data-handling
16/17 December 1996	Lessons in successful school improvement
3 February 1997	Using ethos indicators in school development
14 March 1997	Accelerated learning
19 May 1997	Pathways to improvement – lessons to date from EPSI
14/15 July 1997	Main findings from EPSI
21 November 1997	
8 December 1997	
24 March 1998	

Workshops for Schools

23 January 1996	Launch
29 February 1996	Writing Task briefing
6 June 1996	Six Conditions – Enquiry and reflection
5 November 1996	Research strategy for supporting school improvement
15 April 1997	Case study and data collection
14 July 1997	Effective governance
8 July 1998	Dissemination

The IQEA Six School Conditions

The Improving the Quality of Education for All project (see Ainscow et al., 1994b) aimed to strengthen a school's ability to provide quality education for all by building upon existing good practice. The IQEA project was based on the assumption that schools are most likely to strengthen their ability to improve when they adopt ways of working that are consistent with their own aspirations as well as the current reform agenda.

The project also used several other explicit assumptions including:

- school improvement works best when there is a clear and practical focus for development efforts; and
- the organizational conditions for school improvement are worked on at the same time as the curricula or other priorities the school has set itself.

At the time of the EPSI programme the IQEA project emphasized six organizational conditions, which schools should focus on if they wished to enhance their capacity to improve. These six conditions were:

1 a commitment to staff development
2 practical efforts to involve staff, pupils and the local community in school policies and decisions
3 leadership
4 effective coordination strategies
5 enquiry and reflection
6 a commitment to collaborative planning

Staff Development

Staff development needs to be a part of school improvement activities. Improving the internal conditions for supporting the professional learning of teachers will have an impact on their teaching and the pupils' learning. Strategies for staff development should be closely linked to school improvement. Also, the development of staff should be concerned with strengthening staff teamwork as well as with the evolution of individual teachers' thinking and practice.

Involvement

Research evidence shows that success, particularly in managing change in schools, is associated with the involvement of staff, pupils, parents and the wider community. A starting point for such involvement is the adoption of clear policies, which encourage participation by various stakeholders.

Leadership

Leadership is a key element in school improvement. However, an emphasis on leadership does not exclude the importance of management, nor does it mean that leadership is confined only to headteachers or senior staff. Leadership at all levels is important. Leadership involves:

- developing and sustaining a 'vision' for the school and in a way that generates staff commitment;
- harnessing staff skills and experience;
- using meetings and group work productively; and
- spreading leadership within the school.

Coordination

To ensure that school priorities are kept in view and implemented, there need to be coordination strategies that enable effective communication across the school, a keen awareness of staff responsibilities, cooperative ways of working and someone, or a small group of staff, who will be responsible for managing the school's improvement priorities on a day-to-day basis.

Enquiry and Reflection

Developing an evidence-based approach to school improvement is vitally important. Schools that are evaluative of their efforts are more likely to be aware of their strengths and limitations and more likely to be able to do something about them. Using school-based data is an essential part of school self-evaluation. Moreover, using these data with a valued external consultant, who can look coolly and critically at the data, the school's interpretation of the evidence and their action plans for responding to the data enhances the benefits of enquiry and reflection.

Collaborative Planning

Schools' improvement plans should be clearly linked to the schools' visions, staff development plans, the schools' enquiries and evidence bases and patterns of involvement. Involvement in the planning process is a vital feature of more effective plans. Moreover, plans need to be flexible and evolutionary, rather than frozen and fixed.

Notes on Contributors

Pete Dudley has been a School Development Adviser since 1995. He has recently been appointed to take a lead role for Key Stage 2 within the curriculum team of the Advisory Service. During the EPSI programme he was a member of the Pupil Data Working Group and played an important role in data handling.

Michael Fielding teaches at the University of Sussex Institute of Education, where most of his work is in the field of professional development, leadership, organizational learning and the development of schools as emancipatory learning communities. He previously worked at the University of Cambridge School of Education. He was involved in the EPSI programme from its inception. His particular interest is in the role of pupil perception data in school improvement and the development of school structures and cultures in which pupils engage in genuine dialogue with peers and adults as part of the mutual process of learning to be and become persons.

Sue Fisher is a School Development Adviser for Essex LEA working with a group of schools. Prior to taking on this role she was a Senior Educational Psychologist. During the EPSI programme she was a member of the Pupil Data Working Group.

Alan Fuller is a Senior Educational Psychologist in Essex and manages a team of psychologists in one area of the county. He has a strong interest in the role of external consultants and was a member of the Pupil Data Working Group during the EPSI programme.

Sue Kerfoot is Head of the Psychology and Assessment Service for Essex County Council. She manages the team of educational psychologists and the team of officers responsible for SEN assessment processes. She was a member the EPSI programme Steering Group.

Paul Lincoln is Director of Learning Services for Essex County Council. He taught for 19 years before joining the local education authority as an inspector. He has held various management posts within the LEA before promotion to his current role. He was chair of the EPSI programme Steering Group and was closely involved with the programme from the outset and throughout the whole enterprise.

Tina Loose is an OFSTED Registered Inspector and a private consultant specializing in school improvement. She has been involved with the EPSI programme from its inception, working in a variety of roles across the whole programme including being a member of the Steering Group and the Pupil Data Working Group. She formerly worked as a primary headteacher in Suffolk and most recently as a senior inspector in Essex.

Gary Nethercott is the Manager of the Special Needs Support Service in Essex, which provides specialist advice to schools and supports children with statements of special educational need. He was a member of the EPSI programme Steering Group.

Judy Sebba is Senior Adviser in the Standards and Effectiveness Unit (SEU) at the DfEE. She is responsible for developing the research strategy and quality of research relating to schools. She is seconded to the SEU from the University of Cambridge School of Education where she was involved in a number of projects including: evaluating the use of School Effectiveness GEST; post-inspection action planning in special and primary schools; school improvement; and inspection and special needs. Judy was the chair of the Pupil Data Working Group for the EPSI programme.

Geoff Southworth is Professor of Education at the University of Reading School of Education, having formerly worked at the University of Cambridge School of Education. He was involved in the EPSI programme from the outset. He has been a primary school teacher, deputy and headteacher. His interests include primary school leadership and improvement. He has published widely on these aspects of education. He is committed to school-based and school-focused research and development and works regularly with colleagues in school, as well as running courses and speaking at conferences.

References

AINSCOW, M. and SOUTHWORTH, G. (1996) 'School improvement: A study of the roles of leaders and external consultants', *School Effectiveness and School Improvement*, **7**, 3, pp. 229–51.

AINSCOW, M., HOPKINS, D., SOUTHWORTH, G. and WEST, M. (1994a) *Creating the Conditions for School Improvement*, London: Fulton.

AINSCOW, M., HOPKINS, D., SOUTHWORTH, G. and WEST, M. (1994b) 'School improvement in an era of change: An overview of the "Improving the Quality of Education for All" [IQEA] Project', paper prepared for American Educational Research Association Annual Meeting, New Orleans, April 1994. University of Cambridge Institute of Education.

AUDIT COMMISSION (1993) *Keeping Your Balance: Standards for Financial Administration in Schools*, London: OFSTED.

BARBER, M. (1996) *The Learning Game: Arguments for an Education Revolution*, London: Victor Gollancz.

BLACK, P. and WILIAM, D. (1998) *Inside the Black Box: Assessment and Classroom Learning*, London: School of Education, Kings College.

CAMPBELL, P., EDGAR, S. and HALSTED, A.L. (1994) 'Students as evaluators: A model for program evaluation', *Phi Delta Kappan*, **76**, 2, pp. 160–5.

CONNOLLY, P. (1997) 'In search of authenticity: Researching young children's perspectives', in POLLARD, A., THIESSEN, D. and FILER, A. (eds) *Children and Their Curriculum*, London: Falmer Press, pp. 162–83.

CORBETT, F., FIELDING, M. and KERFOOT, S. (1996) 'The role of Local Authorities in school improvement in the future: The key contribution of LEA advisers', paper presented to the Annual Conference of the British Educational Research Association.

DFEE (1997a) *Excellence in Schools*, Education White Paper presented to Parliament by the Secretary of State for Education and Employment, July, London: Stationery Office.

DFEE (1997b) *From Targets to Action*, London: Department for Education and Employment.

DFEE (1998a) *Effective Action Planning after Inspection: Planning Improvement in Special Schools*, London: DfEE.

DFEE (1998b) *Excellence in Research on Schools*, A review by the Institute of Employment Studies, University of Sussex for the DfEE, London: DfEE.

DUDLEY, P. (1997) 'How teachers respond to data', paper presented at the annual conference of the British Educational Research Association, University of York, September.

ELLIOTT, J. (1990) 'Educational research in crisis: Performance indicators and the decline in excellence', *British Educational Research Journal*, **16**, 1, pp. 3–18.

ELLIOTT, J. (1996) 'School effectiveness research and its critics: Alternative visions of schooling', *Cambridge Journal of Education*, **26**, 2, pp. 199–225.

ESSEX COUNTY COUNCIL (1997) *Setting and Achieving Challenging Targets*, Chelmsford: Essex County Council.

ESSEX COUNTY COUNCIL LEARNING SERVICES (1999) *The Essex Quality Framework*, Essex County Council.

FIELDING, M. (1997) 'Beyond school effectiveness and school improvement: Lighting the slow fuse of possibility', *Curriculum Journal*, **8**, 1, pp. 7–27.

FIELDING, M. (1998) 'Students as researchers: From data source to significant voice', paper presented at 11th International Congress for School Effectiveness and School Improvement, University of Manchester.

FIELDING, M. (1999) 'Communities of learners: Myth: Schools are communities', in O'HAGAN, B. (ed.) *Modern Educational Myths*, London: Kogan Page, pp. 64–84.

FULLAN, M. (1991) *The New Meaning of Educational Change*, London: Cassell.

FULLAN, M. (1992) *Successful School Improvement*, Buckingham: Open University Press.

FULLAN, M. (1993) *Change Forces: Probing the Depths of Educational Reform*, London: Falmer Press.

FULLAN, M. and HARGREAVES, A. (1992) *What's Worth Fighting For in Your School?* Buckingham: Open University Press.

GIPPS, C. (1990) *Assessment: A Teacher's Guide to the Issues*, London: Hodder and Stoughton.

GOLDMAN, G. and NEWMAN, J.B. (1998) *Empowering Students to Transform Schools*, Thousand Oaks, Calif.: Corwin Press.

GRAY, J. and WILCOX, B. (1995) 'In the aftermath of inspection: The nature and fate of inspection report recommendations', *Research Papers in Education*, **10**, pp. 1–18.

HARGREAVES, A. (1994) *Changing Teachers, Changing Times*, London: Cassell.

HARGREAVES, D. (1995) 'Inspection and school improvement', *Cambridge Journal of Education*, **25**, pp. 115–23.

HARGREAVES, D. (1996) 'Teaching as a research-based profession: possibilities and prospects', Teacher Training Agency Annual Lecture.

HARGREAVES, D.H. and HOPKINS, D. (1991) *The Empowered School*, London: Cassell.

HOLLY, P. and SOUTHWORTH, G. (1989) *The Developing School*, London: Falmer.

HOPKINS, D., AINSCOW, M. and WEST, M. (1994) *School Improvement in an Era of Change*, London: Cassell.

ISEP (1996) 'Improving School Effectiveness Project: Primary Pupil Questionnaire', in THOMAS, G. et al.

References

KEELE UNIVERSITY (1994) *Pupil Survey of School Life*, Centre for Successful Schools, Keele University.

KELLNER, P. (1997) *Times Educational Supplement*, 19 September.

KUBR, M. (1983) *Management Consultancy: A Guide to the Profession*, International Labour Office.

LEARMONTH, J. and LOWERS, K. (1998) 'A trouble-shooter calls: The role of the independent consultant', in STOLL, L. and MYERS, K. (eds) *No Quick Fixes: Perspective on School in Difficulty*, London: Falmer Press.

LEVACIC, R., GLOVER, D., BENNETT, N. and CRAWFORD, M. (1998) 'The rationally managed school? Headteacher practice and preparation for school-based management within a state control framework', unpublished paper presented at the ESRC seminars on School Leadership, Milton Keynes.

LOOSE, T. (1997) 'Achievement culture', *Managing Schools Today*, May, p. 23.

LUNDBERG, C. (1997) 'Towards a general model of consultancy: Foundations', *Journal of Organisational Change Management*, **10**, 3, pp. 193–201.

MACBEATH, J. (1998a) 'Just think about it', *Times Educational Supplement*, 18 April, p. 13.

MACBEATH, J. (1998b) '"I didn't know he was ill": The role and value of the critical friend', in STOLL, L. and MYERS, K. (eds) *No Quick Fixes: Perspective on School in Difficulty*, London: Falmer Press.

MACBEATH, J., BOYD, B., RAND, J. and BELL, S. (1996) *Schools Speak for Themselves*, London: National Union of Teachers.

MACGILCHRIST, B., MYER, K. and REID, J. (1997) *The Intelligent School*, London: Paul Chapman.

MESSICK, S. (1989) 'Meaning and values in test validation: The science and ethics of assessment', *Educational Researcher*, **18**, 2, pp. 5–11.

MILES, M.B. and HUBERMAN, A.M. (1984) *Qualitative Data Analysis: A Sourcebook of New Methods*, Newbury Park, Calif.: Sage.

MILES, M., SAXL, E. and LIEBERMAN, A. (1988) 'What skills do educational "change agents" need? An empirical view', *Curriculum Enquiry*, **18**, 2, pp. 159–93.

MILLETT, A. (1998) 'The Keele Improving Schools Network Seminar', report in the *Times Educational Supplement*, 12 June, p. 28.

MORTIMORE, P., SAMMONS, P., STOLL, L., LEWIS, D. and ECOB, R. (1988) *School Matters: The Junior Years*, Wells: Open Books.

NIAS, J., SOUTHWORTH, G. and CAMPBELL, P. (1992) *Whole School Curriculum Development in the Primary School*, London: Falmer Press.

NIAS, J., SOUTHWORTH, G. and YEOMANS, R. (1989) *Staff Relationships in the Primary School: A Study of School Cultures*, London: Cassell.

OFSTED (1998) *School Evaluation Matters*, London: Office for Standards in Education.

OFSTED and DfEE (1996) *Setting Targets to Raise Standards: A Survey of Good Practice*, London: Office for Standards in Education.

POLLARD, A., THIESSEN, D. and FILER, A. (1997a) *Children and Their Curriculum*, London: Falmer Press.

POLLARD, A., THIESSEN, D. and FILER, A. (1997b) 'Introduction: New challenges in taking children's curricular perspectives seriously', in POLLARD, A., THIESSEN, D. and FILER, A. (eds) *Children and Their Curriculum*, London: Falmer Press, pp. 1–12.

PRYOR, J. (1995) 'Hearing the voice of young children: Problems and possibilities', paper presented to the Annual Meeting of the British Educational Research Association, University of Bath.

REYNOLDS, D. (1998) 'Annual TTA Lecture', London: Teacher Training Agency.

ROBSON, C. (1993) *Real World Research*, Oxford: Blackwell.

ROSENHOLTZ, S. (1989) *Teachers' Workplace: The Social Organisation of Schools*, London: Longman.

RUDDUCK, J., CHAPLAIN, R. and WALLACE, G. (eds) (1996) *School Improvement: What Can Pupils Tell Us?* London: Fulton.

SCHEIN, E. (1987) *Process Consultation, Volume 2: Lessons for Managers and Consultants*, London: Addison-Wesley.

SCHEIN, E. (1988) *Process Consultation, Volume 1: Its role in Organisation Development*, 2nd edn, London: Addison-Wesley.

SEBBA, J. and LOOSE, T. (1996) 'Post-inspection action plans: Problems and possibilities for primary school improvement', paper presented to the British Educational Research Association Annual Conference, University of Cambridge School of Education mimeo.

SEBBA, J. and LOOSE, T. (1997) 'Examples of schools' approaches to collecting data', paper presented at the British Educational Research Association Annual Conference, York, University of Cambridge School of Education mimeo.

SEBBA, J., CLARKE, J. and EMERY, B. (1996) *Enhancing School Improvement through Inspection in Special Schools*, London: OFSTED.

SooHoo, S. (1993) 'Students as partners in research and restructuring schools', *Educational Forum*, **57**, pp. 386–93.

SOUTHWORTH, G. (1996) 'Improving primary schools: Shifting the emphasis and clarifying the focus', *School Organisation*, **16**, 3, pp. 263–80.

SOUTHWORTH, G. (1997) 'Emphasising evidence-based developments in teaching and learning in primary schools', paper presented at the British Educational Research Association Annual Conference, York, University of Cambridge School of Education mimeo.

SOUTHWORTH, G. (1998) *Leading Improving Primary Schools*, London: Falmer Press.

SOUTHWORTH, G. and AINSCOW, M. (1996) 'Working with schools: Puzzles and problems in process consultancy and school improvement', paper presented at a symposium on School Improvement and School Effectiveness: Towards a New Synthesis, AERA Annual Conference, New York.

STEINBERG, S. and KINCHELOE, J. (1998) *Students as Researchers*, London: Falmer Press.

STOLL, L. and FINK, D. (1998) 'The cruising school: The unidentified ineffective school', in STOLL L. and MYERS, K. (eds) *No Quick Fixes*, London: Falmer, pp. 189–206.

References

STOLL, L. and MORTIMORE, P. (1995) 'School effectiveness and school improvement', *Viewpoint*, **2**, London Institute of Education.

THIESSEN, D. (1997) 'Knowing about, acting on behalf of, and working with primary pupils' perspectives: Three levels of engagement with research', in POLLARD, A., THIESSEN, D. and FILER, A. (eds) *Children and Their Curriculum*, London: Falmer Press, pp. 184–96.

THOMAS, G., DAVIES, J.D., LEE, J., POSTLETHWAITE, K., TARR, J., YEE, W.C. and LOWE, P. (1998) 'Best practice amongst special schools on special measures: the role of action planning in helping special schools improve', a research report to the DfEE, University of the West of England.

TIMES EDUCATIONAL SUPPLEMENT (1997) 'Take children's views seriously', *Times Educational Supplement*, 5 December, p. 20.

TURNER, A.N. (1988) 'Guiding managers to improve their own performance', *Journal of Management Consulting*, **4**, 4, pp. 8–12.

TURNER, S., ROBBINS, H. and DORAN, C. (1996) 'Developing a model of consultancy practice', *Educational Psychology in Practice*, **12**, 2, pp. 86–93.

WEATHERILL, L. (1998) 'The "Students as Researchers" Project at Sharnbrook Upper School and Community College', *Improving Schools*, **1**, 2, pp. 52–3.

WILLIAM, D. (1996) 'National Curriculum assessments and programmes of study: Validity and impact', *British Educational Research Journal*, **22**, 1, pp. 129–41.

WEST, M. and AINSCOW, M. (1991) *Managing School Development: A Practical Guide*, London: Fulton.

Index

able pupils, mathematics targets for 42
achievement culture 84
acting on behalf of pupils 119
action plans 14, 15–16, 18–19
  EPSI 147–8
  post-inspection 156–7, 167
  programme teams support 132
action-orientated response 97–8
advisory support
  LEA 126
  see also school development advisers
agency, pupil 121
analysis of data 158–9, 169–70
  on EPSI advisers 143–4
  with programme pairs 96–7
  on pupil interviews 112–16
  see also data handling
assessment 59–60, 162
  in targets 36, 57
  see also Key Stage tests; reading
    tests; writing assessments; Year
    4 assessments
attitudes 163–4, 215
  see also pupil perceptions
auditing 192–3
average level data 102–3, 213

barriers to the formal method 78–9
behaviour, pupil 37, 44, 112
benefits
  anticipated 15–16, 132–3
  summary 16–23
  to LEA 22–3
  to schools 20–2
boycott of national tests 93, 97
budgets 78, 167

classroom observations 19, 59–60,
  161, 197
co-supervision 130
Code of Practice for LEAs 105, 139,
  141, 159, 174–5
collaboration, teacher 197, 221
collaborative culture 83–5
collaborative work, pupils' 39, 164
complacency, programme challenges
  131
conceptually clustered matrix 113
conditions rating scale 17–18, 81, 91,
  95, 130, 169, 198, 219–20
  see also staff perception data
conferences 61
confidence, professional 135, 136,
  170–1
confidentiality 98, 114
consultancy 139–51
  models of 140–3
contextualized analyses 33
  see also value added
coordination 168, 220
coordinators, curriculum 36, 46, 194
criterion-referenced assessment 93
criticism, reaction to 114–17
cultural model 79–82, 85, 98, 105
culture 19, 83–5, 130, 172, 187, 191,
  197, 205
curriculum backwash 101–2
curriculum coordinators *see*
    coordinators

data
  analysis of *see* analysis of data
  collection *see* data collection

effectiveness 159–60
performance 27–32, 176
pupil *see* pupil data
pupil perception *see* pupil
  perceptions
qualitative *see* qualitative data
quantitative *see* quantitative data
in school improvement 160–71
schools use of 13, 17–18, 92–5,
  96–100, 160
sources of 92, 143–4
value added *see* value added
data collection 12, 155, 158–9
and action plans 156–7
programme teams in 131, 146, 148
for pupil perspectives 108–12
schools collect 1–2, 11
success of 169
in targets 56
data handling
skills 18, 72, 78, 105
software for 21–2, 72, 96
teacher involvement in 192–3
see also analysis of data
delegation of financial resources 125
dependency, avoiding 150–1, 191
see also ownership
deprivation, value added data and 33
DfEE
Code of Practice for LEAs 105, 139,
  141, 159, 174–5
and five-stage model of evaluation
  and improvement 77
measures adopted by 102
and self-evaluation 78
see also government
differentiation, school improvement
  and 71, 193–5
difficulties, schools in 33–4, 41, 80
Director of Education 200
doctor-patient consultancy model 141

Early Reading Research 179
Education Schools Act (1992) 125
educational change 201–2, 208

educational psychologists 1, 128–9,
  149
English
as a focus 34, 94
Key Stage 2 tests 26, 28–30, 63
in targets 43, 52
see also reading; writing
enquiry and reflection 13, 18, 176,
  220–1
EPSI advisers
consultancy and 143–9
see also programme pairs
EPSI programme 1–6
aims, targets and success criteria
  11–12, 209–12
data-driven approach in 72
and educational research 198–202
end of programme conclusions
  186–91
issues investigated 13–14
LEA strategies following 174–85
multiple perspectives 5–6, 12
overview 9–23
pupil data used in 87–91
Essex LEA
benefits to 16, 22–3
cultural changes in 191
and data handling software 21–2, 72
focus 15
heads want closer ties with 70
impact of EPSI on 175–81
intervention 105–6
post programme 174–85, 190–1
in process consultancy 139–51
and pupil data issues 104–6
role of 9, 125–7, 174–5, 181–5
in EPSI 11, 12, 200
and school improvement 125–38,
  211–12
staff *see* LEA staff
targets 210–11
value added project 100, 162, 177,
  213
Essex Local Education Authority *see*
  Essex LEA

Essex Primary School Improvement
    Research and Development
    Programme *see* EPSI
    programme
Essex Quality Framework for Schools
    100, 177, 178–9, 180, 183
Essex schools 27, 28, 29, 30–3, 34,
    102
  in EPSI programme *see* schools
evaluation 156–7, 167–8, 207–8
  in targets 46
  see also self-evaluation
evidence-based approach 7, 17, 64, 75,
    76, 82, 204, 207
expectations, pupil 216
expertise, knowledge and 135, 151
external advisers 140, 141
external resource
  for data handling 72
  programme acts as 70, 132
  for school improvement 206–7

feedback
  of pupil interview data 112–16, 117
  of reading test data 96
  of staff perception data 95
five-stage model of evaluation and
    improvement 77
focus
  choosing 11–12, 64
    problems with 166
  English as 94
  and heads 70, 77, 85–6
  key point in improving schools
    191–2
  LEA focus 15
  post-programme 28
  role of programme teams in 131
  team focus 136
formal model of school improvement
    77–82, 85, 98, 105, 195–8,
    204, 207, 208
future directions
  school improvement 120–1
  transformative education 121

Goodhart's law of economics 101
government 9, 174
  and educational change 201–2
  policy
    on formal model 204
    on responsibility 206
  see also Code of Practice; DfEE
governors 165, 189
grant maintained status 2, 125
group interviews, pupils' 109–10
group work *see* collaborative work

headteachers 69–86, 189
  comments on targets 35, 36–58
  leadership of 204–5
  and pedagogy 19–20
  on programme teams 134–5
  use of staff perception data 95
  see also leadership

improving learning for all 175
Improving the Quality of Education
    for All project *see* IQEA
improving schools *see* school
    improvement
incentives in pupil attitude survey
    215–16
independence, teachers' 82, 83
independence in learning 38, 41, 45,
    50, 51, 54
indicators, Goodhart's law of
    economics and 101
instability of schools 64–5
intervention, LEA 105–6
interviews
  end of programme 186–7
  with LEA staff 133–5
  with pupils 109–16
  with schools and advisers 143–4
investigational work 49, 164
involvement 220
  parental 43, 165, 216
  of programme pairs 144–9,
    151
  student 215

IQEA (Improving the Quality of
    Education for All) project 72,
    91, 130, 142, 198, 219–20

Key Stage 1 tests 63
Key Stage 2, focus on 2–3, 13, 17
Key Stage 2 tests
    average level data 102–3, 213
    data from 25–35
    improvement in results 63, 161–2
    methods of expressing data 89
    pupils attaining level 4 102–3, 213
    see also value added
Key Stage tests
    boycott of 93, 97
    introduced without research 201–2
    Key Stage 1 tests 63
    Key Stage 2 *see* Key Stage 2 tests
    SATs results in targets 42, 57, 58
knowledge and expertise 135, 151

LEA staff
    expertise of 2
    interviews with 133–5
    and pupil perceptions 117
    purpose of programme for 1
    training for 184
    workshop programme for 217
    see also programme pairs
leadership 10, 176, 204–5, 220
    see also headteachers
league tables 9
    see also performance tables
learning
    emphasis placed on 74–5, 82, 83,
        176, 195
    improvement in 21, 161, 162,
        163–4, 166
    individual and whole-school 182
    programme investigates 14, 18–19
    quality of 60, 62, 209–10
    see also pupil learning outcomes
learning about pupil perspectives
    118–19
learning strategies 50

Learning Support managers 23
LEAs
    Code of Practice for LEAs 105, 139,
        141, 159, 174–5
    in EPSI *see* Essex LEA
    role of 105, 125–7, 140
levels, National Curriculum 17, 27,
    94
    average level data 102–3, 213
    pupils attaining level 4 102–3, 213
link school development advisers
    129
listening skills, pupils' 39
local management of schools 125

main findings 24–64, 202–8
    and headteachers 70–7
mark schemes for writing assessments
    93, 94
mathematics 30–1, 34, 63
    in targets 42, 48, 49
measure fixation 101
measures, agreed 102–3, 161–2,
    213–14
    see also assessment
mid-Key Stage assessment *see* Year 4
    assessments
monitoring 192–3
    and evaluation 156–7, 207–8
        costing 167–8
        in targets 46
    lack of, for teaching 75, 82
    programme investigates 14, 19
    in pupil attitude survey 216
    see also evaluation
motivation
    of pupils 163–4, 175
    of staff 14, 20
moving schools 10
multi-disciplinary teams 1, 128, 130,
    131–7, 151, 184, 190
    see also programme teams
multi-disciplinary working 176–7
multiple perspectives, EPSI offers 5–6,
    12

National Curriculum 2, 3
    as criterion-referenced assessment 93
    introduction of 9, 125, 201
    levels *see* levels
    tests *see* Key Stage tests
national framework for school
        improvement 5
negative responses, reaction to 114–17
networking 136, 176

OFSTED (Office for Standards in
        Education)
    emphasis on quality of teaching 83
    inspections by *see* OFSTED
        inspection
    introduction of 125
    Key Stage 2 concerns 2–3
    pupil interviews by 117
    and school improvement 77, 78
OFSTED inspection
    influence of 71–2
    reports *see* OFSTED inspection
        reports
    and school with difficulties 41
    school revisits 59–63, 159, 173
    and teacher motivation 14, 20
OFSTED inspection reports 27, 80, 193
    and action plans *see* action plans
    lack of clarity 18, 156
    perceived as external 91–2
    and programme focus 11–12, 15–16
    use of 166–7
OFSTED Performance and Attainment
        (PANDA) summaries 92
open-ended questions in targets 45
organizational cultures 81
    see also cultural model
ownership 149–50
    see also dependency

pace of school improvement 80, 184–5
parental involvement 43, 165, 216
pedagogy 82–5
    improving 14, 19–20
    increased dialogue on 168–9

and pupil data 74–5
    see also teaching
performance data 27–32, 176
performance tables 27, 93, 98
    see also league tables
planning
    collaborative 221
    by pupils 51
    by teachers 38, 44, 51, 53, 56, 221
political context 9, 174
power, children's views on 118
PPs *see* programme pairs
presenting pupil perception data 113–14
primary schools 2
    and pupil data 87–106
        threefold typology of engagement
            118–19
    reasons for focus on 2–3
    see also EPSI programme
problem-solving, improvements in
        164
process consultancy 139–51
    compared to other types 141
professional cultures 130, 187, 197
professional development, programme
        teams and 22–3, 151
programme pairs 11, 128–9, 189
    assist with action plans 19, 21,
        166–7
    and methods of feedback 95
    and process consultancy 139–51
    and pupil perspectives 95, 110–16
    reports of 35, 36–58, 70, 165
    stages of involvement 144–9, 150
    workshop programme for 218
    see also LEA staff
programme teams 128–32
    professional development 22–3, 151
    views and conclusions of 186–91
    see also multi-disciplinary teams
pupil attitude survey 215–16
pupil attitudes *see* pupil perceptions
pupil data 87–106
    tool kits for, LEA developing 21–2
    use by headteachers 72–6

use by schools 13, 17–18, 92–5,
    96–100
use in the EPSI programme 87–91
use in practice 91–6
see also data
Pupil Data Working Party 12, 88, 108,
    155
Pupil Individual Reading Profile 163
pupil learning outcomes
    data 18, 89–90
    improvement defined in terms of 11
    lack of, on OFSTED reports 156
    in targets 50
pupil perceptions 107–21, 215–16
    data 18, 90, 205–6
        indicates improvement 51, 163–4
        use in practice 95, 99–100
    effect on staff 73–4, 114–17
    and school improvement 116–21,
        205–6
pupils
    behaviour of 37, 44, 112
    discussions with, in OFSTED
        revisits 60–1
    interviews with 109–16
purchase of information consultancy
    model 141

QCA benchmarks 92
qualitative data
    findings 35–58, 64
    mixed with quantitative 98–9
    semi-structured interviews for
        110–12
    types of data collected 24
quality of learning 60, 62, 209–10
quality of teaching 10
    OFSTED emphasis on 83
    in OFSTED revisits 60
    in targets 45, 56, 209–10
quantitative data
    findings 25–7, 63–4
    Key Stage 2 tests 27–35
    mixed with qualitative 98–9
    types of data collected 24

questions
    pupils' comments on 119
    research 16–23, 181–5

reading material, dislike of 163
reading and targets 43, 56, 57
reading tests 89, 96, 99, 161–2, 214
recognition, pupil attitude survey and
    215–16
recording and reporting in targets 36,
    56, 162
reflection, enquiry and 13, 18, 176,
    220–1
reporting, recording and, in targets 36,
    56, 162
reports
    end of programme 143
    OFSTED *see* OFSTED inspection
        reports
    by programme pairs 35, 36–58, 70,
        165
research
    action research approach 82
    and EPSI programme 13, 16–23,
        181–5, 198–202
    pupil perspective problems 120–1
    pupils, improvements in 40, 164
    in teaching 72, 130, 142, 176
research culture 97
research skills, pupils' 40
researchers, students as 119–20,
    121
resource allocation 167
resource selection, pupils' 39
responsibility, student 215

samples for pupil perspectives
    108–9
SATs results *see* Key Stage tests
school culture 130
school data 13, 17–18
school development 10
school development advisers (SDAs) 1,
    16, 22, 23, 128–9, 149
school effectiveness 100, 137

school improvement
  continuous potential for 175
  data in 160–71
    triangulation of 103–4
  and differentiation 71, 193–5
  evaluating 155–73
  future directions 120–1
  and headteachers 69–86
  key points 191–8
  and LEA 125–38
    consultants 139–51
    strategies following programme 174–85
  ongoing nature of 5
  as opposed to development 10
  pupil perspectives in 107–21
  research on 10–11
  and school effectiveness 100
  success criteria, defining 157–8
  see also EPSI programme
schools
  avoiding dependency 150–1, 191
  benefits to 15–16, 20–2
  and data
    common measures agreed 213–14
    Key Stage 2 performance 26–35
    qualitative findings 35–58
    use of 13, 17–18, 92–5, 96–100, 160
  in difficulties 33–4, 41, 80
  in Essex 27, 28, 29, 30–3, 34, 102
  instigating change 149–50
  OFSTED revisits 59–63, 159, 173
  and programme pairs 144–9, 150
  programme teams in 131–2
  starting points 25
  workshop programme for 218
  see also school improvement
science 31–2, 63, 75
SDAs *see* school development advisers
secondary schools 2, 10–11, 107, 119, 196
self-esteem 44, 175
self-evaluation 72, 190, 192–3, 204
  see also evaluation

self-improvement 6, 21, 88, 206
self-managing organizations 21
semi-structured interviews
  for pupil perception data 110–12
  with schools and advisers 143–4
SEN *see* special educational needs
senior educational psychologists 1, 128–9, 149
shared attitudes and beliefs 215
skills, required by LEA 183–4
SNSS *see* special needs support staff
software, data handling and 21–2, 72, 96
special educational needs (SEN) 53
  see also special needs support staff (SNSS)
special needs support staff (SNSS) 1
  special educational needs managers 16, 22
  team leaders 128–9, 149
  see also special educational needs (SEN)
staff
  LEA *see* LEA staff
  teaching *see* teaching staff
staff development
  and conditions rating scale 219–20
  for moderation and assessment 94
  programme is source of 189–90
  see also training
staff perception data 90–1, 95, 99
  see also conditions rating scale
Standards and Frameworks Bill (1998) 105
Steering Group 12, 21, 108
study skills, improvement in 164
success criteria 11, 209–12
  defining 157–8
  in the future 61
  results 160–71
suspicions, use of data and 97

targets 12, 96, 209–12
  post-programme 27
  reports on 36–58

setting 9, 59, 177–8
  programme pairs assist 146–7
  for pupils, but not teachers 74–5
teacher cultures 19, 83–4, 191, 205
Teacher Training Agency (TTA) 83
teaching
  effect of programme on 61, 161,
    163
  focus on 74–5, 176
  key point in improving schools 195
  problems addressing 82–4
  quality of *see* quality of teaching
  research in 201
  skills targeted 50
  strategies for improving 166
  see also pedagogy
teaching staff
  and data 170–1, 192–3
    pupil, response to 73–4, 97–8,
      114–17
    skills with 72, 78
  enquiry and reflection 13, 18, 176,
    220–1
  importance in primary development
    194
  self-esteem 44
  turnover 64, 78–9, 174, 194–5
  understanding of programme 61
teaching to the test 101
team focus 136
teamwork by staff 168
themes of enquiry for pupil
    perspectives 108–9
theory and practice division 200–1
tool kits for pupil data 21–2, 183
tracking school improvement 198
training
  for data handling 18, 105
  for LEA staff 184, 207
  see also staff development
transformative education 121
triangulation of data 103–4, 112
TTA (Teacher Training Agency) 83

University of Cambridge School of
    Education (UCSE) 1, 11, 12,
    100, 129–30, 186

value added 32–3, 34, 63, 102–3,
    213
  confidence in 98
  improvement in 161–2
  schools value 93
value added project 100, 162, 177,
    213

Warwick University, Early Reading
    Research with 179
working group for pupil perspectives
    108–9
working practice, implications of
    multi-disciplinary approach for
    135–7
working with pupils 119
workshop programmes 130, 217–18
writing
  assessment *see* writing assessments
  in targets 55, 56, 57
writing assessments 17, 89–90, 91,
    93–4, 99, 214
  backwash effect 101
  criteria for 74–5
  improvement in 161–2

Year 4
  assessments in *see* Year 4
    assessments
  emphasis on 17
  pupil perspectives 109, 110, 115,
    163
Year 4 assessments 76, 91, 105
  schools invited to use 1–2
  writing 89–90, 91, 93, 99, 214
Year 6
  attainment *see* Key Stage 2 tests
  pupil perspectives 109, 110, 115,
    163